EARTHQUAKES AND GARDENS

CLASS 200 NEW STUDIES IN RELIGION

EDITED BY Kathryn Lofton AND John Lardas Modern

Awkward Rituals: Sensations of Governance in Protestant America
Dana Logan

Sincerely Held: American Secularism and Its Believers
Charles McCrary

Unbridled: Studying Religion in Performance
William Robert

Profaning Paul
Cavan W. Concannon

Making a Mantra: Tantric Ritual and Renunciation on the Jain Path to Liberation
Ellen Gough

Neuromatic: Or, A Particular History of Religion and the Brain
John Lardas Modern

Kindred Spirits: Friendship and Resistance at the Edges of Modern Catholicism
Brenna Moore

The Privilege of Being Banal: Art, Secularism, and Catholicism in Paris
Elayne Oliphant

Ripples of the Universe: Spirituality in Sedona, Arizona
Susannah Crockford

The Lives of Objects: Material Culture, Experience, and the Real in the History of Early Christianity
Maia Kotrosits

EARTHQUAKES AND GARDENS

Saint Hilarion's Cyprus

VIRGINIA BURRUS

The University of Chicago Press
Chicago and London

The University of Chicago Press, Chicago 60637
The University of Chicago Press, Ltd., London
© 2023 by The University of Chicago
All rights reserved. No part of this book may be used or reproduced in any manner whatsoever without written permission, except in the case of brief quotations in critical articles and reviews. For more information, contact the University of Chicago Press, 1427 E. 60th St., Chicago, IL 60637.
Published 2023
Printed in the United States of America

32 31 30 29 28 27 26 25 24 23   1 2 3 4 5

ISBN-13: 978-0-226-82322-5 (cloth)
ISBN-13: 978-0-226-82456-7 (paper)
ISBN-13: 978-0-226-82455-0 (e-book)
DOI: https://doi.org/10.7208/chicago/9780226824550.001.0001

Library of Congress Cataloging-in-Publication Data

Names: Burrus, Virginia, author.
Title: Earthquakes and gardens : Saint Hilarion's Cyprus / Virginia Burrus.
Other titles: Saint Hilarion's Cyprus | Class 200, new studies in religion.
Description: Chicago ; London : The University of Chicago Press, 2023. | Series: Class 200: new studies in religion | Includes bibliographical references and index.
Identifiers: LCCN 2022021773 | ISBN 9780226823225 (cloth) | ISBN 9780226824567 (paperback) | ISBN 9780226824550 (ebook)
Subjects: LCSH: Jerome, Saint, –419 or 420. Vita S. Hilarionis Eremitae. | Hilarion, Saint, approximately 291–approximately 371—Homes and haunts—Cyprus. | Earthquakes—Religious aspects. | Earthquakes—Cyprus—Paphos. | Excavations (Archaeology)—Cyprus—Paphos. | Earthquakes in literature. | Mountains in literature. | Gardens in literature. | Paphos (Cyprus)—In literature. | Paphos (Cyprus)—History—To 1500.
Classification: LCC BR65.J473 V58 2023 | DDC 281.9/5693—dc23/eng/20220610
LC record available at https://lccn.loc.gov/202202177

*For Mary Lee Powell Burrus
(April 13, 1935–October 13, 2020)
and Charles Sidney Burrus
(October 9, 1934–April 3, 2021),
who gave me
a spirit of adventure
and a sense of home.*

———————

CONTENTS

List of Figures ix

PART ONE: POINTS OF DEPARTURE

Memories 3
Three Notes on Method 7
Setting Out, with Jerome 9

PART TWO: PAPHOS

Poetry and Place 37
Curating Earthquakes 54
Life in Ruins 72

PART THREE: THE MOUNTAIN

Geographies of the Remote 93
Entropic Gardens 114
Literary Cartographies 131

PART FOUR: CODA

An Ocean of Possibility 151

*Acknowledgments 157   Notes 161
Bibliography 185   Index 197*

FIGURES

1.1	Preface to Jerome's *Life of Hilarion*. Madrid, Real Academia de la Historia, codex 13, folio 19v. Tenth century. 11
1.2	Rosamond Purcell. *Book/nest*. Photograph, 1990s. 27
2.1	Aphrodite of Trikomo. Limestone sculpture. Cyprus, about 500 BCE. 49
2.2	Aphrodite of Soloi. Marble sculpture. Cyprus, first century BCE. 50
2.3	Rock of Aphrodite. Paphos, Cyprus. 52
2.4	Cyprus stamp with Aphrodite of Soloi and Rock of Aphrodite. 1979. 52
2.5	Skeletal remains of earthquake victims. Kourion, Cyprus, fourth century. 60
2.6, 2.7	Sissel Marie Tonn, with Jonathan Reus. *The Intimate Earthquake Archive*. Ballroom Marfa, Marfa, Texas, 2018. 65
2.8	David Brooks. *Repositioned Core (Byproduct)*. Ballroom Marfa, Marfa, Texas, 2018. 68
2.9	*Equation of Time Cam, 01999*. Ballroom Marfa, Marfa, Texas, 2018. 68
2.10	Agia Kyriaki surrounded by ruins of the fourth-century Chrysopolitissa basilica. Paphos, Cyprus. 76
2.11	Marble column in the Chrysopolitissa basilica. Paphos, Cyprus. 78
2.12	Maarten van Heemskerck. *Landscape with Saint Jerome*. 1547. 82
2.13	Hieronymus Cock after Maarten van Heemskerck. *Saint Jerome in a Landscape with Ruins*. 1552. 82
2.14	Ledelle Moe. *When* exhibition, Massachusetts Museum of Contemporary Art, North Adams, MA, 2019–20. 85

2.15	Ledelle Moe. *Remain. When* exhibition, Massachusetts Museum of Contemporary Art, North Adams, MA, 2019–20. 86
2.16	Ledelle Moe. *Study for Untitled. When* exhibition, Massachusetts Museum of Contemporary Art, North Adams, MA, 2019–20. 88
2.17	Stone of Aphrodite. Old Paphos (Kouklia), Cyprus. 88
2.18	Saint Paul's Pillar. Paphos, Cyprus. 88
3.1, 3.2	Ryan Dewey. *Copper Boulder*. Tenna, Graubünden, Switzerland, 2018. 105
3.3, 3.4, 3.5	Thomas Schütte. *Crystal*. The Clark Art Institute, Williamstown, MA, 2015. 106
3.6, 3.7	Tessa Kelly and Chris Parkinson. *The Mastheads Studios*. Pittsfield, MA, 2017. 110
3.8	Saint Hilarion. *Menologion of Basil II* (Codex Vaticanus 1613/0150). Constantinople, about 1000. 120
3.9	Masanobu Fukuoka (1913–2008). Shikoku, Japan. 123
3.10, 3.11	Duisburg-Nord Landscape Park. Duisburg, Germany. 124
3.12	Hilarion's Castle. Kyrenia, Cyprus. 138
3.13	Episkopi Rock with Saint Hilarion's Church. Episkopi Village, Paphos, Cyprus. 140
3.14	Abraham Ortelius. *Wanderings of Ulysses*. Map inset, 1597. 143
3.15	Estienne Michalet. *The Deserts of Egypt, the Thebaid, Arabia, Syria, etc.* Map, 1692. 143

I
POINTS OF DEPARTURE

The life of a saint is a composition of places.

MICHEL DE CERTEAU

MEMORIES

HERE IS HOW I REMEMBER IT: the windows on both sides began to rattle like teeth. So loud! My god, they're going to explode, I thought, shoving the stroller into the middle of the street. The ground lurched. Not a fire, then—something else. And a big one! I was not so much afraid as astonished.

I wound my way along shuddering roads, feeling oh so wide awake, while the baby slept. And why shouldn't he? I thought. The world is new to him; the earth itself is rocking him. It was only when we were inside our second-floor flat that fear hit me full force. I huddled under a doorway, clutching my son. Buildings can fall: the awareness had arrived with the force of revelation. This one might come down around my ears, around his dear little ears, I thought. But it didn't. Not then and not during any of the aftershocks, real or imagined, that sent us back under the doorway in the days and weeks that followed.

Eventually I came to trust the ground again, to trust that my home would stay standing. But I knew *in my body* something I hadn't truly known before. *The earth is a moving thing.* For a few long seconds, its movements had become perceptible to me; its pace had accelerated to match my own. The moving earth and I were temporarily operating in the same timescale, meeting in the same place. It was terrifying.

The epicenter of the 1989 Loma Prieta earthquake was about sixty miles south of San Francisco, where I then lived. The quake registered 6.9 on the moment magnitude scale and as high as IX in some places on the Modified Mercalli intensity scale. What does that mean? Like the more familiar (but now outdated) Richter, moment magnitude, calculated mathematically with the aid of measurements from seismographic instruments, indicates how much work an earthquake does in pushing one piece of rock past another. A 6.9 earthquake does a lot of such work: according to a US Geological Survey publication, in the Loma Prieta quake "the Pacific plate moved 6.2 feet to the northwest and 4.3 feet upward over the North American plate."[1]

The Modified Mercalli intensity scale measures something a bit different: namely, the effect of an earthquake (how hard it shakes things) at a given location. In contrast with moment magnitude, this measurement is distinctly subjective, not only because it is location-specific but also because its measuring "instruments" are primarily the variegated bodies of humans and their built structures. At the locations where its effects were most strongly felt, the Loma Prieta earthquake reached an intensity level of IX. That means that its shaking was violent, and the damage it caused was heavy: entire buildings and freeways collapsed.[2] While it may be possible to quantify such levels of destruction in monetary terms, for example, the intensity measurement favors qualitative evaluations, such as "violent" and "heavy." Tellingly, the US Geological Survey solicits online feedback under the heading "Did you feel it?" Indeed, the question of how widely and how strongly a given earthquake registers in human perception largely determines the distinctions between the first six out of twelve levels on the intensity scale. For the higher levels, where the register of human perception has been saturated, the local impact of the earth's movement is read in the suffering of built structures.

Philosopher Michel Serres, who also lived through the Loma Prieta earthquake and its aftershocks, experienced his body quite explicitly as an intensity measuring instrument. He counted up the levels: "Three, I sleep, the body unaltered. No, four's not serious. Six and up, I run and protect myself." Jolted into a state of hypervigilance, he was as acutely attuned to Earth's movements as to those of a lover. "At that time, my body transformed into a sensitive seismograph that had no need of any machine to estimate precisely how and how much the Earth was shaking. Eminently adapted, my sensation caresses and follows the fissure's trembling." This attunement, which stays with him, at least to some degree, verges on identification: "Since then, my body thinks like the Earth."[3]

Might we imagine a built structure counting up, as Serres did, and taking the count higher for us? Five, I sleep, the body unaltered. No, six is not serious, assuming I'm reasonably well constructed. Seven, I am starting to crack. Eight, I gape and tilt. Nine, I begin to collapse. Ten and over, I am *down*. (A building cannot run and protect itself. Neither can humans trapped under it.)

Among the structures that experienced extremely high levels of intensity in the Loma Prieta earthquake was the Central Freeway spur north of San Francisco's Market Street, a double-decked viaduct that sustained failures to both columns and joints. The northern segment of the freeway, too badly damaged to be repaired, was demolished in 1992. The part immediately south of the demolished segment was finally taken down in 2003, after more than a decade of highly charged political debate about whether to renovate or remove it.

Between 2010 and 2013, when the area was partly redeveloped for housing, something remarkable happened in the ruins of this freeway: thousands of volunteers transformed a vacant 2.2-acre lot that had been the site of the freeway's on- and off-ramps into a thriving green space known as Hayes Valley Farm. The urban farmers created soil on top of the old concrete, using more than eighty thousand pounds of recycled cardboard along with two hundred cubic yards of organic matter, and established permaculture gardens. They grew an orchard of trees in pots. They raised bees, built a greenhouse and an outdoor oven, ran a café and educational programs, made art, showed films, and more. In the three years that it operated, Hayes Valley Farm produced more than 168 projects, developing a distinctive style of shared governance that allowed multiple initiatives to flourish and cross-fertilize.[4] A quake taught this freeway to think like the earth.

Loma Prieta is lodged in my own memories. It gives me one beginning to my story. But here I pursue an earthquake from the deeper past; I track the fallen monuments and resurgent gardens of a more distant city. The goddess of love once reigned in that city; the Christian saint Hilarion once passed through it, seeing only ruins—ancient Paphos, on the island of Cyprus.

How does one come to know an earthquake that is more than 1,600 years old? Historical seismologist Emanuela Guidoboni writes evocatively of drawing on "the long memory of the inhabited world."[5] Much of that long memory is lodged in literary or documentary evidence of a sort familiar to all historians; but if it is distinctly "human memory," we must read it "as though man was a very special 'seismograph.'"[6] One can also discover "earthquake effects" in an ancient building or archaeological site, Guidoboni notes;[7] material artifacts can be encountered as seismographs too, then. The intensities that they measure, as well as their stratigraphic timescales,[8] may be different from those of human seismographs, however. Moreover, in the case of a built structure, the instrument and its recorded measurement—the seismogram—are one and the same. The effect of the earthquake is written directly on the body of a building.

For Hilarion, our Christian saint, the toppled buildings of late fourth-century Paphos were just such a seismogram, recording the intensity of a mighty quake. We see them through his eyes, a trace of memory recorded by a very special human seismograph—Jerome of Stridon, Hilarion's hagiographer. Perhaps the memory was always Jerome's, rather than Hilarion's. Perhaps it was even his literary invention, but that makes little difference to us here and now. What matters is what the text and the landscapes it evokes know and remember, and what they might still have to teach us—not only about Paphos but also about the mountaintop garden several miles inland from the city, where Hilarion eventually settled. All we have to go on is two small fragments of writing and the mental images that come with them. This book will construct itself around those fragments, those images; it will grow itself from their seeds.

The earthquake that Jerome recorded through his representation of the buildings of Paphos was for him both literal and figurative. If this present book is a kind of seismogram, as well as a kind of plant, the intensities that it registers are, similarly, both those of a literal earthquake (felt differently in different places and by different bodies) and those of a metaphorical character. In both cases, however, they are intensities that are felt and known in the body, and they are intensities that allow the body to leap its own bounds, so to speak. They are intensities through which the body comes to think like the earth.

THREE NOTES ON METHOD

LIKE MOST BOOKS, THIS ONE wants to do several things at once.

First, it is an exercise in place-centered or "geocritical" reading of a notoriously human-centered genre,[1] the Saint's Life. Focusing on Jerome of Stridon's *Life of Saint Hilarion*, I initially planned an extended sojourn on the island of Cyprus, where Hilarion is said to have spent his last years. Travel to Cyprus would have enabled me to read the text not only *for place* but also *in place*. Motivated by ecological concerns, I wanted to think about how direct, embodied experiences of landscapes interact with literary experiences, about the kind of agency exercised by places as such, exceeding their textual mediations.[2] I hoped not only to visit key sites on the island but also to talk to local seismologists and geologists, botanists and archaeologists, monks and gardeners, poets and artists, multiplying perspectives. However, plans necessarily changed when a global pandemic rendered international travel impossible. Questions shifted their focus. I now ask what it means to develop a relationship to a place—in this case, a fourth-century Mediterranean island—that is not only long ago and far away but cannot be reached at all. How can we do this while taking the materiality of place with utmost seriousness, refusing to let it be reduced to a *mere* literary artifact, and at the same time leaning into the ways that literature and other arts allow us access to what is otherwise inaccessible? How, finally, can "sheltering" hermit-like in our own places become a resource for knowing other places?

Second, the book is a meditation on destruction and resilience, on ruination and the resurgence of life, and also on grief and consolation. These topics can be deeply personal: I wrote the book while grappling with the deaths of both my parents during (but not directly because of) a pandemic. They also point to phenomena that are massive in scale and deeply impersonal—what Timothy Morton calls "hyperobjects," of which pandemic and global warming are salient examples;[3] so too are tectonic shift and photosynthesis. Earthquakes and gardens are concrete manifestations of destruction and resilience that anchor us in the *Life of Hilarion* while also drawing us beyond the text. Operating on both literal and metaphorical planes (Morton himself describes the discovery of hyperobjects as a "being-quake"),[4] they open onto more-than-human worlds that are at once distant and close, vast and intimate, in all their poignant precarity and surprising persistence. What do those worlds have to say to us here and now?

Third, the book is a methodological experiment in the close reading of small bits of text. It fosters a disciplined attentiveness that balances narrow focus with free-floating curiosity. Under the pressure of a highly selective reading, the text falls to pieces. This occurs all the time. But what happens, I wonder, when we actively encourage that process of textual decay, releasing the relics into a wider world of dialogue and discovery, where they may be transformed while also (perhaps) becoming more intensely themselves? Catherine Michael Chin suggests that we engage past remains by creating resonance chambers that amplify our artifacts and the traces of worlds that still cling to them, thus bringing them into closer contact with our own fragmentary selves and worlds.[5] In later chapters, I shall juxtapose fragments of Jerome's text with other texts, objects, and works of art to which they seem drawn by affinity. Some of these are historically related to Jerome's world, while others are not. Some come from Cyprus, while others are drawn from the environments in which I write. These eclectic juxtapositions are intended to function as resonance chambers, in Chin's sense. Since I am the one staging them, my own experiences and sensibilities will inevitably be strongly in play. These are not only close readings, then. They are also intimate readings that require me to give something of myself and invite you to do so too.

SETTING OUT, WITH JEROME

HERE AT THE START, I shall offer a reading of the *Life of Hilarion* in its literary and historical contexts, while beginning to dislodge a few passages of the text from their contextual moorings. This initial interpretive venture will serve to introduce the text, along with some of the themes and topoi that will preoccupy us in this book—not least earthquakes, gardens, and ruins. More than that, it will perform a first stage in the process of fragmentation that this close, place-centered reading entails. It will launch us on the journey that is the rest of the book.

Jerome wrote the *Life of Hilarion* in Bethlehem around the year 390 CE, and he dedicated it to a Roman friend—"*nonna* Asella, honor and dignity of virgins."[1] He was not the first to write of the saint, who had died some twenty years earlier. "The holy Epiphanius, bishop of Salamis in Cyprus, who had many exchanges with Hilarion, wrote down his praise in a brief letter that is read by the masses," he reports in his prologue. Epiphanius's letter does not survive, and although he counted the bishop as a friend and ally, Jerome hints that this is no great loss. "It is one thing to praise the dead with commonplaces, another to relate his characteristic virtues," he observes (*Life of Hilarion* 1).* Epiphanius knew Hilarion personally,[2] but Jerome (who did not) considers himself better equipped to write an account that would present the ascetic in his distinctive guise as saint and exemplar.

More than an act of literary one-up-manship or even ascetic instruction

---

*Throughout this book, I use the Latin edition of Jerome's *Life of Hilarion* from Edgardo M. Morales and Pierre Leclerc, eds., *Jérôme: Trois Vies de Moines*, Sources Chrétiennes 508 (Paris: Les Éditions du Cerf, 2007), 212–99. Translations are my own, but I refer the reader to Carolinne White's translation in *Early Christian Lives* (London: Penguin Books, 1998), 89–115, which I also consulted. My in-text references to the *Life* follow the traditional section numbers used by White, in accordance with the edition of *Patrologia Latina* 23.

(though it is also those things), Jerome's text is a kind of postcard, linking people and places: acquired by Jerome in Hilarion's beloved Cyprus, where he visited Epiphanius on his way from Rome to the Holy Land, it was inscribed and mailed from Jerome's new home in Palestine, near both Hilarion's birthplace and the site of his second and final burial. Addressed to Asella, the hagiographical portrait was surely intended to be read by other friends in Rome as well. Eventually it would circulate far more widely, of course. In so doing, it called attention to its own spatial networks, triangulated between Rome, Palestine, and Cyprus. It also disseminated a portrait of a saint strongly defined by his own complex and ambivalent relationship to place as such.

Born in Thabatha, a Palestinian village just south of the city of Gaza, Hilarion, the child of polytheists, "flourished as a rose, so to speak, among thorns," as Jerome puts it (2). As a youth, he was uprooted from his native place, however. Sent to study with a grammarian in Alexandria, he heard tales of the famous hermit Antony and traveled to the Egyptian desert to learn from the holy man's exemplary asceticism. A few months of such face-to-face discipleship sufficed: Hilarion ended his apprenticeship when he could no longer bear the presence of the many others who were likewise drawn to Antony's desert dwelling. (This aversion to crowds would recur throughout his life.) He returned to the region around Gaza at age fifteen, taking up residence in a desert that had not yet been colonized by monks or overpopulated by their admirers (3). He lived there for fifty years, ultimately attracting disciples and drawing miracle-seeking crowds himself. And yet stability of place is not Hilarion's defining achievement, as Jerome depicts him. In a restless search for both solitude and a place that would feel like home, Hilarion spent the last fifteen years of his life outside Palestine, frequently on the move, always poised for flight. It was in Cyprus that he finally settled on a remote mountaintop outside Paphos, held in place, if only just barely. It was in Cyprus that Jerome encountered his memory.

This late ancient postcard has been sitting on my own desk for many years, though it took me some time to recognize it for what it was (fig. 1.1). The *Life of Hilarion* is Jerome's sending, but it is also Hilarion's. It draws us to Cyprus as a place of both exile and homecoming, of both ruins and new emergence, of stone- and plant- as well as human-being. It draws us to Cyprus as a place of dying and of becoming.

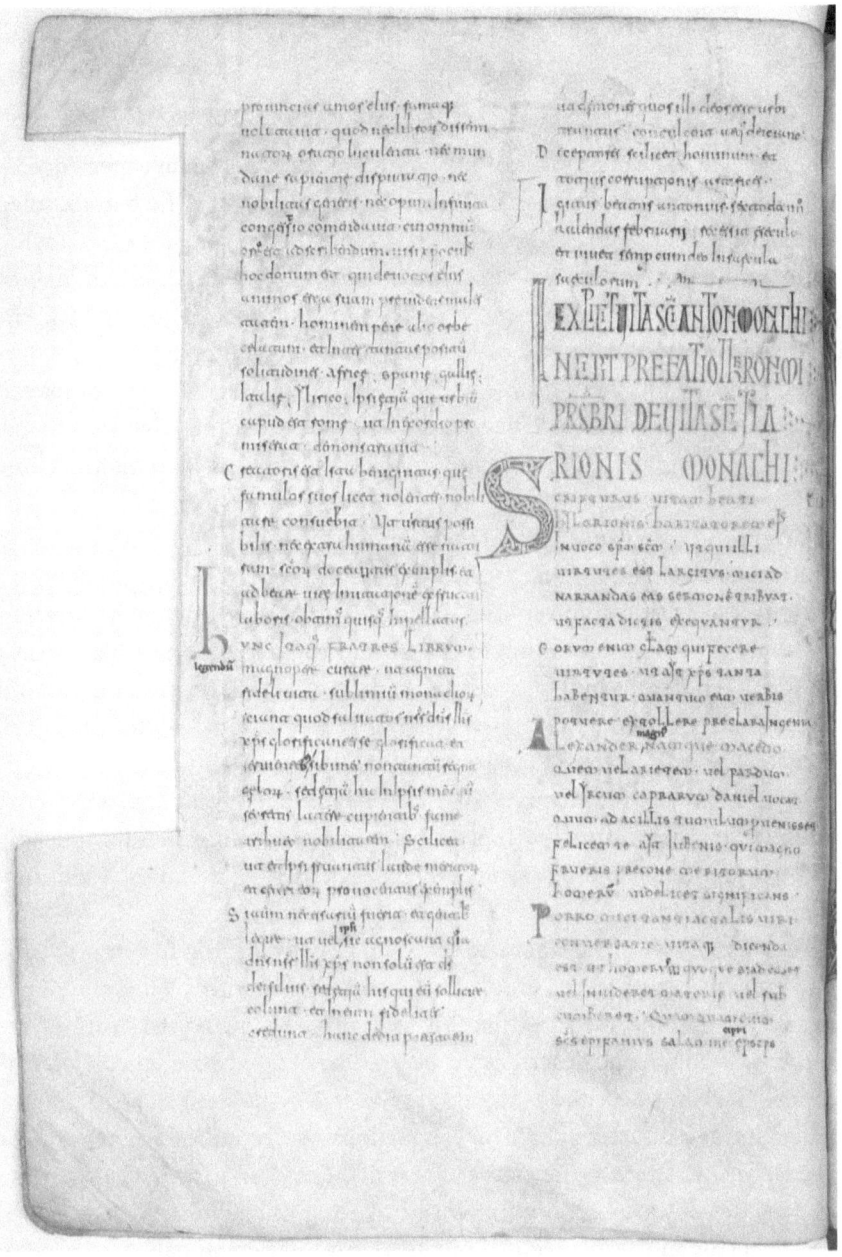

FIGURE 1.1 Preface to Jerome's *Life of Hilarion*, on manuscript page missing a part of its margin. Madrid, Real Academia de la Historia, codex 13 (folio 19v). Tenth century. Photograph courtesy of the Real Academia de la Historia.

GETTING THERE: EARTHQUAKE AND FLOOD

Hilarion came to Cyprus as an outsider. Apart from his youthful sojourn in Egypt, he had spent most of his life in Palestine when he experienced a psychological crisis at age sixty-three: the monastery that he had founded and led for many years began to feel to him like a prison (29). Craving solitude, he finally fled two years later, following the death of his mentor Antony, whose dwelling place he desired to visit once again (30–31). His travels, which took him well beyond Egypt, would end on a mountain outside Paphos, a journey of some 360 miles that might have been completed in less than a week.[3] But Hilarion did not yet know that Cyprus was his destination, and his route was circuitous, to say the least. It took him some eight years to get there.

Traveling over land, he followed the coast to Egypt, turning inland to visit Antony's hermitage in the eastern desert (30–32) and proceeding from there to the ascetic communities of the western desert, where he lingered for some time before heading to the Libyan coast to continue his journey by sea (33–34). Still moving west, he sailed to Sicily, settling in an inland retreat until his cover was blown (35–37). When he took to the seas again, he headed north to the "barbarous nations" on the Dalmatian coast, stopping in the town of Epidaurus. There hoped-for anonymity was once more thwarted by his seemingly irrepressible miracle-working: he slew a deadly serpent that was plaguing the area by first enchanting it and then setting it aflame (38–39).[4]

Just as Hilarion was about to leave Epidaurus, fleeing his own notoriety, a massive earthquake shook "the entire world," with a tsunami following swiftly. Jerome specifies that this took place following the death of the emperor Julian. As he describes the event, "the seas exceeded their bounds" so that "ships were carried away and suspended on the steep slopes of mountains." It was a disaster of biblical proportions—a second god-sent flood, or (worse yet) a return to the primal chaos of Genesis 1:2. The "roaring surges and masses of waves and mountains of swirling waters hurled at the shore" struck terror in the people of Epidaurus, and understandably so. Having already seen whole towns destroyed, they feared the same fate awaited them. With nowhere else to turn, "they approached the old man, and as if they were advancing into battle, they stationed him on the shore." Put into place like a military talisman, Hilarion did not disappoint. Drawing the sign of the cross in the sand three times, he raised his arms and faced down the towering sea, which gradually (and with seeming reluctance) subsided. The marvelous feat only increased the holy man's already considerable local fame as a dragon-slayer. Years later, mothers in the region still told the story to their children, Jerome reports (40).

Perhaps Jerome heard the tale from those mothers firsthand; after all, he hailed from Dalmatia himself. But echoes of another story of an Adriatic Sea surge can also be heard through his telling, putting such a straightforward transmission into question. That story is known through the mediation of later writers, the ninth-century Byzantine chroniclers Theophanes and George the Monk. Like Jerome, Theophanes records an earthquake that took place "throughout the whole world." Describing the effects of the associated tsunami on the city of Alexandria, he adds that "sailors reported that, while sailing in the Adriatic, their ship was caught up and then rested on the sea bed; after a short time the water returned again and refloated them" (1.56). George's narrative similarly focuses initially on Alexandria but subsequently broadens its scope; like Theophanes, George notes that "in some seas, including the Adriatic and the Aegean," waters retreated, leaving ships stranded, and then returned, raising them again (462/689). It seems clear that the two Byzantine accounts are independent of each other but share a common source. Crucially for us, that source (or one from which it ultimately derives) also appears to have been known by the late fourth-century historian Ammianus Marcellinus,[5] who finished his *History* around the same time that Jerome was writing his *Life of Hilarion*. The source must have been familiar to Jerome too, in some form.[6]

Working within this tradition, Jerome localizes the narrative by placing Hilarion in a specific town on the Adriatic coast, while Ammianus universalizes it by dropping the reference to the Adriatic Sea altogether. "The entire stability of the weight of the quaking earth was shaken," the latter writes, giving us not only the year—"in the first consulship of Valentinian and his brother" (Valens)—but also the exact day and time of the disaster—July 21, 365, just after dawn—while avoiding any mention of place (26.10.15–18). Not until the very last sentence of his lengthy and vivid ecphrasis of the tsunami does Ammianus provide any geographical specificity at all: "Other huge ships, thrust out by the mad blasts, perched on the roofs of houses, as happened at Alexandria, and others were hurled nearly two miles from the shore, like the Laconian vessel near the town of Methone which I saw when I passed by, yawning apart from long decay" (26.10.19). Ammianus's first exemplum decenters but still preserves a trace of what seems to have been originally an Alexandrian-centered narrative; it aligns closely with Theophanes's observation that in Alexandria the waves carried ships onto the roofs of buildings and parallels Jerome's report of ships suspended on mountaintops. The second exemplum—involving a coastal town in the Peloponnese—constitutes Ammianus's own signature or seal on the account, lending the veracity of eyewitness to an otherwise perhaps unbelievable narrative. It also pronounces Ammianus's judgment on his own age. Following the death of the emperor Julian (361–363), the ship of state founders and falls apart, as civil war threatens with the usurpation of Procopius (365–366), while the inundation of barbarians looms on the horizon: Ammianus will conclude his history with the Goths' defeat of the Romans at the Battle of Adrianople in eastern Thrace (378). Natural disasters are typically portentous events for late ancient writers, but Ammianus's earthquake is as much allegory as omen.[7]

Might we say the same of Jerome's earthquake? Hilarion's departure from Palestine is overdetermined, attributed narratively to his desire for solitude but correlated chronologically with both the death of his teacher Antony of Egypt in 356 (*Life of Hilarion* 29) and, more loosely, the pagan Julian's ascendency to imperial rule in 361 (33). At least one of his disciples expected him to return to Palestine after Julian's death on June 26, 363 (34); instead Hilarion embarked on a series of sea journeys, which took him first to Sicily and then to the Adriatic coast, as we have seen (35–39). Thus the "universal" earthquake that Jerome describes does not appear to have taken place immediately after Julian's death but only in the general aftermath: his narrative implies that the year may be 364.[8] Yet it matters to Jerome to connect the quake with Julian, even as he places his hero in its midst.

In linking the earthquake and tsunami with Julian's death, Jerome, like Ammianus, alludes tacitly to yet another prior text, Libanius's funeral oration for Julian, in which the famous rhetorician poetically attributes the recent shaking of the earth to earth's mourning for the emperor: "Like a horse tossing its rider she has destroyed ever so many cities—in Palestine many, in Libya all. The greatest cities of Sicily lie in ruins, as does every city in Greece except one: Nicaea the lovely is laid low, and our loveliest of cities is shaken and can have no confidence for the future" (*Oration* 18.292–3). Gathering several earthquakes into one hyperbolic account to demonstrate the broad scope of the earth's grief over Julian's death, Libanius writes prior to the tsunami that Jerome and Ammianus describe. Nonetheless, he establishes a precedent for their treatments, one to which Ammianus alludes approvingly, Jerome critically. For Jerome, Julian's reign, not his death, brings about destruction and chaos, and Hilarion is the dragon-slayer and earthquake-tamer whose actions punctuate the defeat of the apostate emperor.[9] No matter if the chronology wobbles by a year or two: such narrative liberties are scarcely unusual. Ammianus himself dates the earthquake to July 21, 365, as we have seen, but places it narratively following the death of the usurper Procopius on May 27, 366, seeking his own punctuating effects.[10] Writing some fifty years later than Jerome and Ammianus, the church historian Sozomen similarly exploits chronological ambiguity, even marking it as such, in order to associate Julian's rule with the destructiveness of the tsunami that devastated Alexandria: "I infer from what I heard that it was either during his reign or when he held the second post of government." Sozomen goes on to note that the anniversary of the Alexandrian earthquake and tsunami "is still commemorated by an annual festival" (*Church History* 6.2).

Is this, then, a mother's artless story or an artful literary performance enacted on a complex field of religious and cultural competition? Perhaps the latter has become a vehicle for the former, placing Jerome the writer in the role of the maternal raconteurs of Dalmatia, "teaching their children to transmit the memory to posterity" (*Life of Hilarion* 40). Like the townspeople of Epidaurus whom he describes, Jerome has planted his hero in front of a vast seismic sea surge drawn from a wider literary context. He has made him the protector of frightened "barbarians" in an area that would (as Jerome well knew) become a bloody battleground within little more than a decade. He has allowed us to imagine stories of danger and survival being told to children, across years of repeated devastation.

Hilarion, the subject of those stories, was (as Jerome tells it) ever a reluctant hero, torn between a deep-seated responsiveness to the vulnerability that he encountered in others and an equally deep-seated desire for peace and quiet. The latter prevailed, at least temporarily. Sneaking away from Epidaurus at night on a small boat, he subsequently boarded a merchant ship that took him to Cyprus in a mere two days (41)—a miracle in itself, as the journey might have been expected to take closer to twelve.[11] By this point, Hilarion had come almost, but not quite, full circle. About seventy-three years old, he would live out his remaining years on the island, dying at age eighty (44–45). Only his corpse would close the loop, returning to Palestine, even as his spirit remained on Cyprus, or so some claimed (46–47).

ARRIVAL: PAPHOS IN RUINS

Jerome's description of Hilarion's arrival on Cyprus offers a concise study in contrasts: "After entering Paphos, the city in Cyprus made famous by the poets' songs,...he dwelled in obscurity two miles outside the city, rejoicing that he was living for a few days in quiet" (*Life of Hilarion* 42). Passing through Paphos quickly, the saint hurried to reach his obscure (*ignobilis*) dwelling place. However, his hagiographer lingers over the famous (*nobilis*) city that Hilarion ignored. Many poets have sung its praises, Jerome observes knowingly, ever the man of letters. But the glories so well celebrated in literature apparently lie in the past. Paphos "has often tumbled down because of earthquakes," he reports; "only by the traces of ruins does it now show what it once was" (42). The city is *lapsa*, fallen—like a woman, perhaps, or a goddess.[12] Its toppled structures are signs of past grandeur and also of past upheaval—architectural seismograms recording the intensity of the earth's motion.

Did the same "worldwide" earthquake that caused the sea to surge in Dalmatia shake Paphos too? If so, Jerome does not make the connection explicit. Indeed, his remark that Paphos had "often" (*frequenter*) suffered damage from earthquakes diffuses the temporality of disaster, contrasting with his vivid depiction of the Adriatic Sea surge as a recent and singular event. There may be literary reasons for this difference, of course: in the first story, Jerome wants to evoke a moment of cosmic (as well as religiopolitical) crisis in which Hilarion intervenes heroically; in the second, he wants to suggest a world of polytheistic worship and culture that has been falling down for some time. At the same time, we can expect that here as elsewhere, Jerome mixes fact with his fiction as he writes the life of this recent saint. If so, what kind of historical context does he invite us to imagine for his striking representation of Paphos in ruins?

Ammianus's description of the earthquake and tsunami that took place at dawn on July 21, 365, entices scholars with its precise dating as well as its author's reputation for objectivity. However, as we have seen, Ammianus does not clearly identify the geographic center or span of the disaster, and even in what appear to be closely related descriptions penned by others, times and locations come in and out of focus and shift, depending on the authors' literary and historiographic aims.[13] Jerome himself refers on three different occasions to earthquakes with tsunamis that occurred in his own lifetime, and if the descriptions match Ammianus's well enough, the dates wobble from 366 to 364 to an indeterminate time in his youth, while the spatial center moves from "cities of Sicily and many islands" to Dalmatian Epidaurus and to Areopolis in either Palestine or the Peloponnese.[14] Are these three different earthquakes, or three different literary focalizations of the "same" earthquake? The challenge of identification increases when we attempt to correlate such highly articulated yet pliable written depictions with the gritty realia of ruins and rocks. As Emanuela Guidoboni notes, "Written sources and archaeological sources are based on two conceptually different timescales."[15] Geological sources widen the gap further. Moving between timescales while dealing with literary texts that are themselves ambiguous, we risk either creating "seismological 'monsters'" in which "the effects of several earthquakes perhaps some distance apart have been drawn together into a single event" or, alternatively, multiplying earthquakes when there may have been only one.[16]

Radiocarbon dating allows earthquake-induced coastal uplifts in Greece and the eastern Mediterranean to be assigned to what seismic geologists refer to as "a narrow period of time approximately between the fourth and the sixth centuries A.D."[17] What is a narrow period for tectonic plates is a broad span for humans. Within this "Early Byzantine Tectonic Paroxysm," as the two-century interval of seismic volatility has been dubbed,[18] individual events can be identified with somewhat greater temporal precision—but only somewhat. An especially dramatic uplift in western Crete, the magnitude of which "would indicate one of the largest earthquakes ever recorded on the earth,"[19] is dated geologically to between 261 and 425 CE.[20] At the same time, coins and (more rarely) inscriptions allow archaeological evidence of earthquake destruction in Crete, Libya, Cyprus, and Sicily to be placed within a range of years centering in the mid-360s; the ubiquitous copper *aes*, or Roman penny, produced with great frequency in this period and deteriorating quickly, "can date stratigraphic horizons with an accuracy of a few months to a few years."[21] Does all of this point to the single, massive "earthquake of the whole world" that Ammianus, Jerome, and others write about? Recent fault modeling renders that doubtful: even an extraordinarily powerful earthquake centered near Crete could not cause the architectural damage found as far away as Cyprus.[22] It has been suggested that Cyprus, not Crete, was the epicenter of the 365 earthquake that Ammianus describes,[23] but given the magnitude of the coastal uplift of Crete it seems likely that there was more than one major earthquake in or around 365—"a main event offshore Crete, a second, probably smaller event offshore Cyprus and possibly another relatively small event between Sicily and Libya."[24] In other words, a seismic sequence clustered in a time period short even for humans offers a working hypothesis that accommodates geological, archaeological, and literary evidence fairly well.[25]

As it happens, aside from the single passage in Jerome's *Life of Hilarion* and one ambiguous statement by Libanius,[26] there are no explicit literary references to earthquake activity in Cyprus at this time. Nor is the geological record revealing.[27] However, archaeological evidence tells a dramatic story. Excavations of the ruins of Kourion, located some thirty miles east of Paphos, indicate that the city was destroyed by a massive earthquake that most likely took place between March of 364 and September of 365, the period to which the latest coins discovered on the site are dated.[28] (Once again, we are indebted to the lowly but ever-present copper *aes*!) The archaeological remains include, poignantly, the skeleton of a mule tethered by an iron chain to a heavy feeding trough, as well as that of a child about thirteen years old, found on top of the animal's hind quarters. "The massive trauma which the child experienced resulted in most of the bones being badly cracked," notes David Soren, who led excavations at Kourion from 1978 to 1987. A bone hairpin discovered near the skull allowed for the child's tentative identification as a girl, a hypothesis later confirmed by dental analysis; the excavators named her Camelia.[29] Subsequent excavations uncovered a man in his fifties, crushed as he took refuge under a doorway, and what appears to be a family—a young woman holding an approximately eighteen-month-old baby, accompanied by a man who seemingly attempted to shelter the two with his own body.[30] According to Soren, Paphos must have been damaged in the same earthquake in which Camelia and the others died; destruction areas in that city "show directional fall to the north and west" that correlates with that at Kourion.[31] This theory may gain further support from Sozomen's report that Epiphanius was "chosen by the inhabitants of Cyprus to act as bishop of the metropolis of their island"—that is, Constantia (former Salamis) (*Church History* 6.32).[32] If Constantia replaced Paphos as the metropolis or provincial capital of Cyprus sometime before 367, when Epiphanius was ordained, might this have resulted from earthquake damage suffered by Paphos just a few years prior? Constantia itself had suffered damage in earthquakes of 332 and/or 342, resulting in the city's rebuilding and rechristening by Constantius II (337–361).[33] Paphos was apparently not so lucky.

In short, it is reasonable to imagine that Paphos suffered from *a* major earthquake, if not necessarily *the* major earthquake described by Ammianus, shortly before Hilarion arrived. Disembarking from a rocking ship, he would have set foot on a shaken island. He would also have found himself once again in the midst of human need. Hearing of the arrival of a miracle-worker, people came to him from Kourion as well as Salamis (Constantia), Lapithos, and other cities on the island (*Life of Hilarion* 42).

But there is a further complication. It is most likely through Jerome's eyes, not Hilarion's, that we view fallen Paphos—in 385, not 364 or 365. This temporal distance from the earthquake may explain why Jerome's description of the ruined city lacks immediacy; it also allows for a little more wiggle room in dating the quake. Jerome left Rome in 385 and, after stopping in Rhegium (modern Reggio Calabria), across the strait from Sicily, took "the course by Cape Maleas [on the Peloponnese] and the Cyclades to Cyprus," as he records elsewhere (*Apology against Rufinus* 3.22 [402]). Thus his own route tracked the one that he would provide for Hilarion when he wrote the saint's *vita* some five years later: Hilarion too was said to have sailed around Cape Maleas and through the Cycladic islands on his way to Paphos (*Life of Hilarion* 41–42). Jerome states that he was received by Epiphanius, who was bishop of Salamis (Constantia), as we have seen. Might he (like Hilarion) have landed first in Paphos, since he was approaching from the west? Alternatively, might he have traveled overland from Salamis to Paphos to visit the holy man's hermitage outside the famous city, much as his friend Paula and her daughter Eustochium are said to have toured monasteries on the island during their ten-day stay with Epiphanius in Salamis later that year (*Ep.* 108.7)? Jerome's nineteenth-century biographer, Abbé Eugène Bernard, has no doubt regarding Jerome's travels. Imagining that his Ulyssean hero would have pursued his researches on Hilarion zealously during his stay in Cyprus, interviewing informants and visiting the hermit's haunts "with a pious curiosity," he assures us that "Jerome saw Paphos too."[34] If he did, he could have seen ruins resulting from the 365 earthquake, albeit many years later. His own memories would have become Hilarion's, two decades after the fact.

But what exactly did Jerome-as-Hilarion see? What do we as readers see? Were tumbled buildings all that remained of the famous city when Hilarion rushed past it? Or did life continue amidst the ruins—human life, animal life, plant life, the life of reassembled things? Did he see children, mules, a "stately carob tree" growing through the rocks,[35] modest shelters raised in the shade of grander ones?

One thing that Hilarion and Jerome would *not* have seen right away was the ruins of Paphos's most famous monument. The poets celebrated Paphos as the home of the goddess Aphrodite, "where her temple stands, and a hundred altars glow with Arabian incense, and fresh garlands emit their fragrance" (Vergil, *Aeneid* 1.415–17). However, even in Vergil's time, the city of

Paphos (more precisely, Nea Paphos or New Paphos), where Hilarion would have disembarked, had long since moved some ten miles west of Aphrodite's sweet-smelling temple, which remained outside the city proper, in Palaipaphos, or Old Paphos, as it was called (modern Kouklia). The temple is known to us mainly from images of its distinctive tripartite facade imprinted on Roman coins minted in Cyprus between the first and early third centuries. These images depict a central structure housing a large triangular object—the famed aniconic stone representing the goddess, "rediscovered" in the late nineteenth century—and flanked by lower porticoes in which two tall censers stand; in front of the shrine is a courtyard with an altar enclosed by a semicircular wall.[36] The complex archaeology of the site suggests that this building in its final phase dates to the first century, when it was reconstructed under the Flavian emperors, perhaps following a large earthquake in 77 CE.[37] The sanctuary appears to have declined in the course of the third century and may have been abandoned by the mid-fourth.[38] If the temple of Aphrodite was still standing at the time of the earthquake that destroyed both Kourion and Paphos circa 365, it would have suffered damage then and would not likely have been rebuilt afterward. New construction in both Kourion and Paphos, when it emerged, bore a distinctly Christian stamp,[39] and even in Palaipaphos, a church dedicated to the Virgin Mary (who is referred to as the Panagia, or "All-holy") would eventually be erected from stones taken from the temple ruins—the twelfth-century Panagia Katholiki, also known locally as Panagia Aphroditissa, in a conflation of Virgin and goddess.[40] But whatever its state, Aphrodite's temple would not have been visible from the port city of Paphos itself when Hilarion arrived.

By invoking "the city made famous by the poets," Jerome collapsed the distance between the "new" Paphos and the goddess's ancient precinct, inviting his readers to see the city of the goddess in the urban ruins. In so doing, he anticipated the longing of later travelers, who often mistook Paphos for the ancient cult site, perceiving traces of the Temple of Aphrodite in the enigmatic remains of other buildings.[41] A watercolor titled "Baffo—ancient Papho in the island of Cyprus," attributed to the eighteenth-century English traveler and art collector John Skippe, provides a suggestive instance of such wishful seeing. Presenting Paphos from the vantage point of a ship anchored just offshore, the painting depicts the headlands that enclose the city's harbor on the left side; peeking out from behind them and standing on the far side of the harbor is a templelike structure. Balancing that structure on the right side of the picture is another prominent building, probably to be identified as Agia Kyriaki (Saint Sunday), a fifteenth-century church built over the northern aisles of the late fourth-century basilica, replacing an eleventh-century church destroyed by an earthquake in 1159. In the middle of the painting, between the two larger buildings, are the modest houses of Kato Paphos (the modern name for Nea Paphos) and a small mosque. Everything is as it might have looked ca. 1760 except the temple, which is entirely the product of the artist's imagination, a fantasy erected from the stones of a ruined castle (Saranda Kolones, or "Forty Columns") built by French Crusaders (the Lusignans) at the end of the twelfth century, destroyed by an earthquake in 1222, and never rebuilt. As Rita Severis puts it, "although topographically correct, Skippe using artistic license allowed his imagination to adorn the view with what was supposed to be there and what lured most of the travelers to visit Paphos"—namely, the temple of Aphrodite. "It was her fame that led him there.... Therefore, where exploration did not fulfil Skippe's expectations the artist's imagination did." Nor was Skippe the only modern visitor who imagined that he glimpsed an ancient goddess among the tumbled columns of a medieval fortress.[42]

As Susan Stewart suggests, ruins "call for an active, moving viewer—often a traveler with a consciousness distinct from that of a local inhabitant—who can restore their missing coordinates and names."[43] Whereas John Skippe and his contemporary travelers were moved by nostalgia for the classical past in their imaginative "restoral" of Paphos's fallen monuments, Jerome's motives and sentiments were more ambivalent. For Jerome, the damage suffered by Paphos was relatively recent, but his evocation of the ruins nonetheless served to consign the city and its "pagan" temple to history, where it could be viewed from a safe distance. Skippe looked at fallen columns and saw a temple; Jerome may have looked at a damaged but still vital city and seen only fallen columns.

"Only those who are belated can observe a ruined form. We may witness ruination but we come upon a ruin," observes Stewart.[44] The ruins of Paphos both connect and distance viewers from the glorious past of the city; they also both connect and distance them from the violence of its destruction. The reminder that the city had fallen *frequently* further blunts the edge of disaster's fury, since presumably it had been rebuilt just as often. If repetition undercuts the finality of disaster, it also offers "a warning to the makers of monuments."[45] Hilarion did not dream of seven-aisled basilicas replacing fallen temples: that lay in the future. Instead, he turned aside from the seductive, fallen city and its monuments. He left the ruins of Paphos to slide into the slow pace of ongoing deterioration. Glories of a different sort would be found elsewhere.

HOME: HILARION'S GARDEN

Hilarion spent two years living on the outskirts of Paphos (*Life of Hilarion* 43), although he had less than a month's peace before crowds arrived from all over the island—"Salamis, Kourion, Lapithos, and the rest of the cities" (42). As we have seen, Jerome contrasts Hilarion's hermitage with Aphrodite's famed but ruined city. Unlike Paphos, Hilarion's residence was obscure, unsung, without proper name or address: "He dwelled, unknown, two miles outside the city" (42). The crowds found the place through demonic navigation: sensing Hilarion's presence, "unclean spirits began to clamor" (42). We might use our own navigation systems, also ghostly in their way, following the routes of Roman roads beyond the ancient city walls—from the north gate toward Marion, the east gate toward Alinospilios, the northeast gate toward Geroskipos or Palaipaphos.[46] However, we would not recognize the hermitage even if we stumbled upon it, for Hilarion left no trace, and Jerome offers no physical description. In fact, he does not refer at all to the place as such. Strictly speaking, it is the holy man, in his activity of dwelling, who is said to be obscure or unknown, not the site. Indeed, the closer we look, the less we seem to see. What was the terrain like? Did the place include a shelter, whether built or natural? Did other humans dwell nearby?

However elusive it may be, this habitation is not "no place," least of all in Thomas More's utopian sense. We might think of it, rather, as a version of what Michel de Certeau calls "lived space." Such space is not mastered and measured from a distance—the perspective of a god or a cartographer—but created and inhabited from within.[47] The contrast that Jerome draws may not be primarily between urban and rural space, for example, but between space that is viewed as a whole from above or outside and "the dark space where crowds move back and forth."[48] It is a matter of viewpoint, then, or rather of having a viewpoint versus being immersed.

It is also a matter of wholes versus fragments, and static versus emergent landscapes. Jerome may seem to offer us a perspective on Paphos that substitutes one totalizing representation, the city of the poets, with its equally totalizing inversion, the city in ruins. However, that view is easily disrupted when we shift our attention from the toppled monuments to the lives that surely continued to move and pulse among the ruins, creating their own pathways and connections. As de Certeau suggests, "Rather than remaining within the field of discourse that upholds its privilege by inverting its content (speaking of catastrophe and no longer of progress), one can...follow the swarming activity."[49] Following that activity reveals Paphos not as a gleaming totality viewed from a distance but as itself a "dark space"—a city of stones reassembled, children and animals roaming, plants pushing up through the cracks. Following the activity also takes us to the mysterious place on the city's margin where Hilarion dwells and crowds arrive and disperse. "Their swarming mass is an innumerable collection of singularities. Their intertwined paths give their shape to spaces. They weave places together."[50]

With his evocation of Hilarion's first dwelling on the island, Jerome has given us a place that falls off the map, invisible and unlocatable even at the second milestone from Paphos. It is a place that can only be known from the inside—touched, traversed, inhabited. It is a place of fragments and evolving connections. Yet we have lost the pathways that weave it together. There Hilarion once cured two hundred people in a single week; some may have been survivors of the earthquake in Kourion. But the place would not hold him. And so footsteps faltered, dreams and memories dissipated. Only the wisp of a story still lingers.

Hilarion's first Cypriot dwelling prepared the way for his second. "A more remote place," even further off the map, it grabbed him in a way that the first did not. Jerome describes it as twelve miles from the sea; thus, he marks the site by its degree of insularity or inwardness rather than by its distance from a precise urban point on a network of coastal roads and sea routes. Tucked away "among remote and harsh mountains that could scarcely be climbed by crawling on hands and knees," it was "an exceedingly frightening and withdrawn place." Nonetheless, it had its charms. Having emphasized its inaccessibility and remoteness, Jerome describes the site in vivid detail entirely lacking in his description of Hilarion's first home on Cyprus. "It was surrounded on all sides by trees and there was also water flowing down from the brow of the hill, a most delightful little garden and many fruit trees.... There was also nearby the ruin of a very ancient temple from which the sound of an enormous number of demons...could be heard night and day." The presence of the demons particularly pleased Hilarion: he liked having his enemies nearby. He stayed there for five years, until his death (*Life of Hilarion* 43).

Aspects of this holy habitat are familiar from Jerome's description of

Antony's Egyptian hermitage, which Hilarion had visited on the first anniversary of the holy man's death soon after he left Palestine. Antony is said to have lived in a palm-shaded valley near a spring-fed stream at the foot of a rocky mountain; there he had planted vines, trees, and vegetables in a small plot, also described as a little garden and an orchard, watered by a pond that he had dug himself. When he felt the need to escape from the presence of his disciples and visitors, he could ascend the mountain along a steep, spiraling path; on the top, two small cells were cut into the rock (31). Hilarion's home recalls this "pleasant place" (recognizable as a version of the classical topos of the *locus amoenus*) but introduces some new twists. First, trees, stream, and garden are located not in a valley but on a mountaintop, rendering the entire place virtually inaccessible, an aspect further accentuated by the inwardness that the island topography affords. Second, Hilarion does not plant the garden but discovers it; indeed, far from cultivating the trees, "he never consumed their fruit as food." Third, the garden is near a ruined temple resounding with the voices of demons, presumably the lingering presences of ancient gods (43).

A temple in ruins, roughly twelve miles from the sea(port)—is Jerome suggesting that Hilarion had taken up residence in Aphrodite's famous sanctuary, located at the eleventh milestone from Paphos? This scandalous possibility hovers over the text, even if the terrain is not quite right.[51] It also shuttles us back to the vicinity of Hilarion's first Cypriot residence: etymology suggests that Geroskipos (ancient Hierokepia, "holy garden"), just over two miles east of Paphos, was the site of a sacred grove dedicated to Aphrodite. A current guidebook notes that the area is still "notable for its many flowers and fruit trees, especially citrus and pomegranate trees—symbols of the goddess."[52] Sacred groves with fruit trees are known elsewhere in the ancient Mediterranean,[53] and citrus and pomegranate trees could have been found in ancient Cypriot orchards as in modern ones. Athenaeus's early third-century *Learned Banqueters* stages a lively conversation about Mediterranean fruits ranging from figs (a variety of which is found in Cyprus, we learn) to apples, pears, quinces, peaches, and citrons, identifying the latter with the "golden apples" of the Hesperides—suitable fruits for the goddess of love. Quoting the comic poet Eriphus, the banqueters also praise pomegranates, noting that "Aphrodite only planted this one tree in Cyprus."[54] Was Hilarion dwelling among the fragrant branches of citron and pomegranate trees, anticipating the habits of later dendrite saints, while recalling those of earlier grove-loving deities?[55] No wonder that he would not eat the bright fruits: they belonged to a goddess. Moreover, eating forbidden fruit was associated biblically with sin. Yet he was pleased to make this sacred garden his home. He relished the provocation of having Aphrodite for a neighbor, of dwelling with temptation.

Having hinted at such a possibility, Jerome recounts a story that subtly remaps the terrain. "One day as Hilarion was leaving the garden, he saw a man lying in front of the gates, his whole body paralyzed." Hilarion asked his disciple Hesychius, who happened to be visiting, who this man was. He learned that he was the "manager of the country-house to whose jurisdiction the garden in which they were located also belonged" (43). Not a sacred grove, then. Apparently, the manager did not mind Hilarion living in the garden of the estate he oversaw—especially not after the old man had healed him of his affliction. Were the house and its garden also in a state of decrepitude, like their overseer and the nearby temple? Were they too haunted by histories now lost to us?

Cyprus had once been known as a densely wooded island. The first-century geographer Strabo cites his predecessor Eratosthenes to this effect: "In antiquity, forests ran riot [ὑλομανούντων] over the plains, so that they were covered with woods [δρυμοῖς] and could not be cultivated." Already in the Hellenistic period, the use of wood in shipbuilding and metallurgy (Cyprus also being famous for its copper) had thinned the forests significantly, yet still humans "did not prevail" over the trees. Thus, those with the desire and ability to "cut out" the trees were granted the "thoroughly purged" land tax-free, we are told (Strabo, *Geography* 14.6.5). Catherine Kearns comments on the "dynamic, and here unexpectedly threatening, efficacy of trees" that must be conquered to make way for the staple crops of wine, oil, and grain. "The physiographical ambiguity of Cyprus is marked by a vegetal politics" that balances "the authorities who managed land use and tax collection" against "the dangerous power of trees to alter the island's *arête*."[56] If the coastal plains were imagined to be cleared for urban life and agricultural productivity, the mountainous interior of the island remained, in the Mediterranean imagination, indistinct and wild.[57] Jerome places Hilarion's retreat, "surrounded on all sides by trees," in that threatening interior, well above the line of civilizing deforestation. True, his garden with its fruit trees had once been a cultivated space, but by the time Hilarion occupied it, it too seems to have been untended for a while (*Life of Hilarion* 43). It was a liminal space, then, both because it mixed domesticated trees with wild ones and because the domesticated trees must have been themselves in the process of rewilding.[58] Unlike Antony, Hilarion was no farmer. He neither cultivated nor consumed the plants in his garden, yet they persisted nonetheless. Unpruned and gnarled, or so we may imagine, the trees still blossomed, leafed out, bore fruit—an arboreal song of praise in the wilderness. Hilarion lived among these trees, he persisted alongside them, his aged body bearing its own fruit of virtue and miracles.

In the meantime, the old man communed with the "multitude of shadows" (43) that also shared his dwelling place. Others feared such ghostly presences, but Hilarion did not. Perhaps he knew that "haunted places are the only ones people can live in," as de Certeau puts it.[59] The silent circulation of stories, memories, and dreams, *and not only those of humans*, mark places as lived-in and make them livable; these too form paths that intertwine, weave, and hold. So strongly were Hilarion's own paths woven into this place that he begged his followers to bury him in the garden immediately upon his death (44). Nestled among the roots, he joined the haunting shades (45). When a disciple subsequently stole his body from the garden and carried it back to Palestine, fragrant and whole (or so he claimed), Hilarion's spirit still breathed with the trees in the garden of Cyprus, "the place he loved more" (46–47).

MEMORY FRAGMENTS

Hilarion's story, as Jerome tells it, has a beginning and an end, as does his journey. This is what historians do: we take shards from the past and piece them together, filling in where necessary to make them part of something whole again. We are the agents of re-collection, of re-membering. We are the storytellers.

But what if the fragments have a kind of agency too? What if they have stories of their own to relate? They may want to tell stories of earthquakes and gardens. They may want to tell stories of places in process, in which the movements of a holy man are only part of the picture.

What if our memories are always pieced together from bits and pieces that are never fully ours, that seek worlds of their own—multiple worlds, even?

We can perceive this possibility most easily with material fragments, perhaps. In a fascinating set of meditations on decay, Caitlin DeSilvey observes that traditionally curated objects "are preserved, most transparently, in order to stabilize memory in material form and to stabilize associated identity formations."[60] She asks what it might mean to depart from this

FIGURE 1.2 Rosamond Purcell. *Book/nest*. Photograph of found object approximately 4 ½ × 10 × 3 inches. Somerville, MA, 1990s. Photograph courtesy of the artist. © Rosamond Purcell.

tradition—"to uncouple memory work from material stability," letting go of "our sense of ourselves as autonomous agents" and instead experiencing memory "as a collaboration with an array of other materials, forces, and organisms," fluid and ever-emerging.[61] Illustrating her point, DeSilvey writes of her discovery of a wooden box in a shed on a derelict Montana homestead where she was working as a researcher and volunteer curator. The box was filled with "a grayish mass of fiber and fragments" among which nestled the remains of a collection of leather-bound books. Immediately she faced a difficult choice: "I could understand the mess as the residue of a system of human memory storage or as an impressive display of animal adaptation to available resources"—book stash or mouse nest, "artifact" or "ecofact," object to be preserved or trash to be discarded (fig. 1.2). Her challenge, as she came to understand it, was to embrace both realities, and to see both as versions of remembering, entangled in natural as well as cultural processes. The little library had released its own memories, in the process of evolving collaboratively into something else, a rodent home: structured sentences had broken down into phrases, words, and letters circulating freely on scraps of shredded paper, and the paper itself was in the process of returning to its fibrous, woody beginnings.⁶² Later, coming upon a similar "stew of paper, fabric, and animal leavings" in a bushel basket, De Silvey composed a poem from the salvaged fragments.⁶³ To remember is also to create and become.

Jerome's text may itself fall to pieces when we accept its invitation to be read in nonlinear and non-totalizing ways, and as it falls to pieces, it too may start to do a different kind of memory work. DeSilvey writes, "Conservation technologies slow or halt physical decay, while interpretive strategies present the objects as symbolic remainders from a static past." Much the same thing is true for a text as object, stabilized and conserved by a critical edition, as well as by a tradition of historically "correct" readings that privilege the text as a whole. But as DeSilvey also points out, conservation strategies "always destroy some cultural traces, even as they preserve others. And decay itself may clear a path for certain kinds of remembrance."⁶⁴ I wonder what paths might be cleared if we remove the constraints of static holism and time-bound historicity from our readings of the *Life of Hilarion*, releasing it into a wider range of its own possible becomings and rememberings.

Yes, Hilarion's story, as I have just retold it, still has a beginning and end, as does his journey. But it is already starting to loosen its grip on the narrative and spatial trajectories that structure the life of the holy man. As we let the *Life of Hilarion* decay, so to speak, textual fragments begin to break free, and the memories of earth, building, and plant mingle with those of humans. Timescales stretch and shrink. Places slide off our carefully drawn maps.

CHORIC GEOGRAPHIES

Jerome writes in Latin of a Greek-speaking island. He refers repeatedly to Hilarion's garden as *locus*—"a more remote *locus*," "an exceedingly frightening and withdrawn *locus*," a *locus* characterized by the "roughness and difficulty" of its terrain (*Life of Hilarion* 43), a *locus* that the holy man cherished (47). This place, this spot, this locality was quite particular. Hilarion loved it at first sight and came to know it intimately. Yet it was also uncanny and forbidding, hard to find, haunted by its mysterious and layered past. Hilarion inhabited the place for five years, and people visited it, despite the difficulty of the ascent and the obscurity of the path. They worried that he would leave, notorious wanderer that he was, but he did not. Indeed, he stayed there until his corpse had been laid to rest in the dirt of the garden. Curiously, ten months passed before his disciple Hesychius could remove his little body, as if Hilarion were clinging to his beloved home even in death—as if he had taken root among the fruit trees. And when his body was gone, his spirit continued to mingle with the other shades.

If Jerome had written in the language of Cyprus, he might have called Hilarion's garden *topos*, a Greek word whose meaning is quite close to that of *locus*; indeed, that is precisely the word that one of his earliest, and most literal, Greek translators chose.[65] As place, "topos is determined, located and known."[66] Capable of being mapped and surveyed, it answers the question "where?" But Greek also has another word for place—*chora*. Although *chora* can sometimes be used interchangeably with *topos*, it is more likely to be invoked to refer to the countryside, as opposed to the city. It also has a distinctive semantic range established by Plato's influential usage in his dialogue *Timaeus*, where it designates a "third kind," neither being nor becoming, that provides "shelter" for "all things that have a beginning" (Tim. 52b).[67] As interpreted by current geographers, the Platonic *chora* "is a more complex and unstable term that characterizes places in process."[68] The meaning of the word is fluid, and so is the spatial phenomenon to which it refers. "Unlike topos, chora does not stand for location."[69] In other words, it does not simply answer the question "where?" In fact, it may not answer it at all: whereas place as *topos* can be mapped and controlled, *chora* points to the indeterminacy and mystery of place, to all that remains withdrawn from our knowing mastery. Like de Certeau's "lived space," *chora* is associated with "home place" or "inhabited place"[70] that is at once familiar and uncanny, ancient and ever new—an indwelled potentiality nourished by ongoing processes of re-membering through which the past continues to be folded into the present. "Memories...carry places, and are carried by places."[71]

Let us call Hilarion's garden *chora*, then (even if Jerome's first translators did not). Let us attune ourselves to the choric geographies of Hilarion's Cyprus. Paphos is fallen, and the holy man's dwelling places cannot be located with any certainty. If the first is said to be two miles outside the city, we do not know in what direction it lies. The description of the second abandons reference to toponyms altogether, orienting the reader only by the island markers of sea and mountain, exterior and interior. Inwardly turned, Hilarion's garden is remote, withdrawn, nearly invisible. But that does not mean that it is utterly isolated or disconnected. It can be reached by a traveler crawling on hands and knees; it can be discovered by touch. If at first glance the place startles with its postcard beauty, that carefully composed image quickly dissolves, as the voices of demons fill our ears and the trees draw us in. Others have been here before us, others live here now. Off the map, we are inundated with memories, in the midst of our own becoming—tree memories, rock memories, earth memories, and more.

DESTRUCTION AND PERSISTENCE

Two biblical specters haunt Jerome's representation of the tsunami that threatens the Dalmatian coast—a return of the flood that god sent to destroy every living creature (Gen. 6:17) and a lapse back into the watery chaos that preceded the divine creation (Gen. 1:2) (*Life of Hilarion* 40). The first suggests a disastrous event, sudden and traumatic, the second an entropic process, gradual and inevitable. Both possibilities frame our interpretation of the ruins of Paphos (42) and of Hilarion's garden and the nearby temple (43). These possibilities are marked, not least, by their divergent temporalities. As Susan Stewart puts it, "Ruination happens at two speeds: furious and slow.... We do not have a sense of a moderate or proper pace for ruination precisely because it is not intended." Sites like Herculaneum and Pompeii "are especially disquieting because they compound the effects of both sudden and slow ruin," she adds. The damage of volcanic eruption—or earthquake, in the case of southwestern Cyprus—is succeeded by that of erosion and weeds. "Their slow ruination has been wreaked upon their already destroyed forms; we are seeing double: the ruin of a ruin."[72] At times it may be hard to sustain this double vision; it may be difficult to know where one layer of ruination ends and another begins, which layer to focus on, or how to feel in response. It may be hard to hear *all* the stories the ruins are telling.

Indeed, our impulse is often to simplify and reduce the complex and layered stories—to subject the ambiguities and excesses of our texts and objects to the certainties of our histories and archaeologies. "The Earthquake That Ended Antiquity" is the headline of archaeologist David Soren's popularizing account of the excavation of Kourion, announcing a story of ruination focused on crisis and transformation; Soren and his co-author argue for "the pivotal point that the disaster occupies in history, the turning away from the ancien régime, the turning toward Christianity."[73] The fourth-century Cyprus earthquake is thus inserted into the familiar story of Rome's fall and Christianity's rise. "After the great earthquake of A.D. 365, Kourion sank into the earth and was completely forgotten for a generation, until a new wave of Christian settlers gradually repopulated the abandoned site."[74] Here the earthquake seems to play a causal role in "ending antiquity" while

SETTING OUT, WITH JEROME   31

also serving as a metaphor for the upheaval brought on by Christianization. A scholarly article by archaeologist Thomas Davis delivers a similarly sensational message: "After the quakes had literally cleared the scene of the physical pagan institutions, the Cypriot Church emerges from the rubble transformed into a dynamic and expansive, international force which is evidenced by the immediate response of church building."[75]

My point is not that these accounts are wrong: Soren's and Davis's work has been crucial for my own understanding of the Kourion earthquake. But there are other possible ways to tell the story. Somewhat surprisingly, perhaps, Jerome does not assign earthquake or flood a divinely wrought or in any way pivotal role in the demise of polytheism. He alludes to a larger literary context that associates such disasters with the reign or death of the "apostate" emperor Julian, but he does not develop the connection. Instead, his account of the Adriatic tsunami focuses on Hilarion's protective response to human vulnerability. When the frightened people of Epidaurus called upon him, the holy man calmed the surging sea, and having performed this miracle, he simply left, seemingly uninterested in converting them to Christianity. Jerome's treatment of the ruins of Paphos is similarly light of touch, and his reference to the apparent "army" of demons that infested the temple ruins near Hilarion's garden is capped by the curious assertion that Hilarion was pleased to have his adversaries nearby.

The lack of explicit triumphalism is thrown into relief by a work more or less contemporaneous with Jerome's hagiography, the *Acts of Barnabas*, which assigns the ruination of a temple on Cyprus to the actions of a first-century Christian miracle-worker. According to this text, the apostle Barnabas and John Mark, the narrator, were walking along the road from Palaipaphos toward Kourion when they came upon a ceremonial procession of naked men and women in a place known for its false worship. "And Barnabas, turning, cursed it [the place]; and the western part [of the sanctuary] fell, so that many were wounded, and many of them also died and the rest fled to the temple of Apollo, which was near the city called sacred" (*Acts of Barnabas* 18). The passage raises several questions, including that of location. The city referred to may be Kourion; and the temple, that of nearby Apollo Hylates ("Apollo of the Woodlands"). Alternately, the "holy city" may be Palaipaphos; and the temple, that of nearby Rantidi, where Aphrodite's consort Adonis/Apollo was worshipped.[76] Either way, the story attributes the partial destruction of a sanctuary whose ruins were likely familiar to fifth-century readers not to an earthquake or neglect but to apostolic chastisement. Jerome's narrative choices are markedly different. Instead of a saint who brings down a temple, he gives us one who dwells near a temple's ruins and consorts with its spirits—an Adonis-like Hilarion, a Hilarion of the Woodlands.

The stories that our fragments tell do not have clear-cut beginnings or endings. They remain in process. Even the biblical flood did not kill every living creature, and not only because of Noah's heroic act of preservation: as the waters began to subside, the greening branch of an olive tree broke the surface, affirming the resilience of growing things (Gen. 7:11). Nor are chaos and decay the enemy of creation: rather, they are its matrix (Gen. 1:2);[77] "Entropy can be best described as possibility."[78] Death and destruction are real and indeed inevitable, as is grief: no created thing lasts forever, and to love is to mourn. But persistence is real, too, and a source of wonder: the tenacity of created things is only matched by the tenacity of our love for them, whether animals, plants, or objects. The structures that we make and tend, and that shape and shelter us in turn, may outlive us by a lot. When they eventually fall, whether quickly or slowly or a bit of both, the story still continues. Ruins do not cease to be homes, whether for plants or holy men, who show up and put down roots even if not invited. At the same time, the materials of made things are broken down and refashioned into new homes, whether for mice or gods: within decades perhaps, the columns of the theater in Paphos made their way into the structure of a Christian basilica. That basilica fell in turn, and another was built in the midst of its ruins; weeds still grow among the rubble. This story of persistence and emergence "trouble[s] the distinction between *making* and *growing*," between natural and cultural processes.[79] Fittingly, Ktisis ("Creation") is represented in a mosaic in a bathhouse in fifth-century Christian Kourion as the bust of an Aphrodite-like figure holding a carpenter's ruler. The image fuses divine and human making—the ongoing transformations of life and art, *eros* and *techne*.[80]

MEDIATING KNOWLEDGE

We know a place by entering its ever-changing landscape, letting our paths become part of its weaving. How, then, can I know Hilarion's Cyprus, long ago and far away? The encounter is necessarily mediated by an ancient text and its wandering holy man. Such mediation has its limits. But it also opens new possibilities of perception and understanding, as we have already begun to see. An ocean of possibility, even.

Bertrand Westphal advocates for place-centered readings that incorporate as many textual perspectives as possible, so as to bring about "the confrontation of several optics that correct, nourish, and mutually enrich each other." As he understands it, the pluralistic point of view that emerges brings us "closer to the essential identity of the referenced space."[81] In practice, that "essential identity," remains elusive for Westphal, and rightly so, it seems to me. But it is not only elusive because, from a human point of view, "the real is always mediated by various forms of textuality."[82] It is also elusive because of the complex and ever-evolving nature of places as such: choric geographies are never fully knowable or mappable. If places are ongoing interweavings of pathways of creaturely emergence and memory, they are not, strictly speaking, representable in literature or any other form of mimetic art. Yet fragments of our experience of places can be powerfully evoked, reflected on, focused, modified, or expanded in literary, visual, and performative media. Such conjured places may be purely imaginary, or they may be known in other ways too, including the mediation of our physical senses: "reality" is a measure of their wider traction in the world, perhaps—the insistence of their materialities, the density of their traces, or the layered texturing of memories they hold.

Jerome's *Life of Hilarion* conjures two especially striking fragments of spatial memory—Paphos and the hermit's mountaintop retreat. These fragments will become more potent when they are released from the human life that binds them together and allowed to circulate freely, engaging with other fragments, some texts, some objects, some drawn from more ephemeral or performative arts. Here mediation is not the problem—as if a literary text could offer no more than a partial, washed-out version of the plenitude of a direct or immediate encounter with place. Mediation is, rather, the solution, so to speak. Jerome's text—the postcard lying on my desk—has things to show us and teach us about places and about being in place, if we heed DeSilvey's call to take up an "entropic heritage practice."[83] Rather than embalming the saint, conserving "his whole body as perfect as if he were alive" (46), as Hilarion's disciple Hesychius did, we can let his (literary) *Life* decay in the garden and see what memories and new creations might emerge in the process. These literary fragments will flourish through an intensification of mediation, as they are placed in dialogue with a range of artistic media—different works, but also different forms of media. These mediations will—or so I hope—amplify the effects of our bits of text, allowing the nonhuman others whose paths are intertwined in our human ones finally to be more vividly present to us, in this place, Hilarion's Cyprus.

The six brief essays or experiments that follow are arranged in two parts, corresponding to both places—Paphos and the mountain—and topics—earthquakes and gardens. Ruins, and the life that grows in them, traverse both parts. The two parts also correspond to, and indeed grow rather directly out of, fragments of text. Let us end here, in pieces, where we will also begin again.

II
PAPHOS

Paphos,
city of Cyprus,
famous from the songs of poets,
which had frequently fallen due to earthquakes,
now only by the traces of ruins
shows what it once was.

JEROME OF STRIDON

POETRY AND PLACE

...*Paphum*	...Paphos,
urbem Cypri	city of Cyprus,
nobilem carminibus poetarum...	famous from the songs of poets...

JEROME OF STRIDON

POETS ARE MAKERS, ETYMOLOGICALLY SPEAKING: to poeticize is to fabricate or create. Poets made Paphos famous in antiquity. But more than that, poets made Paphos what it was, in part, just as Paphos left its imprint on their verse. As Bertrand Westphal observes, a geographical place and its artistic representation "are interdependent and interactive. This relationship is dynamic, subject to constant evolution."[1] Some of the most generative songs of the ancient poets still echo in our own ears, though their sounds and linguistic contexts continue to evolve and shift, as do the interactions of their images with the "real" places of embodied experience.

To approach a poem or any other text geocritically, from a place-centered perspective, may result in its fragmentation, as we have seen: some parts are highlighted and amplified, while others fade into obscurity and silence. Poetry lends itself to this process with particular ease, for it always stands in close relationship to the fragment, though the relationship takes many forms.

In ancient poetry, meter divides lines of verse from one another, while also breaking each line into rhythmic "feet" separated by tiny audial fault lines. Homeric epic in particular bears the marks of a history of composition from small, repeatable units that conform to those metric patterns.[2] In this context, iteration marks the fragment as such, whether iteration of a metric pattern or of a specific combination of words. Thus, the *Odyssey* sings:

> Straightaway to Cyprus came laughter-loving Aphrodite,
> to Paphos: there, her sanctuary and fragrant altar,
> and there the Graces bathed her and anointed her with oil
> immortal, such as gleams upon the ever-existing gods,
> and they wrapped lovely garments around her, a wonder to behold.
>   (*Odyssey* 8.362–66)

The Homeric *Hymn to Aphrodite* sounds a similar note:

> To Cyprus she [laughter-loving Aphrodite] went and entered her
>   fragrant temple,
> to Paphos: there, her sanctuary and fragrant altar.
> There, going in, she closed the shining doors,
> and there the Graces bathed her and anointed her with oil
> immortal, such as gleams upon the ever-existing gods—
> immortal, sweet, filled with fragrance it was.
> And she wrapped all her beautiful garments around her body well.
>   (58–64)

Repetition both defines and isolates the unit of poetry. It binds Paphos, the temple, the incense-burning altar, and the bathing and anointing of the goddess together in memory. At the same time, it detaches the condensed scene from its larger framing, rendering it both open and mobile. Paphos is a place to which Aphrodite may retire from the humiliation of illicit love exposed, as in the *Odyssey*, or in preparation for a seduction, as in the *Hymn*. The place-bound performance of her toilette is a fragment that can be repeated endlessly and is always in search of a narrative context.

In its Homeric form, the fragment performs a kind of spatial zoom-in: "To Cyprus, to Paphos: there, her sanctuary and fragrant altar...." In quick succession, Cyprus is displaced by Paphos, and Paphos by the goddess's sanctuary and altar. Aphrodite's sacred precinct thus comes to stand in for the whole island. Approached from afar, through a series of narrowing frames, the sanctuary looms large as a place of sensuous intimacy, appealing to smell and touch as well as vision. The altar is fragrant with the scent of incense. The goddess's body is anointed with divine oil and covered in clothing that delights both skin and eye.

The first-century geographer Strabo takes note of this literary technique and its effect on spatial representations. He comments directly on Homer's propensity to repeat the name of a place or people by referencing a part. The occasion for his reflection is the following passage from the *Odyssey*: "Having wandered about Cyprus, Phoenicia, and Egypt, as well as Ethiopia, I reached Sidon and Erembia and Libya" (Strabo 1.2.31; cf. *Od.* 4.81). "Speaking of Phoenicia, he also names Sidon, its capital city," Strabo observes (Strabo 1.2.33). Homer, in the voice of his speaker Menelaus, thereby employs a customary *schema*, or figure of speech, Strabo argues, noting further that such repetition, in which a part substitutes for the whole, can serve to call attention to the particular part, allowing more detailed description to be introduced (1.2.33). To illustrate his point, Strabo introduces a series of *exempla* drawn from the *Iliad*:

> He urged the Trojans and Hector to the ships. (Strabo 1.2.33; cf. *Il.* 13.1)
> For the sons of magnanimous Oeneus were no more;... and fair-haired Meleager was dead. (Strabo 1.2.33; cf. *Il.* 2.641)
> He came to Ida and to Gargarus. (Strabo 1.2.33; cf. *Il.* 8.47)
> He possessed Euboea, Chalcis, and Eretria. (Strabo 1.2.33; cf. *Il.* 2.536)

Here Hector is one of the Trojans, Meleager one of Oeneus's sons; Gargarus, a mountain in Ida; Chalcis and Eretria, cities in Euboea. In each case, an apparent addition to a list or sequence proves in fact to be a synecdochal iteration that narrows and deepens the focus.

Homer is not the only poet to use this figure of speech, according to Strabo. He goes on to introduce a verse of Sappho's poetry that names both the island of Cyprus and its capital city. By invoking Cyprus, the citation circles back geographically to the beginning of the Homeric line that initially provoked the geographer's discussion of spatial synecdoche: "Having wandered about Cyprus, Phoenicia, and Egypt..." (*Od.* 4.81). The Sapphic verse is so fragmentary as to be scarcely legible: "ἤ σε Κύπρος ἤ Πάφος ἤ Πάνορμος [You either Kypros or Paphos or Panormos.]"[3] But its incomplete state is not unusual. Whether due to the technique of citation, as in this case, or to the decay of papyrus (and in one case, pottery) that preserves it, Sappho's poetry is famously transmitted in a fragmentary form in which art and accident are sometimes difficult to distinguish. The entropic process that has conditioned the survival of this literary corpus as a collection of palpably incomplete texts has sometimes colluded to intensify their condensed, allusive power, a feature especially appealing to modernist sensibilities. "How I would love to know how Sappho's Fragment 31 ends," writes Judith Schalansky, in a performance of longing for lost things.[4] Anne Carson makes the most of the allure of the fragmentary, titling her edition and translation of Sappho's work "If Not, Winter"—an enigmatically open-ended line from Fragment 22—and allowing each of Sappho's poetic fragments to float alone in the blank space of a full page.[5] "Poetry, more than any other literary form, has come to be associated with the pregnant void, the blank space that breeds conjecture," notes Schalansky. "Intact, Sappho's poems would be as alien to us as the once gaudily painted classical sculptures."[6]

Translating fragments is especially challenging, due to the lack of context. Carson's rendering of the Sapphic fragment in Strabo, cited above, conforms to August Meineke's still widely followed 1852 edition of Strabo, without trying to force sense on the partial verse. Rather, its possible meanings are left open and unresolved. However, other English translators have tended to follow the emendation suggested by the sixteenth-century editor Isaac Casaubon, reading *panormos* as an adjective rather than a place name.[7] Thus H. C. Hamilton translates the verse as follows (omitting to translate *se*):

> Whether Cyprus, or the spacious-harbored Paphos.[8]

Horace Leonard Jones goes further, filling the remaining gap with the conjectured verb "holds":

> Either Cyprus or Paphos of the spacious harbor holds thee.[9]

Regardless of which version of the text one follows, "you" (*se*), which appears in the accusative case, is probably to be understood as the direct object of a missing verb, one that Jones does not hesitate to supply. But who is the "you" addressed? Is it Aphrodite, as elsewhere in Sappho's poems? Often Sappho addresses the goddess directly and imperatively, in the vocative case (*su*):

> ...You [*su*]
> be my ally. (frag. 1)

> In this place you [*su*] Kypris taking up
> in gold cups delicately
> nectar mingled with festivities:
>   pour. (frag. 2)[10]

Sometimes, however, the poet references the goddess as "you" in the accusative case, whether in indirect command or narration:

...I beg you [se]. (frag. 1)
...And fine birds brought you [se]. (frag. 1)[11]

In the fragment preserved by Strabo, Cyprus appears to be in the subject position, Aphrodite (if it is indeed she) in the object position: *Cyprus, Paphos,...you. Cyprus, Paphos*, birthed, nurtured, drew, held, housed, honored *you*, O goddess. The possibilities multiply, as the fragment seeks supplementation.

The synecdochal movement inscribed in the Homeric fragments—*to Cyprus, to Paphos*—seems to be reflected not only in the Sapphic fragment but also in the manuscript tradition of Euripides's *Bacchae*. In the second choral ode of the tragedy, the female followers of Dionysos express their longing to be transported elsewhere:

> Would that I could go to Cyprus,
>   to the island of Aphrodite,
> where dwell the love-gods
> who charm the hearts of mortals,
> and to Paphos, which the hundred-mouthed
> streams of an alien river
> water without rain. (402–408)

Most scholars agree that the description of Paphos refers to the Nile, which presents a geographical problem, given the distance that separates Paphos from the famous river.[12] Thus Paphos should probably be emended to Pharos, an island in the Nile delta with Dionysian associations.[13] But to what should we attribute the seemingly blatant error that crept into the manuscript tradition? Perhaps it was the iterative force of the Homeric fragment that caused a scribe to write Paphos in place of Pharos and allowed the change to stick so stubbornly. To Cyprus, to Paphos, we long to go, borne on the desire of a persistent verse!

By the time Strabo recorded Sappho's verse, and perhaps by the time Euripides's verse had transformed itself as well, the Homeric fragment had also hopped across a linguistic border. The Latin of Vergil's *Aeneid* takes us immediately to Paphos as the site of the goddess's temple.

> She herself to Paphos goes, borne aloft, and revisits her abode
> joyfully, where her temple is, and a hundred altars

glow with Sabaean incense, and are fragrant with fresh garlands.
(1.415–417)

Here Vergil has not merely translated but intensified the Homeric description. The incense-burning altar is now a multitude, and the fragrance of incense, exotic in its explicit orientalism, is augmented by the scent of flowers, an addition that is no surprise in this notably plant-attuned poet.[14]

Jerome certainly has Vergil's lines in mind, among others, when he describes Paphos as "a city of Cyprus famous from the songs of poets." The extravagance of Vergil's description of a hundred garlanded altars burning makes the contrast even more vivid when Jerome reports that "only the traces of ruins now reveal what it once was." Whether those traces are to be understood as the ruins of New Paphos (the city) or of Old Paphos (the sanctuary site) is unclear, as we have seen. City and sanctuary had been distinct since the founding of New Paphos in about 320 BCE. However, the distinction collapses when Paphos is seen through the lens of the poetic tradition, in which the city is virtually equated with the goddess's sanctuary for which it was famed. This archaizing view proves surprisingly enduring. By the medieval period, pilgrims and other travelers simply assumed that New Paphos, the only Paphos in evidence, was the site of the sanctuary, mistaking other urban ruins for the goddess's temple, as we have seen. Even after the ruins of the sanctuary at Old Paphos were discovered in the sixteenth century, the tendency to conflate the two persisted, leaving modern archaeology to attempt to set the story straight.[15] If Jerome knows the difference, he does not acknowledge it here. What matters in his text is not which ruins we see but all that we as readers do not see or smell or feel. Aphrodite's Cyprus, her Paphos, her sacred precinct, is no longer fragrant with the scent of incense and flowers; its hundred altars are all cold, its monuments toppled.

Elsewhere in late ancient literature, the Paphos of Homer and Vergil still flourishes, however. Writing roughly a decade after Jerome pens his Saint's Life, the Latin poet Claudian evokes a Cyprus of revivified myth, vibrant and lush, thriving not in the past but in the poetic present.[16] In Claudian's poem, which celebrates the marriage of the emperor Honorius and his bride Maria in 398, it is winged Amor, rather than Venus herself, who approaches the goddess's dwelling from across the sea. Venus's domain is set on a plain atop a rugged mountain "inaccessible by human foot" (*Epithalamium de nuptiis Honorii et Mariae* 50) and so vast that it simultaneously overshadows the Ionian mainland to the northwest and faces the island of Pharos and the Nile delta to the southwest. From this vantage point, Euripides's (corrupted?)

text does not seem so far-fetched after all: the mountain of Cyprus and the mouth of the Nile gaze upon each other across the sea. Old Paphos may be the implied location of the mountain. Later in the poem, Venus's mount, the sea-monster Triton, is said to come ashore on the "Paphian sands" (148), and Venus herself says to Maria, "For you I left my Paphian abode and Cyprus," thereby reversing the Homeric move from whole to part (254).[17] Here, however, the city is not named, and the setting, like that of Hilarion's garden, seems remote rather than urban or even exurban, lofty rather than coastal or even near the coast. Moreover, the impression given is less of a move from the whole to the part—Cyprus, Paphos, sanctuary—than of a collapse of the whole into the part, as if Venus's precinct were coterminus with the island itself. The zoom-in effect is still in play, but it is achieved not by a progressive narrowing of the spatial field, as in the Greek poems, but by movement through space, in an elaborate ecphrasis of the sanctuary that "progresses sequentially from the encircling to the encircled"—that is, from wall to grove to palace.[18] And the scene of Venus's toilette at which we eventually arrive does not evoke a sense of intimacy so much as of awe. Indeed, as Michael Roberts puts it, "The whole movement of Claudian's description, moving from periphery to center, is contrived to increase the reader's sense of Venus' majesty." He adds, "The progression is reminiscent of the organization of imperial palaces, or Christian basilicas."[19] The approach has the air of a processional.

Venus's mountain enjoys an eternal spring, we read, in a passage laced with allusions to poetic convention and canon.[20] Enclosed, within golden fences, "her lands are vibrant and, although subjected to no cultivation, they blossom perpetually," writes Claudian (60–61). Only the most tuneful birds flit among the trees, and the trees themselves are redolent with pleasure. "The leafing branches live for desire [*in venerem*] and in turn every happy tree loves [*amat*]: the palms nod in mutual marriages, poplar sighs poplar-struck, and planes whisper to planes and alder to alder" (65–68). Springs flow. Nymphs, cupids, and other minor deities revel. At the center is Venus' domicile, gleaming with gold and precious gems, and fragrant with gardens of herbs and flowers—as Alan Cameron puts it, "positively reeking with all the rarest odours."[21]

The over-the-top rhetoricity of Claudian's description is typical of late ancient poetry, as is the allusive, bricolage-like style.[22] Both features contribute to an aesthetics of the fragment. However surprising it may initially seem that descriptive excess should be aligned with the fragmentary, excessiveness does indeed go hand in hand with fragmentation: too much is the ally of too little in resisting wholeness. Late ancient ecphrasis—the rhetorical technique of producing vivid word pictures—operates by breaking an image down into as many parts as possible, enumerating details to often overwhelming effect in a highly structured play of repetition and variation—not a forest but palms, poplar, planes, alder, and not a tree but a multitude of branches and leaves. As Roberts notes, "It was as though texts were put under a microscope, magnifying the constituent parts at the expense of the whole."[23] At the same time, through this very process of magnification, description becomes detached from any larger context of narration or argumentation. Each ecphrastic segment is a miniature world unto itself, like a jewel or a flower. "The art of the poet was akin to that of the jeweler—to manipulate brilliant pieces...and to throw them into relief by effects of contrast and juxtaposition," writes Roberts. "The poet strives for an impression equivalent to that of a flower-covered meadow in spring."[24] As Jaś Elsner and Jesús Hernández Lobato put it, late ancient poetry "privileges the part over the whole and breaks up the literary/artistic experience into a kaleidoscope of sharp close-ups."[25] It is parts all the way down and up. Each fragment is, in principle, infinitely divisible and also infinitely combinable.

Reading Claudian's passage alongside Jerome's, we note striking similarities as well as obvious differences. If Claudian overwhelms totality with excess, what of Jerome? As we have seen, the latter simultaneously invokes and erases the poetic tradition, in a highly condensed fragment of text—"Paphos, city of Cyprus, famous from the songs of poets, which...now reveals what it once was only by the traces of ruins" (*Life of Hilarion* 42). Having consigned the Paphos of the poets to the past, Jerome directs his readers' attention to his hermit's dwelling place, located in the neglected ruins of a temple, "among remote and harsh mountains that could scarcely be climbed by crawling on hands and knees" (42). Claudian effects a similar spatial and literary displacement, but it is Venus's sacred precinct, traditionally associated with Paphos, that is transported to an unnamed and inaccessible mountaintop, described in lavish language. Both gardens are untended yet fertile, although we are told that Hilarion does not eat the fruit of his trees. Both gardens flow with springs and are encircled, albeit with trees rather than golden walls in the hermit's case. Both gardens are near a temple, although Hilarion's temple is in ruins, and both are haunted by spirits, although Hilarion describes these as demons rather than deities.

It may seem that Claudian's particular "art of the fragment" gestures nostalgically toward a restoral of lost wholeness through a performance of ecphrastic plenitude, while Jerome's depiction of ruins shatters worldly wholeness in order to overcome and replace it with the fullness of eternity's totalizing bliss. Yet I would suggest, alternatively, that the performative inexhaustibility of ecphrasis in Claudian's text keeps his description of Venus's sanctuary open and unfinished, while also unmooring it from both the prior poetic tradition and the immediate rhetorical context—namely, the celebration of the marriage of Honoris and Maria.[26] At the same time, Jerome's highly episodic style of narration and his minimalist, even apophatic, representation of Paphos as the ruination of poetic description likewise resists closure or wholeness. We might say that both Claudian and Jerome push poetic iteration past its limit: it is not repetition, as with the epic tradition, but the dramatic subversion of repetition that here marks the literary fragment as such, via either the excesses of descriptive variation that threaten to explode the poetic tradition or the austere negation of the poetic canon itself. On the one hand, Claudian's lavish description, as well as his wanton allusiveness, mimic the boundless growth of the vegetal realm, which is ever incomplete: there is no end to it. The goddess's fertility, embodied in the landscape of a *mons veneris*, overtakes the island, and Paphos is lost in the luxuriant growth. On the other hand, Jerome's ruined description insists on the finality of fragmentation without rendering the fragment static or sterile: the remains of Paphos give way to the remains of a garden where the holy man thrives, flourishing like a weed—one fragmentary being among others.

However different they may be, both landscapes—Claudian's as well as Jerome's—open themselves to futures yet unknown, indeed never to be fully known. The Paphos of these late ancient poets is caught up in larger processes of becoming-other, processes that evade the teleologies of both history and theology: Christianization never unfolds exactly as we might expect. Claudian's religious affiliations are uncertain. And the Christian poets of sixth-century Constantinople whose works are preserved in the Cycle of Agathias invoke the ancient goddess of love with perhaps surprising frequency. Referring to her as "the Cyprian" or "the Paphian" while honoring her presence in local places, they thereby translate her island abode to the baths and bedrooms of Christian Byzantium.[27] As for Jerome's text, the Paphos that is "famous from the songs of poets" remains open for reinterpretation and reappropriation. The author who elsewhere imagines himself divinely judged and condemned for reading Cicero and Plautus (*Ep.* 22.30) does not control this passage: that Jerome remains outside the margins of the fragment that speaks of the generativity of poetry and place. True, Jerome has not sung the poets' songs for us in his *Life of Hilarion*, but we hear them anyway, echoing through his text. *To Cyprus, to Paphos*. A fragment repeats itself persistently, traveling across texts, across centuries. It exceeds itself, erases itself, falls apart, comes together again, each time a little bit differently, attached to new contexts. Someone enters Paphos, again and again—a goddess, a saint, a supplicant or pilgrim, an exile or refugee. They arrive from afar but discover themselves at home, neither strangers nor natives, in the city made famous by poets. *There*, remains of the past, at once literary and architectural and vegetal; *there*, futures in the making.

Of course, poets continue to sing today of Cyprus, of Paphos, of the goddess's sacred precinct. They sing in the tongues of Greek, Turkish, English, and more. Their Cyprus is "Mother Mary's and Ummu Haram's, Aysaaba- and Zoi-women's, a Christian saint's and a Muslim saint's small country," in the words of Turkish-speaking poet Fikret Demirag (1940–2010).[28] That is to say, it is the domain of Christ's mother and Mohammad's aunt, of women with both Turkish and Greek names, of saints both Christian and Muslim. But that is not all. Demirag does not hesitate also to claim "coquettish, mind bender Aphrodite [who] came out to your shores from the waves of the ancient and wise Mediterranean," as part of his own complex Cypriot heritage.[29] In *From Limnidi's Fire Until Today*, he works his way forward from the prehistoric era of his island home's past, depicting empires sweeping through Cyprus like hurricanes—Assyrians, Egyptians, Persians, Macedonians, Romans. New religions arrived with them. "Reading secrets that echoed in old Baf's streets," Demirag reports that "a new young tree loaded with commentary of belief / sprouted from the soil with an unbelievable speed / stretching its branches to Sergius Paulus." (A note explains that when "Apostle Barnabas visited Baf [Paphos], the capital of Roman Cyprus, he persuaded the Roman governor Paulus to adopt Christianity."[30]) Later, Byzantines, Franks, Venetians, Ottomans blew in too. "With a prayer they hit your shores, making your soil shiver. [...] An Ottoman hurricane!"[31] Excavating the island's layered history, Demirag produces what postcolonial literary scholar Bahriye Kemal refers to as a "spatial palimpsestic archaeology of Cyprus."[32] As Kemal argues, his work exposes histories of colonialism, most recently British, while also disrupting the nationalistic discourses that keep the partitioned island in a political deadlock. Rather than looking for a single, definitive narrative of origins, the poet celebrates the rich fusion of religious and cultural traditions that have shaped Cyprus: "Oh You: icons and writings of *Bismillah ir-Rahman ir-Rahim* and statues of Aphrodite."[33]

In "Requiem for Trikomo," Demirag's younger contemporary, the Anglophone poet Stephanos Stephanides (b. 1951), reaches for memories more intimately personal if also richly layered, recalling a Cypriot childhood crowded with images of goddesses, including those of the cinema:

> In my smallness I catch sight
> Of fractured Aphrodites and redolent Madonnas,
> And on screens wavering with night breeze
> I filch glances of the sacred in ruinous passion
> Melina's husky melody in black and white[34]
> Sophia wet and surging from the blue
> Rescuing my totem the dolphin
> And the boy ready to ride away[35]

According to Herodotus, a bronze statue once commemorated a dolphin's rescue of the ancient Greek poet Aion from drowning (Herodotus 1.23–24). That tradition may have inspired the gold statue supposedly discovered at the bottom of the sea by Phaedra, a Greek sponge diver played by Sophia Loren in the 1957 film *Boy on a Dolphin*. Like a boy or a poet on a dolphin, Stephanides was carried away from Cyprus to Britain as a small child. Thenceforth he lived between and among islands, as he describes it in both poetry and memoir. Cyprus, and specifically the village of Trikomo, is a place from which Stephanides has departed and to which he is continually returning, in memory as well as in flesh, crossing both seas and barbed-wire partitions. *To Cyprus, to Trikomo*.

In "Between Sweet Well Water and the Salty Sea," Stephanides writes of

> the wet touch of island memories
> lingering like aged shadows of
> goddesses who dropped their buckets deep
> to cool well water [...]
> or who rode the foam to travel far [...]
> goddesses frozen like little statuettes
> the Aphrodites du Trikomo in the Louvre[36]

Here he discovers divinity in the old women of the village who drew water for him to drink, and also in women like his mother, who left the island for distant shores. Once flesh and blood, they are now like figurines gathered in the shrine of the poet's memory. Stephanides imagines them as so many "Aphrodites of Trikomo," with reference to the archaic limestone sculpture of the goddess discovered near the village and now housed in the Louvre—wide-eyed, sturdy, and decorous, in contrast to her more voluptuous Hellenic representations (fig. 2.1).[37]

In another work, "Postcards from Cyprus (Made in India)," Stephanides collaborates with photographer Anandana Kapur: "I hail a friend from far away / Anandana the blissful one, / To send me visions of an eye land."[38] Kapur's eighteen photographs of Cyprus, which "She / framed as postcards / (made in India)," elicit his poetic response, itself a kind of contemplation or beholding, at once Greek *theoria* and Sanskrit *darshan*.[39] Stephanides is a self-proclaimed θεωρός, or seer, converting images into "words [...] celebrating their *nostos*," or homecoming.[40] Writing (on) Kapur's postcards, he sends them back to Cyprus. His own geographical location, like Kapur's, is unclear; or rather, both artists are implicitly nomadic, dwellers of between-spaces. At once native and stranger to Cyprus, Stephanides is not the only one who has returned from afar. In Kapur's photos "an abundance of Aphrodite revenants" is revealed:[41] the goddess returns too, again and again.

In one photograph, we see a plaster bas-relief copy of a now-iconic, first-century BCE marble sculpture of the goddess from Soloi, inscribed "Aphrodite of Cyprus"; thighs, pubic area, and breasts are lit from below, suggesting that the figure may be prone and possibly no more than souvenir-sized (though the scale is difficult to read).[42] This is no random image. The Soloi Aphrodite has become the poster child of the Cyprus Tourism Organization, conveying the allure of legible Greekness (figs. 2.2, 2.4). "Nudity combined with marble instantly evoke the artistic canon of the Greek World," as Christine Morris and Giorgos Papantoniou note. "In addition her fragmentary condition (missing her arms and lower legs) evokes the romantic idealization of the fragmented body or ruined site."[43] In Kapur's photographs, the "stony grey" color of the plaster replica of the Soloi goddess is echoed in adjacent images of "glazed and wooden / Mannequins erect in lingerie" standing in a storefront labeled "NO BORDER Underwear"; one is headless and positioned in a window over a garbage can.[44] Is sex, however tawdry, exploitative, or even abusive, one place where the "wiry borders" of a partitioned state and capital city—Nicosia—come down?[45] Another photograph shows an old woman crocheting lace in a shadowy and otherwise empty arcade. This image faces a photograph of boxes of sugar-dusted fruit candies displayed on a sunny sidewalk in front of a store called (like the candies)

FIGURE 2.1 Aphrodite of Trikomo, also known as Lady of Trikomo. Archaic Cypriot, around 500 BCE. Limestone with polychromy, 97.5 × 47 × 24 cm. Musée du Louvre, Paris, France. Photographer, Franck Raux. © RMN-Grand Palais/Art Resource, NY/Art Resource.

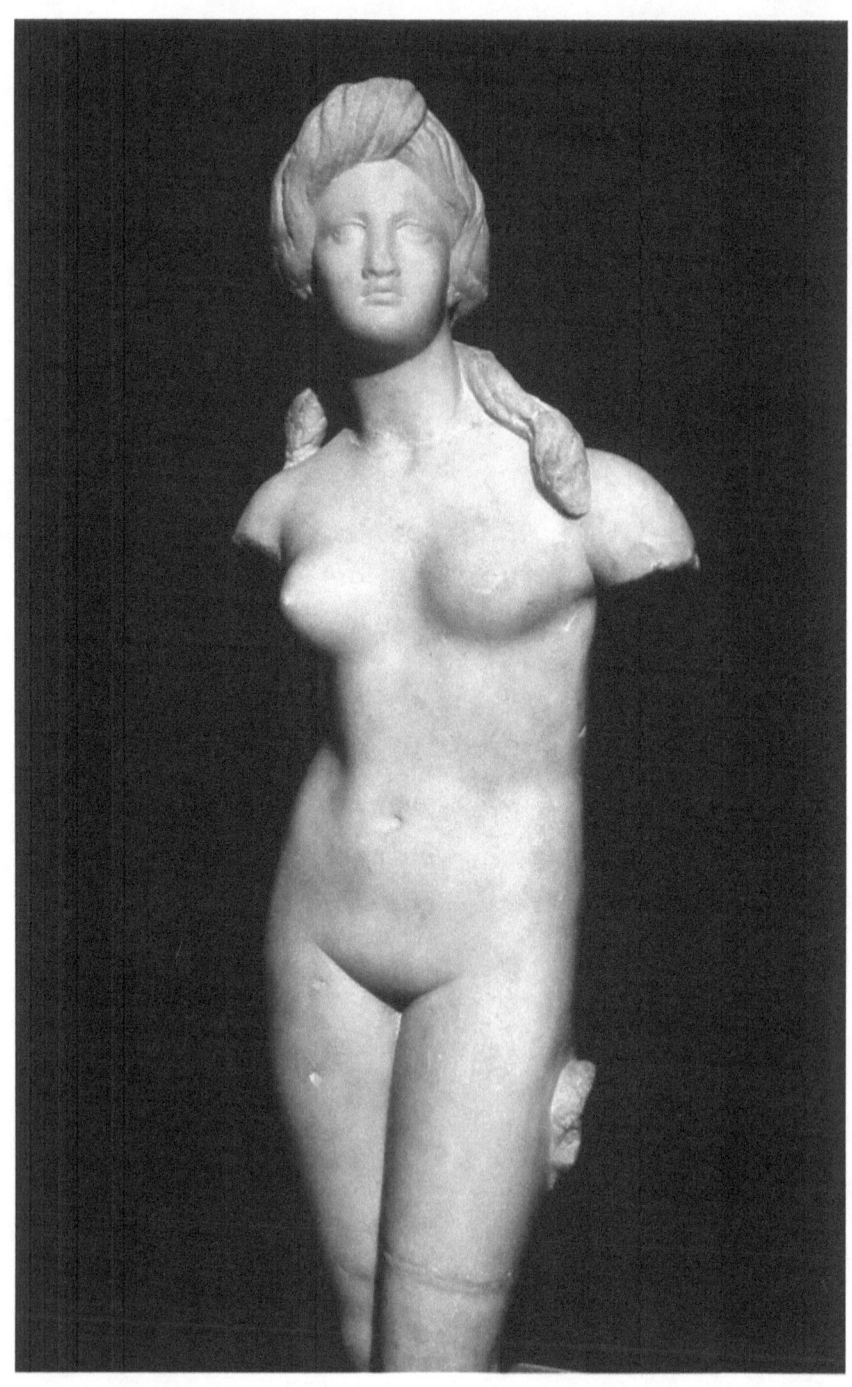

FIGURE 2.2 Aphrodite of Soloi. Soloi, Cyprus, First century BCE. Marble. Archaeological Museum, Nicosia, Cyprus. © HIP/Art Resource, NY.

"Aphrodite Delights"—treats "too jellied and excessive for the old and weary," as Stephanides writes.[46] "Aphrodite Delights," a specialty of Geroskipos near Paphos, are elsewhere on the island called "Turkish Delights," just as Aphrodite herself is elsewhere referred to as "Venus," in careful avoidance of Greek nomenclature; like the Soloi goddess, the candies are primarily packaged for tourist consumption.[47] Below the photograph of the lace maker, another shows a young Asian woman who echoes her seated posture and working hands while engaging a young girl (her daughter?). Next to this is a photograph of an altar holding both a cross and a vase of sacred basil, a plant said to have been brought to Cyprus from India by the Roman empress Helena, mother of Constantine, as Stephanides explains.[48] Like Stephanides himself, the goddess has returned to Cyprus from all over the globe.

Indeed, she is everywhere, diverse in her incarnations and significations. Travelers since the medieval period have sought her in the coastal city of (New) Paphos. Modern archaeologists have relocated her inland in the ruins of Old Paphos, or Kouklia, and elsewhere. Contemporary tourists are invited to see her rising from the sea by the "Rock of Aphrodite," a romantic site near Paphos that has become an icon of Cyprus as a whole (figs. 2.3, 2.4).[49] But the poets are able to see the wider spread of the Cypriot divinity, in "fractured Aphrodites and redolent Madonnas" (Stephanides),[50] in "icons and writings of *Bismillah ir-Rahman ir-Rahim* and statues of Aphrodite" (Demirag),[51] in women of the villages, in women haunting the border zones of a partitioned capital, in women who have left, to dream of return.

"He proceeded to Cyprus.... Having then entered Paphos,... he dwelled in obscurity" (*Life of Hilarion* 42). As Jerome describes it, Hilarion reaches Cyprus by sea. He disembarks at Paphos. And he continues on, only stopping when he is a few miles beyond the city gates, relieved to have gained a bit of peace and quiet. In this he is not unlike the goddess herself, ever returning to Cyprus, to Paphos, to the safe haven of her famous sanctuary outside the city. Indeed, the saint becomes part of the goddess's poetic iteration, caught up in her fragmentary dissemination across Cypriot space and history, as it was performed in antiquity and continues to be performed by contemporary writers. This would not be the first time Aphrodite appeared in disguise, cloaked in the veil of mortality, though it might be one of her best disguises yet.

FIGURE 2.3 Rock of Aphrodite. Paphos, Cyprus. © Joana Kruse/Alamy Stock Photo.

FIGURE 2.4 1979 Cyprus stamp with Aphrodite of Soloi and Rock of Aphrodite. Photograph courtesy of the Cyprus Department of Postal Services.

To recognize the goddess in the saint is not only to acknowledge the fecund force of desire that he both embodies and attracts, drawing crowds within a few weeks of his arrival.[52] It is also to attend to the saint's particular attachment to Paphos as sacred landscape and connective hub—a place of sea-borne comings and goings, meetings and minglings. Lacking relics or shrine on the island, just as the goddess now lacks altar and sanctuary, Hilarion is all the more present in the place through the literary relics of Jerome's enigmatic text, condensed, distilled, and fragmentary—not, in the end, an erasure of the Paphos of the poets so much as a radical reinscription. To Cyprus, to Paphos, we go still, carried by the winds of a church father's imagination.

CURATING EARTHQUAKES

...*Paphum*
urbem Cypri
...*quae frequenter terrae motu*
  lapsa

JEROME OF STRIDON

...Paphos,
city of Cyprus,
...which had frequently fallen due
  to earthquakes

HOW MANY TIMES HAD PAPHOS suffered damage from earthquakes by 364 CE, when Hilarion may have arrived, or by 385, when Jerome visited Cyprus and first conceived the story of the saint? Often enough, evidently, that the city had a reputation for such disasters, and recently enough that the damage was still evident. Such seismic activity is not surprising, from the perspective of contemporary theories of plate tectonics. Paphos sits on the northern edge of the Cyprian Arc, where the north-drifting African and west-drifting Anatolian plates meet, an inherently vulnerable zone. In addition, a tear-fault runs roughly perpendicular to the arc near Paphos; this fault produced a magnitude-6.8 earthquake as recently as 1996.[1]

The field of seismotectonics is young, and the seismological data on which it is partly based also lacks historical depth: while relevant measurements began to be collected in neighboring countries as early as 1896, Cyprus first installed its own seismological station in 1984.[2] And even one hundred and twenty-five years are but a blink of the eye when it comes to the creeping—and occasionally jolting—movements of the earth's lithosphere. The detection of long-term patterns that might help predict future trends—a central concern of seismology—requires assembling catalogs that give witness to earthquakes that predate the use of seismographic instruments by centuries or even millennia. The beginnings of such a project can be dated to 1457, when the Renaissance humanist Giannozzo Manetti composed *De terraemotu*, recording a hundred seismic events in the Mediterranean region, together with their ancient and medieval sources.[3] It continues into the present, as with the "Advanced National Seismic System Earthquake Catalog" on the United States Geological Survey website, a worldwide database searchable by earthquake magnitude, date and time, and geographical region.[4]

At the risk of leaning into an already overused word,[5] we might think of the earthquake catalog not only as a scientific instrument but also as part of the art of *curating* earthquakes. Evidence is collected, culled, preserved, and displayed in such a way as to highlight a certain phenomenon, create a certain effect, or tell a certain story. In the case of catalogs of historical earthquakes that are dependent on written sources, the relevant passages from the sources are listed and sometimes even cited in full. The result is a compilation of textual fragments whose differences are partly flattened and ambiguities glossed over, so as to produce a clear and well-ordered archive. The fragment from Jerome's *Life of Hilarion* regularly appears in such compilations, although, tellingly, it is not always assigned to the same earthquake.[6]

As historical seismology has developed in the twentieth and twenty-first centuries, following the invention of the seismograph, increasing sophistication in the critical use of historical sources has sometimes been in tension with the implementation of quantitative parameters for classifying earthquakes. If the former tends to highlight the uncertainty of the evidence our sources provide, the latter calls for precise numerical estimates of seismic intensity and magnitude, in addition to date and epicenter location. In 1965, Nicholas Ambraseys published "The Seismic History of Cyprus," cataloging dates, locations, and intensities for earthquakes prior to 1900. In this article, the renowned seismologist confesses, "My chief difficulty has been the assessment of the intensities of these earthquakes."[7] Relying primarily (but not exclusively) on "the degree of damage to public buildings and the human reactions to the shock," as recorded in his historical sources, he assigns numerical intensities to most of the forty-six recorded earthquakes, while acknowledging that his assessments "are purely subjective and that personal differences in this estimation, even under otherwise equivalent circumstances, could exist."[8] Twelve of the seismic events that he records are said to have affected Paphos, with dates ranging across three millennia, from 1500 BCE to 1567 CE, and at intensities ranging from VI ("strong") to X ("extreme"), on the I to XII Modified Mercalli scale.[9] Ambraseys's account of fourth-century earthquakes in this article is now somewhat dated, a reminder of how rapidly the field of historical seismology is still evolving on all fronts—geological, archaeological, and literary. He reckons that an earthquake circa 367 in Kourion, near Paphos, reached an intensity level of VII ("very strong") or VIII ("severe").[10] However, David Soren, who led archaeological excavations at Kourion in the 1980s, has suggested that the maximum intensity of the earthquake that likely destroyed both Kourion and Paphos in 365 (not 367) CE was between IX ("violent") and XII ("enormous catastrophe") in both places.[11] At Kourion the shock waves were strong enough to lift and hurl an eight-hundred-pound stone feeding trough.[12] Based on literary as well as archaeological sources, Emanuela Guidoboni similarly estimates that the intensity at Paphos was between IX ("violent") and XI ("catastrophe").[13]

Seismologists sometimes also attempt to estimate the overall strength of historical earthquakes, a parameter referred to as magnitude. For example, Terry C. Wallace proposes that the earthquake that destroyed Kourion would have had a magnitude of 7.25 on the Richter scale.[14] However, the experienced intensity of the earth's shaking in a given place—a subjective measurement, as Ambraseys emphasizes—is more directly accessible than a quake's objective magnitude, in the case of historical earthquakes. More typically, then, it is the intensities that are cataloged. And often it is the intensity that tells the story that matters, regardless of when the earthquake took place. As Michel Serres writes after experiencing an earthquake in California in 1989, "At 7.2 [on the Richter scale], the Loma Prieta quake which I suffered from but which delighted me, caused some material damage and fifty-seven victims, whereas two hundred and fifty thousand Haitians died in Port-au-Prince, recently, for less intensity on the Richter scale."[15] More accurately, more than two hundred and fifty thousand Haitians died in the 2010 quake for comparable *magnitude*—7.0 versus the 6.9 officially assigned to the Loma Prieta quake. It was precisely the *intensity* of the earth's shaking that was so great in Haiti, due to the shallow depth of the quake, the effects of which were further amplified by "human, collective, political, economic social conditions—poverty, for example," as Serres notes.[16] As I write, Haiti has just been shaken again by 7.2 quake, in the midst of a tropical storm and enormous political turmoil. How to quantify such convergent forces?

As we have seen, earthquake intensity is customarily measured by an earthquake's effects on human bodies (the lower, more sensitive end of the scale) and human-built structures (the higher, less sensitive end) in specific places. The scale tops out when the effects on buildings have been saturated:

"XII. Damage is total." It is in part because of their special relationship to architecture, as well as geology, that earthquakes are such strongly spacial and spatializing events. They mark places and are themselves defined and contoured by place. Human bodies, moving between places, can sense and record the intensity of earthquakes in those places, without necessarily being fatally or even deeply affected by that intensity; seismographs serve as technological extensions of such human power, lending both precision and locational stability to the task. Buildings, on the other hand, have no choice but to suffer in feeling and remembering. The sensation and record of earthquakes is written on their bodies, up to the point of complete ruination. When humans suffer significantly from earthquakes, it is usually a secondary effect of the damage to the built, or in some cases the natural, environment: their bodies are vulnerable to being struck or crushed by displaced objects (including water).

There is, then, a terrifying intimacy to the standard measurements of earthquake intensity, exposing both the sensitivity and the vulnerability of human beings and their built worlds. *Terrae motus*: the earth moves. Its surface gapes, slides, buckles, trembles, jerks. It moves other beings in turn. How forcefully does the quaking earth move a human, whether directly or through other objects that it puts in motion? How acutely does the human feel its motion physically? How strongly does the human react emotionally? How much intellectual or cultural activity is incited? How much rebuilding takes place? These may all be considered questions of intensity, posed from a human perspective. Of course, it is possible to look elsewhere too: humans and their dwellings are not the only beings that sense and remember the intensity of the earth's movements. Rocks also have stories to tell, and so do trees. More firmly rooted in the earth than most built structures, trees are also more supple and adaptive, thus potentially more tenacious and articulate in their memories. Whether living or dead (in the case of a "ghost forest"), a forest can be a kind of archive, particularly eloquent with respect to the dating of earthquakes, and thus to calculating their frequency and likely recurrence in a given place.[17]

While the frequency of earthquakes is distinct from their intensity, frequency can collude with intensity, as Jerome's text invites us to consider. We might even say it can intensify intensity. Buildings that have already been shaken may be quicker to collapse when shaken again. And humans who have experienced one earthquake tend to become more attuned subsequently to the sensation of terrestrial tremors: we recall Serres's claim that his experience of the Loma Prieta earthquake in California "transformed [his body] into a sensitive seismograph."[18] Thus humans and other beings may be affected physically, emotionally, and imaginatively by the cumulative number and frequency of earthquakes experienced, as much as by the intensity of a particular quake. And earthquake-prone areas like late ancient Paphos (as Jerome presents it) are shaped by such shared, repeated experiences; the earth's movements become part of the collective knowledge and affect of the place, whether traumatized or resilient.

Earthquake catalogs record and display, with minimalist economy, the unpredictable rhythms and intensities of shock that are inscribed in Paphos's past. The following excerpt of Paphos-specific entries from Ambraseys's 1965 Cypriot catalog would no longer be considered historically accurate, much less complete; for starters, Ambraseys wrongly assigns a 342 CE quake centered near Salamis, on the opposite side of the island, to Paphos,[19] and his catalog lacks reference to the Kourion-centered earthquake that also affected Paphos circa 365 CE.[20] But both completeness and accuracy are illusory goals in this case, and Ambraseys's catalog speaks eloquently to a spatial experience punctuated by upheaval and haunted by memories much longer than those of any single human. As a place, Paphos knows that there are no unshakable foundations and that change, whether gradual or sudden, is inevitable.

1495 BC	Paphos (?)
26	Paphos (VII)
15	Paphos (IX)
6?	Paphos (VII)
342 AD	Paphos (X—)
394	Paphos (VII ?)
1144, May 19	Paphos (VII ?)
1183	Paphos (VIII)
1222, May	Paphos (IX)
1481, May 3	Paphos (VI)
1481, Dec 18	Paphos (V)
1567, Dec	Paphos (VI)[21]

Catalogs are, of course, only one way of curating historical earthquakes, and they are not the most obvious. Museums are the traditional sites of curatorial work. The American Museum of Natural History in New York City, for example, includes a set of earthquake exhibits in the Hall of Planet Earth, one of which is devoted to America's most active and famous earthquake zone, the San Andreas Fault, located on the boundary between the Pacific and North American plates. A placard in front of an exhibit of a fault scarp warns that earthquakes are "inherently unpredictable." Another placard, labeled forthrightly "Can we predict earthquakes?" answers its own question mostly in the negative, noting that "the majority of earthquakes...strike unannounced, causing tragic loss of life." Yet the goal of seismological measurement remains predictive, even from the perspective of this museum. Another exhibit features a recorder "showing real-time ground shaking at stations in Alaska, Arizona, and Japan." There a placard reads, "Recording both large and small earthquakes helps us understand the structure of Earth and points to where earthquakes are likely to occur in the future."[22] Earthquakes always arrive as a shock, yet they imprint the historical record—seismological, geological, archaeological, and literary—with a forcefulness that opens up sight lines into the future. Curating the past, these museum exhibits also raise the question of how we anticipate and prepare for the unpredictable.

A museum in Episkopi in the district of Limassol in Cyprus frames the question more intimately. Focusing attention not on "Planet Earth" but on one very particular place on that planet, the Local Kourion Archaeological Museum is housed in two rooms of a former residence and dig house. One room contains Bronze Age finds from Kourion and the surrounding area, while the Main Exhibition Room includes later finds, most notably from the Sanctuary of Apollo, the so-called Earthquake House, and the Christian basilicas constructed in the aftermath of the earthquake.

As the museum website notes, "The skeletal remains of inhabitants of the city who lost their lives in the 4th century earthquakes constitute one of the most impressive exhibits of the room."[23] Displayed in a low, glass-covered case in the center of the room, three delicately entangled skeletons lie partly embedded in dirt, mimicking the state in which they were found in 1986 amidst the ruins of a house that had collapsed in a massive earthquake around 365 CE (fig. 2.5). The skeletons have been identified as those of a young man, a young woman, and an eighteen-month-old baby, as we have seen. The woman is holding the baby, and the man is close behind her, arms reaching as if attempting to shield them both. Two rings were found near the man's hand, one of plain iron, the other of bronze, the latter inscribed with the Greek letters chi-rho and alpha-omega—distinctly Christian symbols.

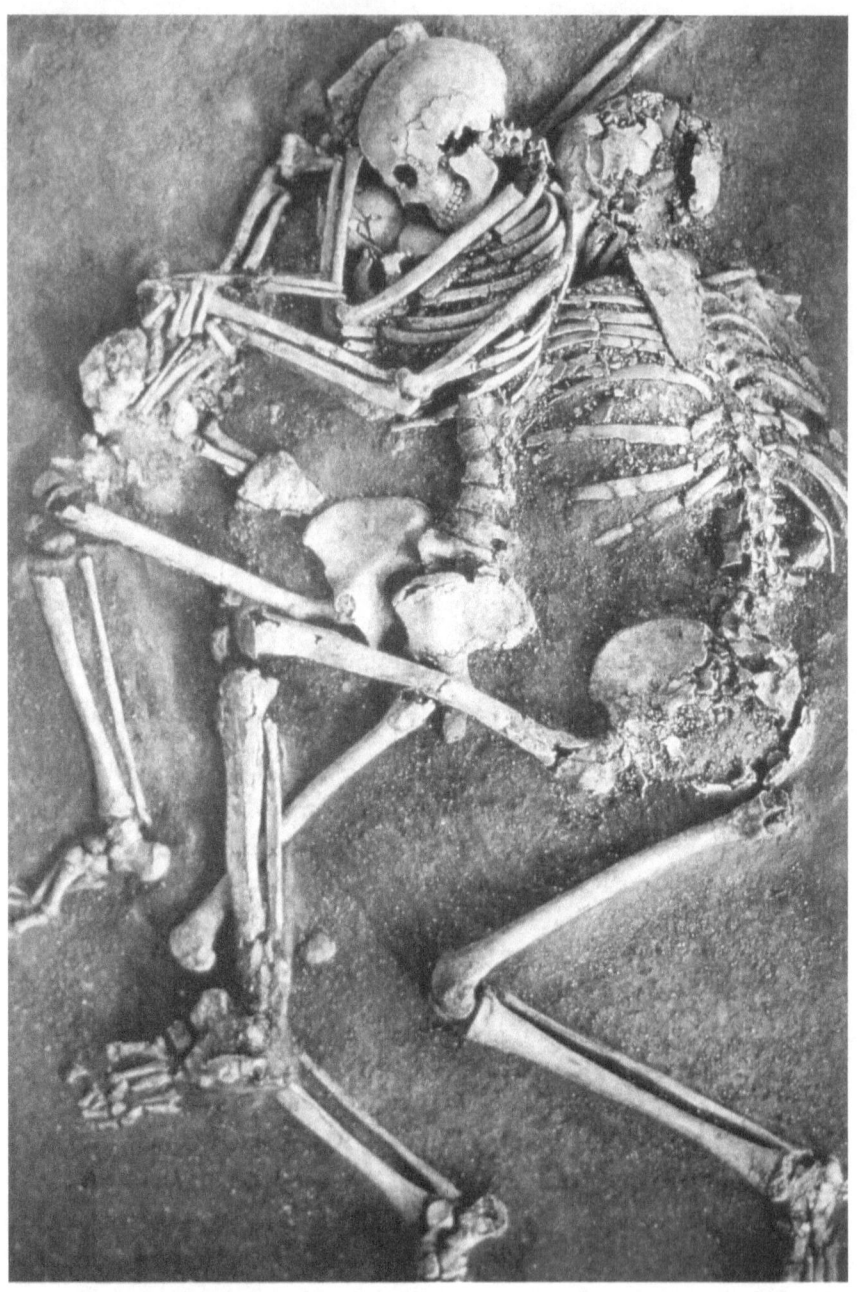

FIGURE 2.5 Skeletal remains of victims of the fourth-century earthquake in Kourion. Kourion Archaeological Museum, Episkopi, Cyprus. Photograph courtesy of the Cyprus Department of Antiquities.

The three present not only as a family but as a Christian family, then.[24] The tableau is deeply poignant. Shocked and frightened, in the instant before falling masonry would have crushed skulls and snapped spines, the last acts of this young family were gestures of care and protection—or so we can easily imagine. The exhibition room contains other delicate, broken things, including locally made clay amphorae found in the house with the earthquake victims, shattered shards carefully glued back together. Fragility is on display, but so too is improbable endurance. The room also contains other Christian things. Are we invited to imagine that this young couple died strong in the conviction that a blessed afterlife awaited them and their child? Perhaps, but our response to that possibility remains open. Here, differently than in the American Museum of Natural History, it is the objects, rather than didactic texts, that carry the message.

Other objects might have been present in the museum but are not, including other skeletal remains. Some of these were long ago carried off by rodents or other scavengers, as was the lower body of the middle aged man crushed to death while seeking protection under a doorway.[25] Others languish in storerooms, too fragmentary to be displayed, as were the mingled remains of a mule and the young girl whom the excavators named "Camelia."[26] Still others have simply gone lost, as the bronze ring with the Christian symbols is reported to have done, leaving a replica on display. Even in museum settings, where the goal is to preserve and conserve, entropy has its way. Things disintegrate and scatter, and sometimes we must find ways to "perform remembrance through transience," whether we want to or not.[27]

Not only the objects but their architectural setting has stories to tell. George McFadden (1907–1953), a wealthy, largely self-trained American archaeologist who funded and effectively headed the University of Pennsylvania Museum's excavations at Kourion between 1934 and 1953, had the house built in 1937–38; it served as his home as well as the dig headquarters. According to his personal assistant, Christofis Polycarpou, interviewed by archaeologist Thomas Davis in 1987, the house was staffed by "a cook, waiter, foreman, and a gardener who doubled as a guard." McFadden also "kept dogs and horses, and would often ride from the excavation back to the dig house."[28] Though his initial choice of the archaeological site may have been motivated primarily by its proximity to a bay well suited to harbor his ninety-foot yacht, McFadden's commitment to the Kourion excavation and to the region more broadly become both strong and personal. He left the house to the government of Cyprus, to be used after his death as a local museum, and under the Department of Antiquities of the Republic of Cyprus, it has functioned in this way since 1969.[29] It also serves as an understated shrine of sorts for McFadden himself, who died in a boating accident in Episkopi Bay shortly before his forty-sixth birthday. Although not open to the public, his bedroom is still preserved, along with books, other personal items, and a photo of him in naval uniform. As Davis reports, "To this day in Episkopi village, people will tell you that the British killed McFadden because he was against the expansion of the Akrotiri garrison." He adds, "It is a measure of the affection he commanded that the residents of Episkopi could not accept that such a good man would have a senseless death."[30] McFadden's obituary, originally published in the *American Journal of Archaeology*, is framed and hangs in the museum. The final line reads, "It is fitting that he should find his end in the Greek and briny sea whence came the goddess of beauty herself to his beloved island—Cyprus."[31]

Following McFadden's death, the site at Kourion was largely neglected until David Soren of the University of Missouri reopened excavations in 1978, initially focusing on the sanctuary of Apollo Hylates, or Apollo of the Woodlands. After a three-year hiatus, having moved to the University of Arizona, Soren returned to Kourion in 1984 with the goal of learning more about the earthquake that had destroyed both sanctuary and city. McFadden's team had opened a trench in 1934 in which they had discovered the skeletons of two earthquake victims whom they dubbed "Romeo and Juliet." Fifty years later, Soren reopened the trench and carried out further excavations for four more seasons in what has come to be known as the "Earthquake House." Among the most dramatic finds were the skeletons of the girl and the mule, discovered in the first season (1984), and the skeletons of the "family" currently on display in the museum, discovered at the very end of the third season (1986).[32] These finds, and the story of disaster that they tell, were publicized by the National Geographic Society, which helped fund the 1985 season of the excavation, deploying photographers, artists, and even film-makers.[33]

The domestic space of the Episkopi museum both echoes and contrasts with the humble, late ancient building whose contents it displays. Soren had hoped to create a museum on the site of the Earthquake House itself, presenting objects in their original context, and indeed he constructed a building for this purpose. However, the Cyprus Department of Antiquities deemed it safer and more practical to display the artifacts in the McFadden house. The architectural context of the museum thus places the objects under McFadden's care, so to speak; it consigns them to a benignly colonial world set in the relatively recent past. McFadden's brief was to acquire objects for the University of Pennsylvania Museum, and in the end some two thousand objects from Kourion ended up in Penn's collection.[34] However, his support for Cypriot involvement in local archaeology and insistence on leaving mosaics in place, for example, bespeaks a certain ambivalence on McFadden's part. His death marked the end of an era, even if the museum setting partly elides this. As Davis notes, "The new post-colonial era of resurgent national pride would soon force museum excavations to focus on recovering data, not objects."[35] Soren wanted to make a reconstructed Kourion a strong draw for tourists, using it as the staging ground for the drama of a disaster that could be said to have "ended antiquity," but the Cypriot authorities resisted what they may have deemed American sensationalism.[36] The current Cyprus Director of the Department of Antiquities has reportedly expressed interest in upgrading the museum display of the earthquake artifacts. What story will this new curation tell, in a distinctly postcolonial moment?

In the meantime, the reverberations of earthquakes are being felt in very different kinds of museum contexts as well. Ballroom Marfa, a non-collecting contemporary arts museum, hosted the exhibition *Hyperobjects* in 2018. The remote West Texas town in which the museum is located was made famous in the 1970s and '80s as a center for minimalist art, when Donald Judd and others were drawn to Marfa by the stark beauty of the desert and the possibilities for large scale installations that the open space afforded. The exhibition was curated by Laura Copelin, then Executive Director of Ballroom Marfa, in collaboration with literary scholar and eco-theorist Timothy Morton. It took its theme as well as its title from Morton's concept of the hyperobject as an entity that is so huge in scale as to defy understanding.[37] Global warming is a prime example, as we have seen; so too is tectonic shift, as well as human-induced faulting of the earth's plates. In the words of the curators, "Hyperobjects create an ecological awareness far beyond normal human comprehension. To understand a hyperobject, we must transform the way we see and experience the universe. In line with this idea, the exhibition sought to create encounters with artworks and non-art objects that de-centered and expanded the scale of human perception."[38]

Housed in a 1920s, white-washed, adobe-style building on one of the main streets of Marfa, the museum's cool interior contrasts with its hot, bright courtyard, which was the site of the installation titled *The Intimate Earthquake Archive*, created by Danish artist Sissel Marie Tonn. Moved by the stories of personal loss, anxiety, and uncertainty conveyed by residents of Groningen, Holland, who had been affected by local earthquakes caused by natural gas extraction, Tonn and her collaborator Jonathan Reus drew on both physical and digital archives of the Dutch Meteorological Institute to create their interactive artwork. Twelve sandstone core samples from the Groningen region were equipped with long-wave radio transmitters that emitted data drawn from specific local earthquakes. In the Texas installation, the core samples were suspended throughout Ballroom Marfa's courtyard (fig. 2.6). When visitors approached them, wearing noise-canceling earmuffs and special vests, compositions of vibrations played out in their bodies, mediated by the vests, which were equipped with both skin- and bone-conduction transducers (fig. 2.7). As Tonn describes the sensations produced by the interface of the vest, "With bone-conduction you have the sensation of sound coming from within the body, and from no particular direction, whereas with haptic transduction of the skin, it's really a tactile experience. These different dimensions combine to create a kind of deep listening experience that's internalised through the body, and this experience is strengthened by the earphones that block out all other environmental sound."[39] The installation was not intended to simulate what an earthquake feels like to a human. If anything, it simulated what it might be like to be the quaking earth. Tonn and Reus's vibratory compositions "move across the body and at the subsurface of the skeleton, producing a composition of tremors on the surface of the body."[40] The human body, skin and bone, becomes a kind of seismograph—an instrument through which the earth can tell the story of its movements.

In an interview, Tonn and Reus discuss their experience of being in West Texas and New Mexico around the time of the Marfa exhibition. "Having grown up in Europe and having lived in the Netherlands for so long, going to the...south-west, you just have this sense of presence of the age of the earth.... It's just so huge, in a way, it's so biblical."[41] Ancient, vast, and seemingly imperturbable, the landscape around Marfa communicates something of the nature of the hyperobjects that gave the exhibition its name. If this landscape contrasts with the relative intimacy of the Netherlands, it also contrasts with the intimacy of the multisensory embodied experience enabled by the interface of the vests. The installation takes something that is too big to conceptualize—tectonic faulting and shifting—and makes it

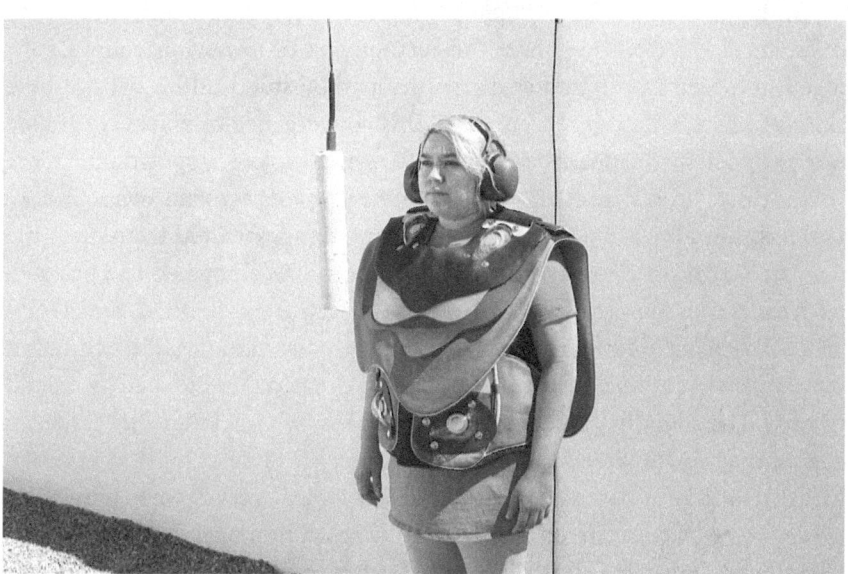

FIGURES 2.6 AND 2.7 Sissel Marie Tonn, in collaboration with Jonathan Reus. *The Intimate Earthquake Archive*. *Hyperobjects* exhibition, Ballroom Marfa, Marfa, Texas, 2018. Photographs courtesy of Ballroom Marfa and the artist. Photographer: Alex Marks.

manageable and accessible, and thereby even more uncanny and disturbing. We feel it in our bones; it makes our skin buzz.

The installation also allows visitors to experience space not as something to be mapped visually and conquered mentally but as something to be navigated viscerally. Visually, the work is not strongly compelling, nor is it intended to be, although the simplicity and starkness of the rock cylinders suspended within tripod frames resonated with the setting of the museum's barren courtyard and the desert beyond. (The effect was enhanced by a second installation that coincided spatially with Tonn's piece—Nance Klehm's "Free Exposure (3 Holes, 5 Heaps)" (2018), a set of dirt works that brought the arid, textured landscape of the desert inside the museum courtyard, conjuring the layered histories exposed by archaeological excavations.[42]) As one moved around the courtyard, visual cues mattered, but the sensations that became primary were the ones mediated by the vest. Space came to be shaped and defined by nodes of vibrational intensity, fostering an almost reptilian awareness.

At the same time, *The Intimate Earthquake Archive* drew very distant and different places close together. The earthquakes of low-lying, rainy Groningen hummed in the bodies of visitors as they stood under the hot blue skies of Marfa's high desert country. This convergence of places was made more explicit by the nearby presence of David Brooks's "Repositioned Core (Byproduct)" (2014–2018), consisting in the deepest segments of a rock core representing nine million years of sedimentation, extracted from one mile deep in Texas's oil-rich Permian Basin (fig. 2.8). The elongated and prone—perhaps toppled?—forms of Brooks's work echoed, extended, and reoriented Tonn's shallower, vertically suspended core samples and reminded the viewer that West Texas, too, is subject to earthquakes induced by oil and gas extraction, in this case, not only drilling but also fracking. On March 26, 2020, a magnitude-5.0 earthquake struck West Texas about halfway between Midland and El Paso; the United States Geological Survey website reports, "This earthquake occurred in an area of known human-caused (induced) seismicity."[43] What is vast is also intimate, what is far away also near, what is deep is also close to the surface. We are all inside this hyperobject of human-made ecological crisis that causes the earth to shudder.

Time, like space, stretched and contracted in this exhibition. A small, highly polished bronze object tucked in the corner not far from Brooks's work caught the eye with the simplicity and elegance of its torso-like twist. The enigmatic object, labeled "Equation of Time Cam, 01999," is a replica of a part of a massive, ten-thousand-year clock being constructed in the West

Texas town of Van Horn by the Long Now, a group co-founded by musician and visual artist Brian Eno; their stated goal is to "foster long-term thinking and responsibility in the framework of the next 10,000 years" (fig. 2.9).[44] Ten thousand years is nothing compared to the nine million years of sedimentation that produced the rock in Brooks's core sample, but it is also one digit more than the millennial units that typically represent the maximum stretch of human historical thinking. That extra digit is enough to bring an earthquake in late fourth-century Cyprus into something like temporal proximity.

The rather elaborate mediation of *The Intimate Earthquake Archive* paradoxically creates a greater sense of immediacy and intimacy than the relatively unmediated encounter with the human remains on display in the history museum at Kourion. The Kourion tableau is moving, to be sure, not least because of the gestures of care and protection that can be almost effortlessly projected onto the mingled bones. Indeed, our empathy may bridge the temporal gap with dizzying ease as we behold this long-ago moment, carefully preserved, frozen in time. But the scene remains on ice. The earth once shook terrifyingly, yet the humans no longer move. Behind glass, they are safe even from scuttling insects, and rodents, and the prying roots of trees; we view them from a measured distance, passive spectators. These bones have, to the extent possible, been taken outside of the ongoing flow of life. They are no longer becoming anything else or more. In contrast, we encounter Tonn's nonhuman, impersonal core samples as active, lively objects that make us feel things in our own bones.[45] Out of place, they bring other places to us, intimately so. They bring Groningen, where earthquakes that are relatively small in magnitude have occurred with such frequency that sturdy farmhouses are reduced to rubble.[46] They may bring Paphos too.

Here another of Tonn's works is also suggestive. Like *The Intimate Earthquake Archive*, *An Education of Attention* (2018–) was inspired by personal stories of earthquakes—in this case narratives gathered from inhabitants of Istanbul, a city that, like Paphos, lies on the edge of the Anatolian plate and experiences frequent seismic activity. As Tonn describes her initial process, "Visiting people throughout the city I collected stories about what they recall noticing before, during and after the earthquake, and how these embodied memories affected the way they perceive potential risks in their environment today." She noticed several recurring themes, in which she discovered four different modes of human attentiveness to their surroundings. "Canary Attention," as she names it, occurs at the threshold of awareness of impending environmental change or danger; "inter-species awareness" consists in

FIGURE 2.8 David Brooks. *Repositioned Core (Byproduct)*. *Hyperobjects* exhibition, Ballroom Marfa, Marfa, Texas, 2018. Photograph courtesy of Ballroom Marfa and the artist. Photographer: Alex Marks.

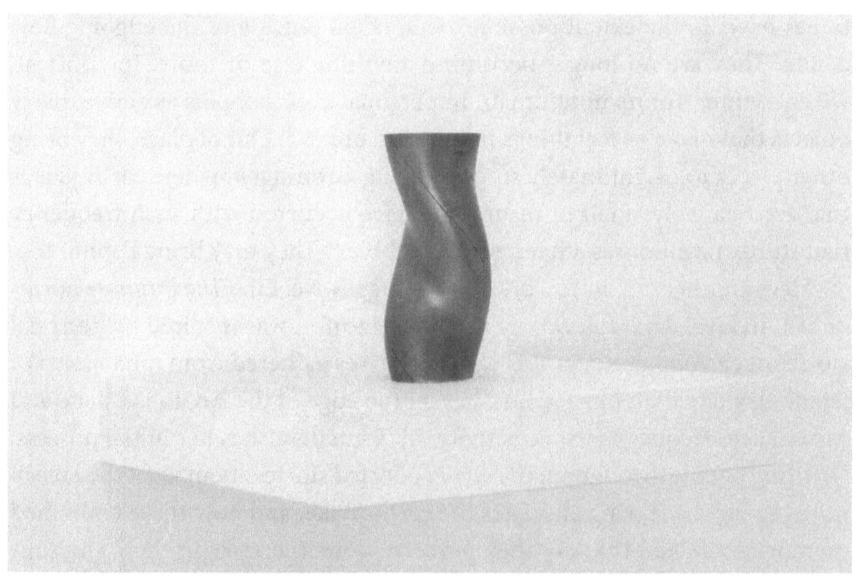

FIGURE 2.9 *Equation of Time Cam, 01999*. *Hyperobjects* exhibition, Ballroom Marfa, Marfa, Texas, 2018. Photograph courtesy of Ballroom Marfa and the Long Now Foundation. Photographer: Alex Marks.

attunement to signs from more sensitive nonhuman creatures that change is underway; "sedimented attention" is a state of alertness instinctively activated by memories of past experiences; and "situated awareness attention" involves a cognitive grasp of elements of the context that shape and potentially intensify environmental change or danger. She assigned to each of these modes of attentiveness a visual code that enabled her to translate the collected stories and experiences into a set of evocatively decorated printed textiles. Suspended vertically, the textiles ripple and tremble gently in response to Istanbul earthquake data transmitted by small speakers embroidered into the fabric.[47]

Tonn's fabric creations evoke more ancient traditions of commemorating earthquakes in Istanbul, dating to a period when the city was called Constantinople and served as capital of the Christian empire of Byzantium. Following significant seismological events in 438 and 447, Constantinople's church year came to include processional liturgies that marked the anniversaries of major earthquakes; by the ninth century, the calendar included nine such commemorations. As Mark Roosien has recently detailed, these commemorative services incorporated readings from the Old Testament on the eve of the anniversary, a procession with penitential hymn-singing that reenacted the evacuation of the city, and New Testament readings centering on the story of Christ's calming of the storm, which the Greek Bible refers to in one case as a "large earthquake" (see Matthew 8:23–27, LXX). Such rituals served to sustain what Tonn calls "sedimented awareness": through annual reenactments of the layered history of a frequently-shaken city, the citizens of Constantinople collectively remembered past traumas and confronted the fact that they could recur in the future. The liturgies also evoked "situated awareness attention" of a certain kind, alerting participants to features of their context that might increase the danger of such recurrence: divine wrath provoked by human sin was known to cause earthquakes, and where sin could not be contained, mercy must be sought through performances of communal repentance.[48] However strange and troubling such theological explanations might seem, Constantinopolitan rituals of earthquake commemoration resonate with Tonn's contemporary art works insofar as they activate memory and attune awareness both to the shaking of the earth and to the implicatedness of humans in that shaking—human vulnerability, and also human culpability.

"Paphos... which had so frequently fallen due to earthquakes" (*Life of Hilarion* 42)—with these words, Jerome's *Life of Hilarion* is (among other things) curating earthquakes, just as both the Episkopi Museum and Tonn's two works do. Offering vivid but fragmentary snapshots, the text does not play on human emotions overtly, nor does it provide much by way of historical context. No narrative arc links fallen Paphos to the tsunami on the Adriatic or the ruins of the garden and temple in the mountains outside of the city. But in each place, if we open ourselves to it, we may feel vibrations—the vibrations of the earth itself and also of the lives that have left their traces, lives of humans, buildings, plants, and more. The stories may not be fully retrievable, but they continue to haunt the fragments of bone, rock, or text that remain.

We might imagine the fragment from Jerome's text as one of Tonn's core samples, coded with data from ancient archives, patient in its suspended state. It awaits our listening bodies, and as we approach, its stories reverberate through our bones and dance across our skin. We must open our own memories to receive these ancient memories more fully. In my case, Adriatic and Mediterranean surges mingle with the waves of the Gulf of Mexico that battered the shore of Texas in hurricane seasons during my great-grandfather's lifetime (he never tired of reminding me that he was present in Galveston for the "Great Storm" of 1900), in my own childhood, and again more recently (Rita, Ike, Harvey). The earth heaved, and buildings jerked and rattled in San Francisco in 1989, where I experienced the Loma Prieta quake while pushing my infant in a stroller on the street, as well as in Paphos and Kourion around 365, where parents' bodies curled protectively around their own children. With the twist of a strange timepiece, we almost converge—but only almost. The past remains the past, and Cyprus is not Texas or the Netherlands—but we can begin to feel its vibrations. We can ask our fragments, as Catherine Michael Chin puts it, not only "*Who are you?*" but also "*Who am I, now that I have met you, now that I know your worlds were here beside mine all along?*"[49]

The relative stillness into which efforts to control the global pandemic recently plunged us allowed scientists to sense the earth's vibrations more clearly.[50] In the midst of upheaval and tragic loss, isolated and often lonely and fearful, we have all been given a chance to do some deep listening to the more-than-human world around us, as well as to human voices often not heard, raised in protest of racism and injustice. This is our moment, distinctly so. At the same time, we carry the past with us and beside us as we engage the moment. Precisely by tuning into that past, perhaps we can become more effectively present to our own world, attentive to the ongoing processes of becoming to which all things are subject. Curating earthquakes is curating violent upheaval, decay, and new emergence.[51] Renouncing stasis as a goal, and accepting unpredictability as a starting point, we may thereby cultivate the insights of an anticipatory history. "History that calls attention to process rather than permanence may...help us to be more prepared for future change."[52] As our texts and artifacts fall apart and are reassembled, the fragments of a livable world may begin to reveal themselves.

LIFE IN RUINS

...*Paphum*	...Paphos,
urbem Cypri	city of Cyprus,
...*nunc ruinarum tantum uestigiis*	...now only by the traces of ruins
quid olim fuerit ostendit	shows what it once was

JEROME OF STRIDON

FOOTPRINTS, TRACKS, TRACES—*vestigia* conjure an urban landscape that hovers between the Paphos of now (*nunc*) and the Paphos of once-upon-a-time (*olim*) (*Life of Hilarion* 42). Rhetorical doubling emphasizes the tenuousness of that ghostly presence. These are not only traces, but "traces of ruins" (42). Even the ruins are not fully present as such; all that remains is "the ruin of a ruin," in Susan Stewart's phrasing.[1] Is this because destruction wreaked suddenly, by the violence of earthquake, has subsequently given way to slow decay, as Stewart suggests? If so, "[t]his process has its limits," as nineteenth-century art historian Alois Riegl noted in a famous essay, "The Modern Cult of Monuments." Even for the most ruin-enamored of viewers, "a shapeless pile of rubble" holds little attraction or meaning. "There must be at least a recognizable trace of the original form, that is, of man's handiwork."[2] A trace of a trace might be enough, just barely, to sustain the legibility of the city's past structures, in the midst of decay tending toward obliteration and oblivion.

But there is another way to understand "traces of ruins." Perhaps the damaged buildings of Paphos that Jerome's Hilarion observes are in the process not only of falling apart but also of coming together again, as the materials move from one context of human "handiwork" to another. For Riegl's "modern man," it appears seemly that human craft and natural decay succeed one another, in an unimpeded and ever-repeating "cycle of becoming and passing away."[3] Honoring the insight, current sensibilities may nonetheless find the binaries too rigid: surely human agency is not asserted against "nature," but rather folded into larger, more-than-human processes of both making and unmaking, and often making and unmaking are part of the same movement. This is the clearly the case when one building is dismantled so that its materials may be incorporated into another, in an act of domination, homage, or simple expediency.[4] In such instances, *spolia*—those stolen or salvaged bits of prior made things—preserve a trace of the ruined structures from which they came, whether this is acknowledged or not. Stewart argues in favor of acknowledgment: "Whether booty or reappropriated forms, *spolia* must be reframed in semantic terms, and along the way, the palimpsest of earlier meanings and uses shines through."[5] Through such a reframing, we come to interpret and value these fragments both for what they have become and for what they once were. We may also be provoked to attend to the often-violent processes at work in the transition from one state to another.

Jerome's literary snapshot of ruins captures a single instant, a moment of flux between times and states. Nodding to the past, he does not show us what the tumbled-down buildings are becoming, but he invites us to imagine. And the ruins of Paphos are with us still, though they have scarcely remained static. Our sense of past possibilities may thus be shaped by present encounters, experienced in person or through the mediation of photography and archaeological description. Excavations are ongoing in the 291-hectare (roughly 720-acre) Paphos Archaeological Park, which has been listed as a UNESCO World Heritage site since 1980. The extensive park includes remains of New Paphos (current Kato Paphos), the necropolis known as the "Tombs of the Kings" to the north of New Paphos, and Old Paphos (current Kouklia) further down the coast to the southeast. As is so often the case, the archaeological artifacts are both suggestive and ambiguous.

Human settlement at Paphos predates the Bronze Age and reaches into the present. Against the backdrop of this *longue durée*, a group of luxurious private houses overlooking the sea, dating to the Roman period, now stand out as some of the city's most impressive remains. With even reconstructed walls rising no more than a few feet above the ground, the floors of these villas are among their most notable surviving features. Those of the "House of Dionysos" are particularly richly and extensively decorated. Built in the late second century, a period of general prosperity in Cyprus, the villa encompasses more than thirty rooms grouped around a central colonnaded courtyard, and at least a quarter of the floors in the two-thousand-square-meter building are covered in mosaics depicting mythological, agricultural, and hunting scenes.[6] At some point in the fourth century—perhaps in the 360s?—the house was destroyed by an earthquake and was never rebuilt, according to archaeologists.[7] Gazing upon this particular structure, we thus seem to behold a city fallen and abandoned.

A nearby villa tells a different story, however. The "House of Theseus" was likewise built in the late second century and damaged in the fourth, but rather than being abandoned, it was rebuilt and expanded. As F. G. Maier and V. Karageorghis relate, "In contrast to the now derelict 'House of Dionysos,' it was gradually reconstructed from the later 4th century A.D. on a vast scale, incorporating elements of earlier buildings on the site."[8] A striking mosaic floor that gives the house its name depicts the youthful hero doing battle with the Minotaur, watched not only by Ariadne but also by figures personifying Crete and the Labyrinth. Created in the third century, this mosaic suffered harm in the fourth century—again, this is attributed to earthquakes—but unlike the mosaics of the House of Dionysos, it was "lovingly restored later in the same century"[9] and ultimately incorporated into the palatial structure that is thought to have been the western residence of the governor of the island in the late fourth and early fifth centuries.[10] The restoration focused on the faces of Theseus and Crete, and Demetrios Michaelides calls attention to the contrast of their strongly drawn but abstracted features with the more subtly rendered faces of the Labyrinth and Ariadne, who appear engaged and responsive as they gaze upon the violent scene unfolding before them. "Despite their wide, staring eyes, Theseus and Crete somehow remain uninvolved with what is going on around them and reflect a shift toward what would eventually become Byzantine art."[11] A sign of things to come, then, this mosaic is as much process as fixed object. And new floor mosaics were created post-earthquake as well, including those in the audience hall, one of which depicts the birth and first bath of Achilles,[12] with iconography paralleling, anticipating, or possibly echoing, Byzantine representations of the birth and first bath of Christ.[13] Here ruination provides the opportunity not only for repair but for renovation and renewal, in a shifting context of cultural hybridity.

It can be difficult to determine the exact time of death of a building. Like the House of Dionysos, the theater of Paphos is thought to have been destroyed by earthquakes and abandoned in the late fourth century, after serving as the stage for performances for some six and a half centuries. During its long life, the building underwent several major renovations, including significant expansion in the mid–second century, and at the end of the third century, modifications were made to accommodate naval spectacles and wild animal performances, using materials from the dismantled stage building to create a containment wall separating the audience from the orchestra. Within a century, all such use was apparently at an end. "Excavations at the theatre demonstrate considerable evidence for the collapse of walls and tumble," reports archaeologist Craig Barker, attributing the damage to the seismic activity referred to by Jerome. "The ruins of the theatre became a quarry site, much of the stone structure (particularly the marble elements) being stripped from the site and reused in the construction of the nearby Chrysopolitissa basilica, just a few hundred metres to the south east of the theatre."[14]

This might seem to be the end of the road for the theater, which surely suffered devastating violence both from the shaking of the earth and from the dismantling and removal of its materials. And yet, in some important senses, the building can be said to perdure, whether measured by continued developments on its site or by the off-site history of its materials.[15] As a quarry, the theater remained both a place and a source of creative activity—a kind of "nurse log" for future growth. Once the worked stone was stripped, the bedrock below the theater was mined. And eventually others moved in. "As stone was removed the remains of the theatre gradually became an industrial zone with evidence of butchery, tanning, lime kilns and semi-agricultural activity well into Late Antiquity."[16] Following its partial destruction, the theater may have ceased to provide a stage for Roman spectacles; it may have been aesthetically compromised; but it did not cease to be a vital structure.

As Barker indicates, not only was the site of the theater effectively remodeled yet again following the earthquake, albeit without any obvious central planning, but many of its stones were also disseminated. Transported just a few blocks away, the granite and marble columns of the theater, topped with Corinthian capitals, were planted anew along the seven aisles of what was to be one of the largest Christian basilicas on Cyprus (fig. 2.10).[17] To the extent that they activated memories and evoked the presence of the theater, we might think of these wandering materials as something like translated saints' relics.[18] As Jerome's contemporary Victricius argued, "There is nothing in relics that is not complete.... The whole can be in the part" (*On the praise of saints* 9–10). Just so, each reused column became part of the spa-

FIGURE 2.10 The church of Agia Kyriaki surrounded by the ruins of the fourth-century Chrysopolitissa basilica. Paphos, Cyprus. © Hercules Milas/Alamy Stock Photo.

tial spread of the theater: even the smallest fragment of the former building might conjure the totality, and the basilica could also be understood to incorporate something of the theatrical in its staging of rhetorical and musical performances as part of the Christian liturgy. Some of the theater's columns still stand now, though visitors may not recognize them as such. Like trunks in a ghostly forest, they surround the much smaller church built on the site circa 1500. This present church replaced an eleventh-century Byzantine church erected when the late ancient basilica, downsized and renovated in the sixth century, had long since fallen into ruins following its destruction by Arab invaders in the seventh century.[19] And if the theater brought some of its architectural DNA into the fourth-century church, did the fourth-century church itself not in some sense project its own life forward into the churches built in its place? Nicola Camerlenghi suggests that we think of such serial or "replacement" buildings on the analogy of a graft: the variety of the built structure might change, "but the new growth would still be imbued with enduring aspects of the site...because the established root system lends stability, offers a physical foundation, and literally feeds the new growth."[20]

Among the stones still located on the layered site of the Paphos church(es), at least two have distinctive stories to tell. The first is a relic in a more traditional sense, though its origins as such are murky. Local legend relates that when the apostle Paul visited Cyprus in 45 CE, he was tied to a pillar and flogged by order of the governor; subsequently, the governor was converted to Christianity and Paul was freed.[21] Like pieces of the "true cross" and other lesser contact relics of antiquity, a worn fragment of a marble column has become a touchstone of memory and a mediator of bodily intimacy with the saintly apostle for current religious tourists (fig. 2.18). A placard helpfully labels the column "St. Paul's Pillar." Without this signposting, it would be difficult to identify which of the columns on the site was associated with the apostle, and at least one stock photograph simply titles the whole forest of columns from the ruined basilica "St. Paul's Pillars."[22]

A second fragmentary marble column holds less interest for tourists, but more for historians (fig. 2.11). This pillar bears its own label: "Eustorgis, may you never thirst."[23] Located near the top of the reused column, the Greek inscription appears to date to the fifth or sixth century. The words bless one Eustorgis, implicitly invoking John 4:14—"Whoever drinks of the water I give them will not thirst"—and John 6:35—"Whoever believes in me will not ever thirst." Perhaps the inscribed column once stood in the nave of the basilica, where a floor mosaic of a deer is glossed with the first verse of Psalm 42 (LXX 41:2): "As the deer longs for the fountains of water, so my soul longs for you, O god." The knowing reader would recall that the next verse begins, "My soul has thirsted for the god of the living."[24] The mosaic has recently been dated to the fifth century,[25] and we might even imagine that Eustorgis commissioned it.

Curiously, this inscription, almost certainly created after the column had already migrated to the basilica,[26] reunites the history of the basilica with that of the theater where the column once stood. For the theater also preserves two apparently contemporaneous inscriptions honoring Eustorgis. One is carved on a broken granite column that had been incorporated into the containment wall in the third century and must have been exposed again in the fifth or sixth, when it was embellished with the words, "Eustorgis raised Cyprus." About twelve feet to the left of the inscribed granite column, a broken marble column was also exposed, and the upper part of the wall between the two columns was removed to provide access to a platform constructed over the first row of seats behind the wall; resting in front of the platform was an old and damaged statue base inscribed, "Eustorgis, lover of building," likely once topped by a recycled statue subsequently melted for the

FIGURE 2.11 Marble column in the Chrysopolitissa basilica, once part of the theater. It is inscribed with the words, "May Eustorgis never thirst." Photograph courtesy of the Cyprus Department of Antiquities.

value of its bronze.²⁷ The language of raising and building is typically applied to public benefactors, and indeed two other inscriptions elsewhere on the island celebrate Eustorgis's generous donations.²⁸ But how are we to imagine Eustorgis's patronage role in the context of a ruin, and what are we to make of this honorific monument crafted from distinctly second-hand materials? The archaeologists who excavated the site suggest that "he meant a great deal for financial and/or other reasons to a small group of quarrymen who had the contract for pulling stone from the site"²⁹ and that "he might have the rights for the stone from the site."³⁰ Another scholar expresses doubts: "This seems to me … too trivial a task for a great benefactor, who was honored for raising Cyprus." Daniela Summa boldly proposes that Eustorgis sponsored renovations in the theater of Paphos as in that of Salamis, both of which may have "still received an audience and had a public function"; an inscription in Salamis suggests that Eustorgis held a rank as high as provincial governor.³¹ Might we imagine that it could have been he who commissioned not only the deer mosaic in the basilica but also the Achilles mosaic, with its Christological intimations, in the House of Theseus?

Part of the basilica's emergence, the theater also continued to evolve on its original site, though it is difficult to track the course of that evolution precisely. Here we encounter buildings not as static objects but as "ongoing processes."³² Perhaps when Hilarion gazed at the shaken city, even the House of Dionysos had more life left in its ruins than we have thought.

Many of us are accustomed to think of ruins as deserted places, in part because Renaissance humanists and their successors taught us to view them that way. Already in antiquity, the possibility of permanent ruination preoccupied the Romans. As Martin Devecka has recently argued, "The Romans knew that cities could die because they had killed a number of them." Indeed, "the Roman Empire was … in many senses built on ruins."³³ Ambivalent fascination with the destruction of Rome, first imagined and then made partly real in the Gothic invasion of 410, reemerged in the sixteenth century and intensified when Rome was once again sacked by Germanic forces in 1527. Stewart traces the creative works of "sixteenth-century scholars, painters, printmakers, and poets" who began to see the violent conflicts of culture and religion in their own era "against a backdrop of Roman ruins that for the first time were viewed not only for the allusions they provided to allegory but also for the ambivalent aesthetic pleasures they offered."[34] Pleasure was interlaced with anticipated profit. An often inscribed sixteenth-century line—"*Roma quanta fuit, ipsa ruina docet*: The very ruins teach how great Rome once was"—echoes Jerome's language while also emphasizing the pedagogical function of ruins.[35] Viewers were invited to discover in fallen landscapes "backgrounds not only to the past but also to the present."[36] The question of precisely what lessons were to be learned remained open: what mattered most, perhaps, was the self-reflective gesture.

Intriguingly, a 1547 painting by Maarten van Heemskerck depicts Jerome himself against a background of ruins (fig. 2.12).[37] Kneeling on stone pavement in the left foreground of the painting, our grizzled author gazes intently at a book while clutching his usual ascetic accoutrements of stone and skull. The saint's upper body is bare, and his red robe and hat are draped on the apse-like curve of a ruined wall in front of him; behind him, at a slight distance, a lion guards the space, following iconographic tradition. Framing both saint and wall, and just barely discernible, is a grotto-like opening in a rocky hillock. Shielded by the hillock, Jerome is turned toward the lower corner of the painting, looking away from the expansive terrain that covers most of the canvas, crowded with broken and toppled monuments from the pre-Christian past. A product of the artist's fantasy, the landscape resembles, but is not identical to, Rome. Van Heemskerck has made allusions to Roman buildings and statues, but he has also brought the monuments together in a new configuration, like painterly *spolia*.[38] Above and behind Jerome, in the upper left register of the painting, is a bronze statue of Hercules wrestling Antaeus. On the right-hand side of the painting, balancing but set slightly back from Jerome, a group of boys play at the base of a marble statue of the Tiber with a wolf nursing Romulus and Remus; the river god, like other sculpted figures in the painting, is depicted at roughly the same scale as the saint.[39] In comparison with Jerome and the statues, the cavorting boys are diminutive. Smaller still are the donkey-drivers who stroll through the middle ground of the picture, heading into the distance. Such apparently incidental figures, known as "staffage," "most often express scale and motion," as Stewart notes. But in sixteenth-century representations of ruins, they do more than that, she suggests, their implied contemporaneity with the viewers inviting identification and allowing them to see themselves "against the backdrop of deep time."[40]

Yet Jerome is neither staffage nor statue, neither sixteenth-century contemporary nor ancient Roman. What are we to make of his presence in this painting? To be sure, the saint was frequently represented in sixteenth-century art, including Dutch paintings, either in his study or in a natural setting—as ascetic scholar or as scholarly ascetic.[41] Hans Holbein the Younger famously painted Erasmus, who published an edition of Jerome's letters in 1516, as a Jerome-like figure of humanistic erudition.[42] By including Jerome in his Roman ruins fantasy, Van Heemskerck introduces another variation on these contemporary themes. The associations are potentially rich, as Arthur DiFuria observes. A reader of Jerome's correspondence would know that he spent several significant years in Rome, where he was closely associated with Pope Damasus, as well as a number of aristocratic women. Later, having left the capital city for Bethlehem, he lamented the sack of Rome in a letter to his friend Principia: "The city that had taken the whole world was itself taken" (*Ep.* 127.12).[43] To link Jerome with the ruins of Rome pictorially was to make him part of their interpretation. Educated viewers might also think of Jerome's letter to the young Eustochium, in which he makes a show of renouncing Latin literary culture in favor of a strictly scriptural curriculum: "How can Horace go with the psalter, Vergil with the gospels, Cicero with the apostle?" (*Ep.* 22.29). Both literally and metaphorically, Rome is a place on which Jerome turns his back, reflective of a culture that Christianity passes through and supersedes. Yet the painting suggests continuity as much as discontinuity, and its layered temporality, in keeping with what Alexander Nagel and Christopher Wood have dubbed the "anachronic Renaissance,"[44] diverges from any strictly linear chronology. Although set apart, Jerome still belongs to the Roman landscape. Part of the city's "deep time," he kneels among fallen structures, a more fitting habitat for a self-denying hermit than the comfort and protection of standing buildings and institutions. Denuded of fine robes and subjected to ascetic austerities, his body is, like the landscape, caught up in a process of ruination, the end point of which is suggested by the skull in his hand. Moral, intellectual, and spiritual goals are the ones that matter. Nonetheless, Jerome's flesh-and-blood figure remains more warmly human than bronze hero or marble god.

Van Heemskerck's composition is known not only as a painting but also in a 1552 print version created and disseminated by his collaborator Hieronymus Cock, an influential maker and publisher of prints (fig. 2.13).[45] The relatively new technique of print-making, "with its precise delineations of surfaces and textures,"[46] lent itself to a kind of detailing reminiscent of Claudian's literary ecphrasis. Each fragment of sculpture or architecture became a study unto itself, as well as a part fit into a larger whole. In achieving these effects, Cock appears to have consulted Van Heemskerck's extensive collection of Roman sketches,[47] reintroducing a degree of literalism that Van

FIGURE 2.12 Maarten van Heemskerck. *Landscape with Saint Jerome*. 1547. Liechtenstein Museum, Vienna, Austria. © Liechtenstein, The Princely Collections, Vaduz-Vienna/SCALA, Florence/Art Resource, NY/Art Resource.

FIGURE 2.13 Hieronymus Cock after Maarten van Heemskerck. *Saint Jerome in a Landscape with Ruins*. 1552. Photograph courtesy of the National Gallery of Art, Washington, DC.

Heemskerck had seemingly eschewed in his painting. Thus the element of spoliation is heightened: as a print, this version of the ruins fantasy is even more obviously and explicitly constructed from fragments of the Roman landscape, rearranged to create novel forms and juxtapositions. The print introduces other small modifications as well: for example, the staffage figures now include two well-dressed sixteenth-century gentleman in apparently animated discussion as they point at the prominent statue of the river god. As Stewart notes, the incorporation of such figures "invites its viewer to take up the same pose of noting and discoursing on the ruins."[48] At the same time, the shift from polychromatic to monochromatic medium lessens the distinction between living and sculpted figures and unifies the field of composition of which Jerome is a seemingly natural part. Finally, one of the most interesting changes involves the figure of Jerome himself. The book at which the saint gazes so intently is presumably the Bible, yet close examination reveals the words *Martinus Hemskircken inve*. ("Maarten Van Heemskerck has invented it") inscribed on its open pages, balancing the signature *Cock fecit 1552* ("Cock made it in 1552") just right of center on the bottom edge. Hieronymus Cock is letting us know that his etching is based on Van Heemskerck's painting of 1547, and in so doing he is identifying himself with his namesake: like Jerome (Latin: Hieronymus), Cock is gazing not at the ruined landscape itself but at Van Heemskerck's image of ruins.[49] The viewer becomes aware of the layers of mediation at work. And Jerome becomes a figure of mediation *par excellence*. Foregrounded, yet very nearly overwhelmed by the crowded background, both chronology and scale place him between the contemporary staffage figures who wander through but do not fully belong to the otherwise deserted landscape, and the statues and buildings that are the *vestigia* of the glories of antiquity. From that position, he both enables and shapes our vision of the Roman past.

Riegl distinguishes the early modern "cult of ruins" (which continued to flourish in the seventeenth and eighteenth centuries, if not beyond) from what he saw as an appreciation of "age value" emerging in the twentieth century.[50] For the former, "ruins were to convey to the beholder the truly Baroque contrast between ancient greatness and present degradation." In contrast to such "Baroque pathos," later modernity cultivates appreciation of "the natural laws inevitably governing all artifacts."[51] Made objects, like the humans who see themselves partly mirrored in them, are inevitably subject to processes of decay, and that is as it should be. Indeed, it is the very transience of things that touches us so deeply, rendering their endurance all the more moving.

Riegl notes repeatedly that visibly aging things trigger an emotional response, one that differs from the more extravagant feelings of pain and regret evoked by ruins in the early modern period. However, he does not give that emotional response a name. Michael Ann Holly does—melancholy. Addressing the field of art history, in terms that nonetheless reach beyond it, Holly meditates on the awareness of loss that permeates our encounters with objects from the past. She suggests that "melancholy is not exclusively the gloomy, sorrowful state" that it is often thought to be; consolation and reparation are enfolded within it. This ambivalence is embodied in the "poetics of loss" that emerges from the confrontation with both the inherent unknowability of past things—those solitary survivors orphaned by history—and the failure of our own words to capture the power and significance of their perduring presence and being. Unknowability is also mystery; failure is the condition that ensures the pleasure and provocation of our inevitably vain attempts to plumb that mystery.[52]

Riegl, who died in 1905, could not have foreseen the degree to which the transience of monuments would preoccupy late twentieth- and early twenty-first-century artists whose works, on his definition, could as yet have no possible "age value." Ledelle Moe's 2019–21 exhibition at the Massachusetts Museum of Contemporary Art (MASS MoCA) evoked the allure and ambiguity of pastness in its very title—*When* (fig. 2.14). The works that comprised the exhibition were laid out in a vast hall, a converted factory building well-scaled to their monumentality: the sculptures were neither crowded nor overwhelmed by a space that seemed alternately both empty and teeming with life. *Memorial (Collapse)* (2019) was stationed nearest the entry and immediately introduced themes and materials that extended to the whole exhibit. In this work, three massive heads lie on their sides, features blurred as if with time. Suggestive of fallen stone-carved statues honoring some culture's "great men," on closer inspection they turn out to be hollow shells pieced together from fragments of concrete, like pottery sherds from an archaeological site restored to a semblance of former wholeness. Is this an iconoclastic message for the makers of monuments? Even the most enduring memorials may be found hollow in their meaning; even the most powerful heroes will someday be brought down. Or is it an iconic witness to

FIGURE 2.14 Ledelle Moe. *When* exhibition, Massachusetts Museum of Contemporary Art, North Adams, MA, 2019–20. Photograph courtesy of the artist.

those lives always already discarded and fallen? As Susan Cross, the curator of the exhibition, suggests, "despite their immense size, these figures seem fragile—like beloved objects broken and glued back together, treasured for the memories they hold." Cross notes that Moe created the series of which these three heads are a part "as a tribute to anonymous victims of violent conflict."[53] Such lives will never be celebrated in granite or marble but are cherished and mourned all the more tenderly and fiercely in their vulnerability.

Two other works were installed in the middle of the hall. *Relief* (2010) consists of a single sprawling figure, again of massive size, suggesting the distorted, metamorphosing body of an animal of indeterminate species—part pig, part turkey, part human too perhaps. (Cross suggests dog or horse!)[54] Nearby was *Transitions/Displacements* (2012), a work consisting of three larger-than life (but nonetheless slightly more intimately sized) horizontal female figures. Contrasting with *Relief*, these figures seem to float peacefully and even companionably; we might imagine them submerged in water or buried in dirt. One of the three is oriented in the opposite direction and appears smaller and younger than the others; her torso is partly covered with a swarm of indeterminate creatures possibly evoking fish, maggots, or birds.

FIGURE 2.15 Ledelle Moe. *Remain. When* exhibition, MASS MoCA, North Adams, MA, 2019–20. Photograph courtesy of the artist.

Beyond these two works, the largest and most striking sculpture was installed near the end of the hall. An eighteen-foot-tall kneeling figure, androgynous but vaguely female, *Remain* (2019) evokes images of goddesses and also of the Virgin Mary (fig. 2.15).[55] Unlike the other sculptures in the room, this one is upright. Their features, as with all of Moe's sculptures, are blurred and communicate both antiquity and timelessness. They seem to wait with infinite patience, staring straight ahead. Cross dubs them a "symbol of life, love, grief, and resilience."[56] Similar to the figure in *Transitions/Displacements*, they are surrounded by a swarm of small, indeterminate creatures suspended on an irregular, latticelike framework; these give the impression of vibrating energy, while at the same time suggesting that the kneeling figure is both disintegrating and coming together out of a multiplicity of fragmented parts—a delicate and complex manifestation of Riegl's "cycle of becoming and passing away."[57] The sense of a multitude was repeated in the work installed behind *Remain*. *Congregation* (2019) consists in a mass of small human heads that seemed to explode across the back wall of the hall, a collectivity both echoing and contrasting with the three massive heads in *Memorial (Collapse)*; Moe mixed soil from the place where each one was made into the concrete material of the object. Throughout the hall one periodically heard the mournful tones of a foghorn from the video installation *Lament (Foghorn)*. Melancholy and loss mingled with the promise of new emergence.

In addition to the main works of the exhibition, Moe also displayed smaller studies, including both sketches and sculptures, that emphasize the aspect of betweenness or metamorphosis that also characterizes her monumental sculptures. Again and again, the line between natural and made objects is blurred, as is the distinction between making and unmaking, creation and decay. *Study for Untitled* (ca. 2008) is a small, lumpish clay sculpture out of which a human figure seems to be slowly unfolding from, or folding into, a fetal position (fig. 2.16). Rounded limbs recall wide-hipped terracotta images of ancient fertility goddesses, such as the Late Bronze Age terracotta figurine from the Sanctuary of Aphrodite in Old Paphos.[58] We are reminded that the Paphian goddess herself was represented by an unshaped, conical stone, depicted on coins and also commented on by bemused writers. Tacitus, for example, notes that "the form of the goddess" is unique, explaining that "the image of the goddess is not according to human likeness; it is a rounded mass rising like a cone from a broad base to a small circumference." Clearly perplexed, he adds, "The reason for this is unclear" (*Histories* 2.2–4). In 1913, the British archaeologist J. L Myers identified a four-foot-high, roughly conical stone found in the area of Aphrodite's sanctuary with this cultic object; the stone is currently on display in the museum at Old Paphos (current Kouklia) (fig. 2.17).[59] As Milette Gaifman points out, "There is no way to assess the validity of this claim." Rather than a "story of survival," what we have is a testimony to "the remarkable force of ancient visual culture," mediated by coins and texts, and experienced through the lens of modern aesthetic sensibilities.[60]

We might think of the stone of Aphrodite at Paphos as the inverse of the trace of a ruin. Like Moe's clay study, it is the anticipation of a made thing, suspended in a state of near-emergence—the fertile potential of materiality itself. And in this it resembles the trace of a ruin, whose limit case is, as Riegl phrased it, "a shapeless pile of rubble."[61] The goddess's stone can be fruitfully compared to *St. Paul's Pillar*, although the latter is moving in the opposite direction, so to speak (fig. 2.18). The fragment of marble column is

FIGURE 2.16 Ledelle Moe. *Study for Untitled. When* exhibition, MASS MoCA, North Adams, MA, 2019-20. Photograph courtesy of the artist.

FIGURE 2.17 (*left*) Stone of Aphrodite. Museum of Palaipaphos, Cyprus. © Hercules Milas/Alamy Stock Photo. FIGURE 2.18 (*right*) Saint Paul's Pillar. Ruins of the fourth-century Chrysopolitissa basilica, Paphos, Cyprus. © Pete Titmuss/Alamy Stock Photo.

also about four feet high, its once-flat top worn down to a rounded shape, almost conical. Like Paul, and Hilarion too, the marble came from elsewhere, to become part of a building on Cyprus. In it we see the remains of a theater, a church, and an apostle's cult, but we also see its stone-self emerging more clearly as it shrinks and sheds its columnar edges, planting itself in the Paphian soil. Aphrodite's igneous stone, also worn smooth, has been part of Cyprus for much, much longer. Like the goddess, it arose from the depths of the sea, a fragment of the oceanic crust uplifted to become the Troodos mountain range some twenty million years ago, as the African plate was already sliding below the Anatolian plate along the Cyprian Arc that runs just off the coast of Paphos. Geologically speaking, Cyprus itself is a kind of a ruin, suspended in a lithospheric process of destruction and becoming. Most of the time the process is far too slow for human apprehension. But sometimes we feel the jolt of the earth's movement; we see the cities falling. More likely, we see them already fallen.

The famous sanctuary of the Cypriot goddess is now gone, but for the barest trace of ruins, disappointing most visitors. Contemplating it now, even in our imaginations, we may find that we are moved nonetheless. Judith Schalansky writes, "Naturally we can only mourn what is absent or missing if some vestige of it, some whisper, perhaps little more than a rumor, a semiobliterated trace, an echo of an echo has found its way to us."[62] Indeed, it may be the ruin of a ruin, the echo of an echo, the trace of a trace that moves us most powerfully. Is the thing disappearing, or is it emerging? we wonder. Perhaps it is both—"a thing that is and is not," as Andrew Hui puts it. "The ruin exists to remind one of what has endured, what has been lost, but most importantly, what is yet to be."[63] And in that moment, melancholy and consolation are inseparable.

III
THE MOUNTAIN

A more remote place...
twelve miles from the sea
among remote and harsh mountains
that could scarcely be climbed by crawling on hands and knees.
An exceedingly frightening and withdrawn place,
surrounded on all sides by trees,
with water likewise flowing down from the brow of the hill,
and a most delightful little garden and many fruit trees...,
but also nearby the ruin of a most ancient temple
from which the sound of an enormous number of demons
could be heard night and day.

JEROME OF STRIDON

GEOGRAPHIES OF THE REMOTE

Secretiorem locum...   A more remote place...
inter secretos asperosque montes   among remote and harsh mountains
quo uix repetando manibus genibusque posset ascendi   that could scarcely be climbed by crawling on hands and knees.
terribilem ualde et remotum locum   An exceedingly frightening and withdrawn place...

JEROME OF STRIDON

THE DESERT FEATURED CENTRALLY in the late ancient Christian imagination, and it stirs us still.[1] A space virtually devoid of life, empty and forbidding, but also pristine and starkly beautiful—such was the geographical destination of the first holy men, and some others as well, seeking radical transformation through the pursuit of solitude and simplicity. We typically associate these desert places with the arid landscapes of Egypt or Palestine, whence Hilarion came. But arguably it is not aridity so much as remoteness that defines the ascetic habitat as such. In this respect, the landscape of Hilarion's Cypriot retreat is part of a larger, late ancient literary phenomenon that we might call *hagiogeography*—the writing of holy habitats—in which remoteness is the crucial but elusive element. By depicting the hermit's desire for distant and withdrawn places, writers of Saints' Lives highlight the widespread allure of remote landscapes that are shaped by the interplay of intimacy and vastness.

"Remoteness is a complex idea," observes geographer Gerardo Bocco. Attempting to unpack that complexity, he posits both an "absolute, geometric dimension" to remoteness and "a relative, geographic dimension."² The absolute dimension yields a typology based on latitude (circumpolar regions), altitude (mountainous regions), continentality (inland regions), and insularity (islands and peninsulas). If most "isolated, ill-connected, poorly hooked settlements are located in regions described by this typology," as Bocca claims, it nonetheless quickly becomes evident that the relative dimension to remoteness is at least as significant as the absolute. "The very notion of remoteness encompasses both dimensions."³ Distance remains a crucial factor, but even in Bocco's absolute typology, it does not operate on a single, uniform scale: a horizontal mile is obviously not the same measure of remoteness as a mile of altitude, for example. And we must also ask: distance from where and for whom? is the terrain rough or smooth, forested, built, or barren? what technologies of transportation and communication are in place? Questions proliferate, already a warning that the relative dimension of remoteness will prove hard to pin down.

Remoteness is as much a product of inaccessibility, even of merely *perceived* inaccessibility, as of distance as such, and it is always experienced and defined from a particular perspective—this much we can say. It also has a highly subjective, affective component. Despite, or perhaps because of, the challenges they present, remote regions have often been "sources of imagination and fantasy," as Bocca observes.⁴ Both the lure and the horror of insular remoteness are especially notorious. As Judith Schalansky writes in her *Pocket Atlas of Remote Islands*, "beyond their actual geographical coordinates, islands will always be places we project onto, places which we cannot get a hold on through scientific methods but through literature."⁵ Whether desert, island, or another kind of place altogether, remote geographies generally carry an ambivalent charge, evoking both danger and safety, the loneliness of exile and the restfulness of retreat—"a place to find peace, to find oneself, and to finally be able to concentrate on the essentials again."⁶

Here as elsewhere, Athanasius's *Life of Antony* sets the standard for later works, including Jerome's, as the text foregrounds the attraction, as well as the ambivalence, of remote places. As a young man of eighteen or twenty, Athanasius's hero Antony begins a journey that will take him ever farther from the Egyptian village in which he was raised (*Life of Antony* 2). He initially pursues his ascetic practice "outside his home" (πρὸ τῆς οἰκίας). No ascetics were yet familiar with "the distant desert" (τὴν μακρὰν ἔρημον), as Athanasius explains; instead they pursued lives of solitude "not distant from their own village" (οὐ μακρὰν τῆς ἰδίας κώμης). Imitating and learning from his predecessors, Antony too takes up a dwelling "outside his village" (πρὸ τῆς κώμης) (3). The preposition *pro*, which might also be translated "in front of," here indicates peripherality or marginality—outsideness—combined with proximity. Repetition emphasizes the significance of Antony's action of withdrawal—"outside the house," "outside the village"—while also acknowledging that the places of withdrawal are "not distant." Already the text establishes its own scales of remoteness, contrasting the relativity of outsideness with the absoluteness of distance. In Antony's next stage of withdrawal, outsideness and distance begin to converge. Having achieved a degree of proficiency in his practice, he moves to "some tombs that happened to be at a distance [μακρὰν] from the village" (8). Relative both to Antony's village and to his place "outside the village," the tombs are "distant." However, they are not yet simply "the distant desert"; they are still distant in relation to something else, the village.

From this point, it will not be Antony's village that anchors measurements of either peripherality or distance—of remoteness, in short—but rather the Nile and its fertile valley. Spatial cues and coordinates become more richly geographical. Moving east, away from both his village and the river, Antony moves ever farther from the well-watered and low-lying lands on either side of the Nile, entering territory that is both arid and rugged. He is at the threshold of the Eastern Desert, a region that he refers to in a moment of transition as both "the desert" (ἡ ἐρῆμος) and "the mountain" (τὸ ὄρος), in a curious and distinctly Egyptian conflation (11).[7] He also moves away from an active conduit of transportation—for the Nile was Egypt's major connective waterway[8]—and into a terrain that is difficult to traverse. Discovering an abandoned fort infested with reptiles (12), he lives there in complete solitude from roughly age thirty-five to fifty-five[9] before emerging "as if from some shrine" to serve as teacher to the others who now also flock to the desert (14). Eventually, however, "being disturbed by the many and not permitted to withdraw [ἀναχωρεῖν] as he wished," he sets out to find a place where he will not be troubled by the presence of so many fellow-monks and miracle-seekers. He is about sixty at the time he makes his next move.[10]

The hermit's initial impulse is to take a boat south, to the region known as the Upper Thebaid, more remote, certainly, with respect to the metropolis of Alexandria and the busy waters of the Mediterranean. However, a mysterious voice tells him that if he wants "to be at rest" (ἠρεμεῖν), he should instead go further east "to the inner desert" (εἰς τὴν ἐνδοτέραν ἔρημον) (49). Rhyming consonants link *ēremein*, "to be at rest," with *erēmon*, "desert": to arrive at the "inner desert" is to arrive at the heart of restfulness. As on most journeys to extremely remote places, maps and roads do not suffice and may not exist at all; one needs the help of locals personally familiar with the terrain. Antony's guides are "Saracens," members of a nomadic people from the Sinai and Arabian peninsulas further east; few others would be passing through the area or know its pathways. "Journeying three days and three nights with them, he came to a very high mountain. And under the mountain there was water most clear, sweet and very cold. Outside there was a plain, and a few untended date palms. Then Antony, as if divinely moved, fell in love with the place," Athanasius reports. "He remained alone in the mountain, no other living with him. Recognizing it as his own home, henceforth he stayed in that place" (49–50). Antony has arrived.

A certain relativity is still honored: in the phrase "inner desert" (49), "inner" might also be translated "*more* interior," and Antony will continue to shuttle between the "inside [ἔνδον, ἔσω] mountain" and the more populated "outside [ἔξω] mountain," in which virtual cities of monks have sprung up.[11] However, a sense of absolute remoteness also characterizes Antony's final dwelling place—absolute not in the sense that distance is absolute for Bocca, because it is objectively measured, but in the sense of representing a limit case, like the North or South Pole. Here the limit is not of latitude but of interiority—what Bocca calls continentality—and that interiority is accentuated by the ruggedness of the land, which first repels and then protectively enfolds the human visitor. The objective distance from waterways or other major transportation routes is significant but not insurmountable, even when amplified by lack of water sources along the way: less than ninety miles separate the traditional location of Antony's monastery from the Nile, traversable along a wide plain between mountain ridges, and ten more miles would bring him to the Gulf of Suez.[12] Nor is the altitude of the mountains in the region extreme: although the highest peak in the Eastern Desert, Shayeb El-Banat, is more than seven thousand feet, the peaks near Antony's monastery are about half that height, roughly on the scale of the Catskill Mountains in upstate New York.[13] Yet for Athanasius's *Life of Antony*, the "inner mountain" or "distant desert" where Antony lives for almost half a century is as remote as it gets.

If the place is restful in the relative absence of other humans, in other ways it thwarts such expectations. Writing of remote islands, Schalansky observes, "There is no untouched garden of Eden lying at the edges of this never-ending globe. Instead, human beings traveling far and wide have turned into the very monsters they chased off the maps."[14] For Antony, the monsters of remote places are wild animals and demons, mirrors of human depravity. The former eat the produce from the little garden that he plants on a scant patch of arable land; "gently prevailing"—a delicate balancing act, to be sure—he asks them to leave the place, and they do so (50). The latter prove less tractable, waging distinctly ungentle psychic war on him, attempting to drive him away, as he did the animals, but he defends himself with prayer and refuses to leave (51–53). The monsters take many forms, and the hermit embraces all of them. Precisely because of its ambivalent character, the remote place gives him something even better than mere peace and quiet—namely, the opportunity to face down his temptations and hone his strength.

Athanasius wrote his biography of the famous desert hermit around 358 CE, just a couple of years after Antony's death at age 105. At almost exactly the same time, some thousand miles away, two young Cappadocians, recently returned from studies in Athens, were corresponding about their own plans to withdraw to a quiet place.[15] In the earliest surviving letter of their exchange, Gregory (known to posterity as the Nazianzen) responds to a now-lost letter from his friend Basil inviting him to join him on his family's estate in Pontus; there, in a remote spot, Basil had already begun his experiments in ascetic life. "I confess that I broke my promise," Gregory begins: he is not able to join Basil full-time, as he initially vowed, due to his obligation to care for his aging parents. "But I will not break it entirely," he adds, proposing that the two of them split their time between Basil's home and his own, "so that all things will be in common, and the friendship on equal terms" (Gregory of Nazianzus, *Ep.* 1). Basil does not appear to have responded positively to this suggestion: Gregory's next letter complains that his friend has criticized him for the area where he lives "and its mud and winters" (*Ep.* 2). Neither the place nor the commute appeal to Basil, it would seem. He seeks rest from his wandering, as he puts it in a subsequent letter to Gregory. "Having only just renounced those vain hopes which I once had in you, ... I left for Pontus in search of a dwelling [κατὰ βίου ζήτησιν]." His search was not in vain. "There indeed the God showed me a spot [χωρίον] exactly suited to my temperament [τρόπῳ]" (Basil of Caesarea, *Ep.* 14).

Place and the life to be lived in it are intimately connected in Basil's mind. Indeed, the word *bios*, which I have just translated "dwelling" means, more basically, "life" or "way of life," and then by extension the place that supports and enables that life. *Bios* thus converges with *tropos*, which encompasses both "temperament" and "way of life," and the particular landscape that Basil encounters in Pontus matches his sought-for *bios* and *tropos* quite precisely, he assures Gregory. "There is a high mountain [ὄρος ... ὑψηλὸν] ... irrigated with cold and clear waters on the north side. At its base a level plain stretches out, constantly nurtured by the moisture from the mountain" (*Ep.* 14). The elements of mountain, water, and plain resonate with Athanasius's description of Antony's dwelling in the "inner mountain." These are not merely literary adornments (though they are also that): globally, more than half of the planet's mountainous areas function as "water towers" for adjacent lowlands, a role particularly crucial in arid and semiarid regions.[16] The waters of Pontus are more profuse than those of Egypt's Eastern Desert, to say the least, and so, correspondingly, is the vegetation. The mountain is "covered with a thick forest." The plain is ringed by "a spontaneously growing forest of varied, many-colored trees" (*Ep.* 14): like Antony's "few untended date palms" (*Life of Antony* 49), they are not planted or cared for by humans. The trees form a kind of wall, and the beauty of the enclosed space exceeds even that of Calypso's island, Basil declares, calling to mind a line from Homer: "A forest grew luxuriant around the cave, alder and poplar and fragrant cypress" (*Odyssey* 5.63–64). "Indeed, it does not fall very far short from being an island," Basil adds, explaining that the Pontic retreat is separated from the land around it by the mountain on one side, deep ravines on two sides, and on another side a cliff dropping down to a rocky, fast-moving river, churning with rapids and whirlpools; thus protected, the dwelling place can only be approached from above, along a high and narrow ridge. Breezes, flowers, and birdsong lend the spot an idyllic character, but Basil pronounces himself largely immune to such charms. "The most pleasing to me of all the fruits it nourishes is the stillness [ἡσυχίαν]." He ends his letter as he has begun, with a jab at Gregory: how foolish he was ever to have taken his friend's proposal seriously and even to have considered trading such a spot for one in Gregory's native region, "that pit of the whole world," populated not by the gentle (and edible) deer, goats, and hares of Pontus but by fierce bears and wolves (*Ep.* 14).

Basil's tone is difficult to read here, and evidently Gregory found it so too. Was the mockery "playful or serious"? he wonders aloud in a return letter. He answers his own question by dismissing it. "It does not matter: only laugh, and be filled with learning, and enjoy our friendship!" he urges his companion (*Ep.* 4). By this point, Gregory has himself spent time at Basil's Pontic retreat and is well able to respond to Basil's letter in kind, matching his literary rendition of a "pleasant place" with a "horrible" one. Delivered in two installments, Gregory's self-proclaimed diatribe mercilessly mocks Basil's Pontic retreat and—even more—Basil's idealizing description of it. The place is "an abode worthy of exile," gloomy, sunless, hemmed in by mountains, and overgrown with thornbushes; the approach is treacherous, the river noisy and violent.[17] Should Gregory, following Basil's lead, falsely name it "Eden" or absurdly compare it with the "Isles of the Blessed"? "Blessed" indeed, he scoffs—no wonder no one visits! (*Ep.* 4). As for the domicile itself, the shelter is rough and damp, the garden barren, the labor required to render the place livable unbearably hard (*Ep.* 5).

With such unflattering depictions, Gregory is clearly having fun while also exacting a kind of revenge for Basil's criticism of his own region. He expresses confidence that Basil will accept the two letters in the jocular spirit in which they are intended (*Ep.* 5). Moreover, Gregory's playful epistolary discourses are followed by a third, this one explicitly marked as "serious" and notably gentler in tone. Now he longs for his time in Pontus, with the hardships, psalmody, prayer, vigils and study, the growing together and single-mindedness of the "brothers," the daily routines and chores (*Ep.* 6). At least to an extent, the two young men appear to have resolved their differences regarding the proper landscape for the pursuit of ascetic virtue.

As with the *Life of Antony*, remoteness is associated in this epistolary exchange with a rugged, inland geography. And here it is even more obviously the case that absolute distance does not tell the full story. Several attempts have been made to locate Basil's retreat, and it now appears that the spot lies on the southern edge of the Pontic Mountains some sixty miles from the coast of the Black Sea, in a bend in the Yeşilirmak River (the ancient Iris), northwest of the village Kaleköy in Tokat, Turkey;[18] there, as in Antony's dwelling place, the peaks are moderate in height, mostly from three to four thousand feet, although further east Kaçkar Daği rises to an impressive 12,917 feet. Most telling, however, of the relative insignificance of distance in configuring remoteness is the fact that the spot was located on the family estate, and Basil's mother lived close enough that she could deliver provisions (Gregory of Nazianzus, *Ep.* 5). Nonetheless, the sense of isolation was apparently real, as both Basil's idealizing and Gregory's satirizing accounts emphasize.

Indeed, Basil could compare the place to an island notorious for its remoteness: no one knew exactly where Calypso's Ogygia was located, but the speculation of some geographers placed it in the Atlantic Ocean, somewhere past Britain (Strabo 1.2.18; Plutarch, *On the Face of the Moon* 26). According to Homer, the island was beautiful enough to captivate even a god like Hermes, but not so beautiful that it could remove Odysseus's sorrow when he endured seven years of involuntary exile on its shores (*Odyssey* 5.55–84). Gregory seems to capture the ambivalence of islands implicit in Basil's Homeric reference when he refers to the Pontic retreat jokingly as both a would-be paradise and a place appropriate for exile. In the end, the two poles converge, as the remote place is valued for both the restful solitude and the challenging hardship that it offers ascetic Christians. Exile *is* paradise, for a monk. If monsters haunt cartographic boundaries, so too do their Doppelgänger, hermits seeking places on the treacherous "edge" (ἐσχατιάν τινα) of civilized territory (Gregory of Nyssa, *Life of Macrina* 3).

Although Jerome would not have been familiar with the correspondence between Basil and Gregory when he wrote his *Life of Hilarion* around 390 CE, he clearly had Athanasius's *Life of Antony* in mind. Hilarion is said to have been Antony's disciple in the Egyptian desert for two months. Like Athanasius's Antony, he tires of the "crowds," but whereas Antony departs for the inner mountain, Hilarion heads back home to take up life in the still-uninhabited desert of Palestine, as we have seen (*Life of Hilarion* 3). Decades later, when he learns of Antony's death, he leaves a now-crowded Palestine for good, and one of his first stops on the journey that eventually ends in Cyprus is Antony's hermitage. In Jerome's description, the worlds of Antony's "outer" and "inner mountains" seem to be collapsed into a single, more compact territory, and also more generously endowed. The plain at the foot of the "rocky and high mountain" is described as containing not just a few but "innumerable" palms shading a stream, and Antony is said to have worked the land well with his hands and his hoe, planting vines, small trees, and vegetables, and excavating a pool for irrigation. High above this plain, two cells are cut into the top of the mountain, which is accessible only "by climbing as if in a spiral and with very arduous effort"; there Antony could retreat when he wanted to escape his disciples and visitors (31). This description of Antony's dwelling partly anticipates Jerome's subsequent depiction of Hilarion's hermitage, as we have seen, especially with its emphasis on the difficulty of the ascent (43).

Hilarion's hermitage also betrays affinities with Basil's Pontic retreat, despite the fact that we cannot posit direct literary influence. Shared literary imaginations, ascetic values, and perhaps also similar geographical familiarities mold kindred landscapes. Like Basil's, Hilarion's retreat is encircled by trees and watered by streams flowing down the side of a mountain or hill: again, we encounter the mountain as water tower. Like Basil's, Hilarion's retreat combines elements of typical, literary "pleasant places" with those of "horrible" ones. Described as "remote and harsh," "frightening and withdrawn," the holy habitat is haunted by demons who might have wandered in from the desert of Athanasius's *Life of Antony*. Yet at the same time, it boasts not only forest and streams but also "a most delightful little garden [*hortulum*] and many fruit trees [*pomaria*], the fruit of which he never took for food" (43). Although the landscape compares favorably with what Gregory describes mockingly as Basil's "gardenless gardens without produce" (Gregory of Nazianzus, *Ep.* 5), Hilarion shows even less interest than do the Cappadocians and the Egyptian Antony in cultivating his bit of land. Basil and Gregory seemingly attempt but fail to revive a ruined garden, while admiring the wild forest, and Antony strikes a similar (albeit more successful) compromise, marking the palm trees as untended while planting a patch of vegetables. But Hilarion will not even eat the fruit spontaneously produced by the trees among which he dwells.

Like both Antony's and Basil's retreats, Hilarion's hermitage is remote primarily because of its interiority and rugged terrain, despite the fact that Jerome tells us quite specifically that it is only twelve miles from the coast (*Life of Hilarion* 43). "It could scarcely be climbed by crawling on hands and knees," we read. And indeed the steep ascent initially discourages visitors quite effectively. "On account of the harshness and difficulty of the location and the multitude of ghosts, as was popularly claimed, no one, or only the rare person, could or dared climb up to him." When people do eventually start to seek Hilarion out, they must overcome "the difficulty of the location and the trackless pathway" (43). Such a description suits the forested Troodos Mountains that cover much of western Cyprus, notable for their distinctive igneous rock formations and copper deposits; the highest peak is Mount Olympos at 6,404 feet. However, Hilarion's hideaway seems not to have been located in the mountains proper but in the hilly region that lies between the mountains and the coastal plain around Paphos. It would have been the particular contours of the local topography, more than the altitude as such, that made the spot so difficult to access. At Episkopi in the district of Paphos, where some locate the monk's place of retreat, a monolithic limestone cliff rises 230 feet above the village. Such a terrain might well create a sense of remoteness, despite the relative modesty of the cliff's 650-foot elevation.

It may seem paradoxical that it should be interiority—Bocca's "continentality"—that conditions the remoteness of this island spot, rather than its sea-girt isolation—Bocca's "insularity." However, island topography often lends itself readily to strong contrasts between coast and interior, especially in the case of larger islands like Cyprus, and a city like Paphos might find itself almost as well connected by sea to Patara in Asia Minor, Alexandria or Pelusium in Egypt, Ascalon or Caesarea in Palestine, as to some points in the interior of the island. Indeed, the inner mountains might seem like another world altogether, albeit one connected with the coastal cities by networks of roads that enabled the transport of copper and timber, for example, from interior to coastal harbor. As Jody Michael Gordon suggests, "When an archaeology of the sea is connected to that of the land, Cyprus' coastal cities appear as coastscape nodes in a larger network of islandscapes that were experienced by a range of peoples who could likely move between the hinterland, the coast, the sea, and even adjacent mainlands, and could actively manipulate their insularity in accordance with whom they interacted. The Cypriot cities of the coast could act as liminal points between the Roman Mediterranean and hinterland areas."[19] In other words, a sea like the Mediterranean could create connection as much as isolation, and on an island as large and complex as Cyprus, insularity is not always what and where it seems to be.

Thus the particular status of Cyprus as an island inflects the remoteness of Hilarion's dwelling, just as the aridity of the Eastern Desert inflects the remoteness Antony's dwelling, and the steep, well-watered valleys of the Pontic mountains inflect the remoteness of Basil's dwelling. And Cypriot insularity reads in a certain way from the perspective of an outsider like Jerome. Catherine Kearns argues that Cyprus holds a distinctive position in the ancient literary imaginary, one that continues to influence even present scholarship. She calls attention to "paradoxical treatments of the island as familiar but unfamiliar, in range but distant, civilized but made up of subjects rather than *polis* citizens."[20] Situated between west and east—for Jerome, between Rome and Bethlehem—at the very limit of the Mediterranean itself, Cyprus was known as a place of betweenness and transit, and it continues to be conceived of as marginal with respect to both Europe and the Middle East. Hilarion himself was only passing through, in his seemingly endless quest for a place sufficiently remote to hold him. Hold him Cyprus did, or very nearly so, not only because of its insular interiority (he had attempted something similar in Sicily but failed) but also because of its peculiar peripherality. Cyprus was a place where a hermit could both find and lose himself, on the edge of every map, at once familiar and strange, near and far in relation to his Palestinian beginning point. And as Schalansky suggests, "An island offers a stage: everything that happens on it is practically forced to turn into a story, into a chamber piece in the middle of nowhere, into the stuff of literature."[21] Cyprus did not give Hilarion, an outsider, a lasting shrine or cult, but it did give him a stage and a story; it helped make him the stuff of literature.

"I feel that remoteness should be a heritage resource that people have access to," writes artist and cognitive theorist Ryan Dewey in 2014.[22] It is a resource all the more valuable when the mesh of our interconnectivity has become so dense, he suggests. The pandemic conditions of 2020–21 and beyond have now significantly affected our experience of both interconnectivity and remoteness. For many of us, distance may seem to have collapsed: everything is equally far and equally near when it arrives on the screens of our computers, and we call it all "remote," even if it has invaded our very homes. "In existence where everything is interconnected, everything plummets haphazardly into the same heap," as philosopher Michael Marder warns.[23] It does not matter if a place is around the corner or across the globe, if you cannot go there but *can* have it come to you—sort of. At the same time, the scope for embodied experiences of geographical remoteness has narrowed dramatically, as we are confined to our smallest living spaces. In this context, access to "real" remote spaces has become a more precious resource than ever. Open-air walks uncoil our bodies, and unfurling beauty comforts our hearts.

Thus pandemic restrictions seem to have intensified the need that Dewey identifies. "Learning to design spaces and paths that evoke notions of remoteness is an important task for helping people encounter a world that lacks the moments of refuge that spatial remoteness provides," he suggests, with an eye to landscape design.[24] Refuge from what? Paradoxically, at least in part, refuge from our own isolation. Dewey proposes that remoteness "brings the larger oceanic sensations of our experience of the size of the earth to the foreground of our attention. It gives us a tool that lets us see ourselves in scale with the earth."[25] To experience the remote is to experience oneself as part of something much, much larger and much, much longer-lived than oneself. But it is also to experience the fact that distances, always both relative and absolute in their measure, do matter, and never more so than in the relational movements by which they are traversed. In spatial terms, with respect to our apprehension of a remote place or object, "either we go to it or it comes to us in one way or another," writes Dewey.[26] For a writer, a landscape architect, or a visual artist, it is all about the "in one way or another."

Dewey's own *Copper Boulder* (2018) uses an object placed in relation to a landscape to evoke complex experiences of remoteness. The work consists of an irregularly shaped, copper, hollow-form repoussé sculpture, approximately three feet in diameter, with a window-like rectangular cut-out in the middle (figs. 3.1, 3.2). Produced on site in Tenna, Switzerland, the sculpture was moved to different locations in the alpine forest during the period of its installation in the summer of 2018. Photographs show it nestled against a tree trunk as if it has just come to rest after rolling down the steep-sided mountain, the copper gleaming brightly against the rich greens and gray-browns of the forest.[27] A video clip shows it burrowed on a slope in a grotto-like space among boulders and ferns.[28] The project proposal states that the emphasis is on sites "with strong verticality";[29] this would seem designed to accentuate the remote character of the terrain and the elusive object set in it. The object both does and does not appear to belong to the landscape, as it both blends and pops visually. Glittering metal extruded from the earth's fiery interior, it has not yet become fully incorporated into the weathered surface. It calls attention to itself in other ways too: the aperture in the middle of the "boulder" not only frames the view of the landscape, making viewers aware of their own act of looking, but also invites them to penetrate beneath surfaces of both space and time.

As Dewey explains, *Copper Boulder* intends to "draw formal comparisons between the economics of resource extraction and the geologic systems of glacial erratics, as both systems have left shaping marks on Swiss geology."[30] The former stretches back to the Bronze Age, when chalcopyrite, a common source of copper, began to be mined in this area, just as ophiolitic copper deposits were mined in Cyprus.[31] The latter draws us into far deeper history: young for a glaciation, the Würm ice age, when the Swiss Plateau was last covered in glaciers, nonetheless dates to between 11,700 and 115,000 years ago. Temporal remoteness is thus part of the experience of *Copper Boulder*, and the slow-moving temporal frame also allows us to travel a distance with the movements of ice and rock. The more recent, if still long-standing, movements of the copper trade draw themselves closer to our own temporal scale, and we may be reminded that it is copper's conductivity that has enabled our networks of electricity and information to flow so swiftly over the last two centuries.

In the meantime, we continue to gaze, and the enigmatic object gleams above on the thickly forested mountainside—copper, known by ancient Latin-speakers as *aes Cyprium*, "the metal of Cyprus." Sometimes it can barely be glimpsed, drawing us up the slope for a better sighting. We may lose ourselves in the landscape of tree and rock, immersed in its vastness,

FIGURES 3.1 AND 3.2 Ryan Dewey. *Copper Boulder*. Copper, hollow-form repoussé. Tenna, Graubünden, Switzerland, 2018. Photographs courtesy of the artist.

for stretches of the climb. And then a line of sight opens up, our eyes glide swiftly across the intervening space, and the thing seems to jump out at us, meeting us at least halfway.[32] Marking the landscape, the object focuses and intensifies our experience of its remoteness, matching distance with a strange kind of intimacy. If we actually reach it—and perhaps we never will—it will only draw us further, opening a window onto another "beyond."

I did not experience Dewey's *Copper Boulder* directly in its dramatic alpine setting, but only visited remotely, so to speak, through the mediation of

FIGURES 3.3, 3.4, AND 3.5 Thomas Schütte. *Crystal*. The Clark Art Institute, Williamstown, MA. 2015. Photographs courtesy of The Clark Art Institute. Photographers: Mike Agee, figs. 3.3 and 3.4 (*above*); Tucker Bair, fig. 3.5 (*page opposite*).

photography, video recording, and my own imagination. (Sometimes such experiences are not simply a hopeless "dump" of sameness.) However, I have lived for almost a year in close physical proximity to another work of art that facilitates a similar experience of geographical remoteness, in the more modestly scaled mountains of the northern Berkshires. Thomas Schütte's *Crystal* (2015) was created and installed following a major redesign of the 140-acre campus of the Clark Art Institute in Williamstown, Massachusetts, in which museum architecture was integrated with landscape via a series of reflection ponds and an upgraded network of trails (figs. 3.3, 3.4, 3.5).[33] Until 2020, *Crystal* was the only work of outdoor art on the Clark grounds, lending it a singular prominence. Conceived as "a small piece of crystal scaled up to architectural proportions,"[34] Schütte's angular, multifaceted structure catches the eye from afar with its unusual shape and hilltop perch above the museum. Carefully sited at the edge of a sloping meadow against a backdrop of woods, it seems to sit directly on the horizon line; it almost floats. Yet *Crystal*, like the cliff above Episkopi, Cyprus, is only a couple of hundred feet above the Clark, on a crest of Stone Hill perhaps half as high as the 1138-foot summit; Stone Hill itself is itself dwarfed by the Taconic, Berkshire, and Green mountains that surround it. Once again, the particular contours of the landscape are more important to a sense of remoteness than absolute distance or elevation.

Drawing the gaze, the sculpture invites approach and even entry, as one side opens to reveal a hollow interior. Those who follow the steep path up from the museum discover that the entryway is not through the open front, which does indeed float just off the ground, but through a closed doorway on the more sheltered back side. Setting foot in the shadowy interior, the visitor's gaze is immediately pulled into the bright, broad vista that opens up dramatically on the opposite side, where a cluster of wild cherry and ash trees is visible in the foreground, a line of mountains in the distance, as figure 3.5 shows. The work was deliberately situated "so that the view from the structure's open side would embrace the natural landscape rather than the Clark campus or Williamstown."[35] Like Dewey's *Copper Boulder*, Schütte's *Crystal* frames a view, but rather than narrowing and focusing vision, it seems to draw it out. As the visitor's eyes sweep across the terrain, their movement activates the dynamism that inheres in the landscape.[36] Whether one is looking at it or from it, the sculpture creates a strong sense of both spacing and connection, in the visual triangulation of object, human, and landscape.

The materiality of *Crystal* also has particular implications and effects. Lined top, side, and bottom with boards of radiata pine, in appearance similar to an unfinished floor, the pale yellow interior, faintly mottled by mildew, links the sculpture with both the forested terrain and the residential architecture of surrounding Williamstown, hinting at temporal processes of growing and making. The exterior is covered with sheets of zinc-coated copper similar to those used in metal roofs, giving the structure a silvery appearance, now dulled by weathering, at once resolutely modern and timelessly elemental. Like most metals in their solid state, both zinc and copper—the metal of Cyprus, again!—are crystalline in structure; thus the outer materials echo the form, which was conceived to be "suggestive of certain types of stone" that are part of Stone Hill's geology.[37] In winter months, when it is often lightly blanketed in snow, the sculpture may suggest the crystalline structure of a snowflake as well. Part of the particular power of *Crystal* is its evocation of both natural and made things: its title tilts toward the former, but its form and materials refuse to resolve themselves, hovering ambiguously between the earthy and the fabricated, sculpture and dwelling.[38] On sunny days, local college students lounge in its shelter, heads bent over books or computers—transient hilltop hermits.

At about the same time that Thomas Schütte's *Crystal* was being installed at the Clark Art Institute, twenty-five miles south, in the small city of Pittsfield, two young architects, both Berkshire natives, were conceiving a project called *The Mastheads*. Launched in 2017, *Mastheads* centers around five small, mobile wooden "studios," 8′ × 8′ × 13′ structures built on roughly the same scale as *Crystal* (figs. 3.6, 3.7). These structures are both more decisively architectural and more explicitly referential than *Crystal*, however. Each "interprets a fragment of the historic structures where five American Renaissance authors wrote while in and around Pittsfield"—Herman Melville, Nathaniel Hawthorne, Henry Wadsworth Longfellow, Oliver Wendell Holmes Sr., and Henry David Thoreau.[39] Now permanently installed on the grounds of Herman Melville's former home, Arrowhead, the studios not only revive historical memories of literary activity in the region, but also revive literary activity in the present. Every July the project hosts monthlong residencies, bringing five emerging writers from across the country to live and work in Pittsfield; each receives one of the studios for their exclusive use as a work space during the residency. At other times, the studios are available for anyone to reserve for single-day use, an opportunity of which I myself took advantage in June of 2021. The initial goal of *Mastheads*, as cofounder Tessa Kelly explains it, was to explore "how we could, as architects, define historic preservation as something other than mere reconstruction."[40] Each structure conjures a culturally rich past without simply replicating it, so as to expand possibilities for the future in a community that (unlike Williamstown) suffers from the economic and cultural impoverishment of its postindustrial moment and condition.

Kelly and her partner Chris Parkinson chose the title of their project to allude to Melville's historic presence in Pittsfield, where he lived while writing his famous novel *Moby Dick*. As Ishmael, the novel's narrator, describes it, "standing mast-heads" was a task crucial to the activity and success of a whaling ship, for it was from the masthead that whales could be spotted. "The three mast-heads are kept manned from sun-rise to sun-set; the seamen taking their regular turns (as at the helm) and relieving each other every two hours."[41] However crucial, the task was frequently carried out poorly. Surprisingly, the problem was not the difficulty and danger of clinging to a perch that lacked even the luxury of the "crow's nests" installed on the masts of northern whalers, but the pleasantness of the experience of standing upon "two thin parallel sticks" a hundred feet above the deck, in warmer climes. "To a dreamy man it is delightful.... There you stand, lost in the infinite series of the sea, with nothing ruffled but the waves.... A

FIGURES 3.6 AND 3.7 Tessa Kelly and Chris Parkinson. *The Mastheads Studios*. Arrowhead (the Herman Melville house), Pittsfield, MA, 2017. © Iwan Baan Photography.

sublime uneventfulness invests you."[42] To such a person, sighting whales is of little interest, Ishmael suggests. Rather than focusing his attention, "standing mast-heads" allows his thoughts to drift freely and far, until he is at one with the vastness of sky and sea. "At last he loses his identity; takes the mystic ocean at his feet for the visible image of that deep, blue, bottomless soul, pervading mankind and nature." Every half-glimpsed creature of the depths "seems to him the embodiment of those elusive thoughts that only people the soul by continually flitting through it." Self is absorbed into ship, ship into sea, sea into "the inscrutable tides of God."[43]

As Kelly notes, Melville here brings together "the intimate and the immense," and the *Mastheads* project draws inspiration from this conjunction. The studios, like Melville's mastheads, "provide only enough space for a single body but open onto vastness, giving the sense of being in the midst of a much larger landscape."[44] As with Schütte's *Crystal*, the sense of expansiveness is achieved through a mixture of siting and sight lines. Installed on a gentle rise just a brief walk from the Melville farmhouse, the studios are situated so that they are invisible to one another, despite their relative proximity. Covered in pine tar, their dark, geometrical shapes seem at home in the landscape, whether set off against the snow of winter or melting into the greening trees of summer; they are as strange and humble as monks. Each structure creates an interior space of intimate enclosure pierced by carefully framed views, both shallow (the nearby woods) and expansive (the more distant mountains); the occupant can decide on the balance of privacy and openness, light and shadow, by manipulating window panels and doors. In addition, the studios conjure the vantage points and views of each of the five writers' work spaces, such as Melville's own study in the nearby farmhouse. There his desk abuts a window looking out onto Mount Greylock, the highest peak in the Berkshires. Melville imagined the mountain to have a whale-like form, discernible from his own second-floor perch, a virtual masthead from which he surveyed the landscape spread out before him, where grasses ripple like waves.

All five of the writers memorialized in the *Mastheads* studios came to Pittsfield and the Berkshires in search of a remote place to pursue their work, Kelly explains. The same is true for current writers who take up temporary residence in the studios. Renouncing certain forms of social and technological connectivity, they gain not only sharpened focus on their own creative projects but also deepened awareness of their connection to the larger, more-than-human landscape in which they find themselves embedded. The studios themselves, simple but arresting in design, call attention to their own woody materiality, and some writers find themselves turning back to basics, eschewing computers in favor of handwritten pages.

Interestingly, Melville's Ishmael constructs an architectural genealogy for the practice of "standing mast-heads," which can take place, he suggests, either "ashore or afloat." The Babylonians, with their famous biblical tower, represent a false start to this history: although they "intended to rear the loftiest mast-head in all Asia, or Africa either," their efforts were destroyed by god before they were finished. This leaves the Egyptians as the earliest "mast-head standers," with their equally well-known pyramids, built as astronomical lookouts, according to Melville. After the Egyptians, Ishmael names "Saint Stylites, the famous Christian hermit of old times, who built him a lofty stone pillar in the desert and spent the whole latter portion of his life on its summit." From there, achievements plummet: "Of modern standers-of-mast-heads we have but a lifeless set"—Paris's Napoleon, Baltimore's Washington, London's Nelson, mere statues set atop towering columns.[45] Thus the Christian hermit, pronounced "dauntless," takes pride of place alongside the Egyptians, in the lineage of masthead-standers claimed by the dreamy whale-spotters. With focus on the stylite, the verticality of remoteness is emphasized, its lofty purchase and sweeping views. And we come full circle to our other mountain-standing ascetics.

Writer and activist Rebecca Solnit gives powerful expression to the lure of remoteness. "For many years I have been moved by the blue at the far edge of what can be seen, that color of horizons, of remote mountain ranges, of anything far away." The blue at the far edge of things can never be reached, however. "For the blue is not in the place those miles away at the horizon, but in the atmospheric distance between you and the mountains," writes Solnit. "Blue is the color of longing for the distances you never arrive in."[46] Referencing Solnit's words, art historian Michael Ann Holly writes of "the enchantments of painted backgrounds" discovered in Northern Renaissance paintings. She traces the attraction of distant landscapes—"the far off, the beyond where serenity resides"—in backgrounds that counterbalance the often horrific events unfolding in the foreground, "in life or in art."[47] This "beyond" is what beckons in more contemporary and interactive works as well, as when we view Dewey's *Copper Boulder* high on the alpine mountainside, or peer through its hollow middle, letting background become foreground. It is what draws us to Schütte's *Crystal* or *The Mastheads* studios, perched on their hilltops; and it is what we see when we enter the intimacy of their enclosures, only to find ourselves absorbed in the distant landscapes framed by their windows, the blue of the horizon still not here but there. Indeed, there is always more: after "where you are not," there is "where you can never go."[48] Anchored in place by architecture that teaches us where and how to look, we encounter a worldly transcendence in the dizzying scale of things, as remoteness "brings the larger oceanic sensations of our experience of the size of the earth to the foreground of our attention," to cite Dewey again.[49] We glimpse, just barely, "the point of view of the mountain," as art historian Estelle Zhong Mengual puts it, adding, "Only the mountain has lived long enough to listen objectively to the howl of a storm."[50]

Hilarion knew the allure of remote places. What made him finally stop in Cyprus, then, rather than continuing his pursuit of the ever-receding blue beyond? Perhaps it was his age. Perhaps it was a room with a view, like Antony's lofty rock-hewn cell, that allowed him to see from the perspective of a mountain—that rendered him indifferent to the howl of a storm, or of the demons of history. That is not to say that he lost sight of the foreground altogether: those in need of healing or advice continued to seek and to find him and to receive his attention. Yet at the same time he let himself be gradually absorbed by the background, vast and ancient, of which he was equally a part. Maybe this is what he had been yearning for all along.

ENTROPIC GARDENS

locum arboribusque hinc inde circumdatum	a place surrounded on all sides by trees,
habentem etiam aquas de supercilio collis irriguas	with water likewise flowing down from the brow of the hill,
et hortulum peramoenum et pomaria plurima	and a most delightful little garden and many fruit trees,
quorum fructum numquam in cibo sumpsit	the fruit of which he never consumed as food,
sed et antiquissimi iuxta templi ruinam	but also nearby the ruin of a most ancient temple.

JEROME OF STRIDON

HILARION MAY HAVE ENJOYED the shelter of a cave or a hut during the last five years of his life. However, Jerome tells us nothing of this. He focuses instead on other features of the old man's habitat—the difficult ascent, the encircling forest, the tumbling waterfall, the garden and fruit trees (*Life of Hilarion* 43). In all of this, the *hortulus*, or little garden, receives particular attention. Diminutive forms suggest that the plot of land was modest in size, and the context suggests that it may have been derelict. Jerome notes in passing that the garden was under the jurisdiction of a nearby *villula*, or farm (43). A manager (*procurator*), presumably a slave, was present on the estate, but Hilarion was initially unaware of him, nor did the manager (who suffered from a paralyzing illness) seem to care that a holy man was living on the property (43). Such a circumstance is not implausible: rural settlements in Cyprus, like cities, declined in the third and fourth centuries.[1] Jerome also reports that the hermit was buried in the *hortulus* at his own request (44–45), that his Cypriot follower Constantia used to visit his burial place (47), that his Palestinian disciple Hesychius came to stay in the *hortulus*, eventually stealing away with his master's body (46), and that miracles continued to occur in the garden even after his body was removed (47).

These fragments of description and narration are enticing. How might we imagine life in a garden that was not only remote but also seemingly untended? What are we to make of the curious fact that Hilarion dwelled in the garden but did not eat the fruits of its trees (43)? Why, finally, was the garden so dear to Hilarion that he wanted to be part of it, even beyond his own death?

When it comes to gardens, "perspective matters," writes plant philosopher Michael Marder. "Are we contemplating gardens from the inside, looking out, or from the outside, prying into them?" Most of us contemplate gardens from the outside, as spectators, even if we are wandering through them. From this point of view, a garden is an enclosure that guards against the encroachment of aliens—undesired plants, insects, birds, rodents—and imposes form on the otherwise excessive growth of even the desired, cultivated plants. "The garden is the form of form, a meta-order bent on preserving order as such," Marder declares. Within its confines "the most diverse beings are primed for appropriation."[2] Through the work of gardening, a piece of land is subjected to human control and possession, yielding ordered beauty and consumable fruits. On such terms, Hilarion's garden would seem to make no sense.

However, when contemplated from within, a garden looks quite different, suggests Marder. Let us imagine that this is how Hilarion saw it. From the midst of a garden we perceive "a mélange of living beings that inhabit or pass through it—grass, bushes, flowers, trees, bees, mosquitoes, birds, spiders, worms, the microorganisms dwelling in the soil, and, last but not least, ourselves." The complete triumph of form over matter toward which the garden tends, when viewed from the outside, would mean the extinction of all life within. "Something of the forest admittedly survives in the garden as well," Marder acknowledges. Indeed, something of the forest—that is, the wild—*must* survive. "The forest breaks through the form of the garden." It breaks through in and as its own materializing, nonformal forms. It breaks through in and as the "ontic exuberance and uncontrollable efflorescence of vegetal life" itself,[3] emerging in the constant exchange between plants, soil, water, air, light, and other living creatures, so many of them invisible to the human eye. Anyone who has weeded and pruned knows that a garden is always threatening its own wilding—not a human-engineered "rewilding" but the irrepressible surge of vitality arising from the plants themselves. The withdrawal of externally imposed form, whether accidental or intentional, complete or partial, allows the garden "to grow from the interactions among its various participants, be they organic or inorganic." Pivoting from dystopia to utopia, Marder adds that a garden freed of formal control "would not figure as property, and certainly not as private property." There would be "no one to guard and plenty of human and nonhuman actors to care for it."[4] There would be no distinction between the garden and its gardeners, one might say.

Would the distinction between the garden and the forest, that emblem of wildness, also disappear? Not quite, if this is still a garden. A garden has its own history, just as a forest does, and that history involves humans, whose traces may persist long after they have left. The descriptor "most delightful" might suggest that Hilarion's garden was originally ornamental in purpose (43). The presence of untouched fruit trees, combined with mention of "the ruin of a very old temple" in the vicinity, further hints at the possibility that the garden was part of a god's precinct—a sacred garden, then (43). However, subsequent clarification that the garden is part of a small farm points more decisively to a productive garden—a kitchen garden, we could call it (43). "Productive gardens were often nestled within the architecture of villas or adjoined them," as the archaeological record shows.[5] And at least one domestic garden excavated at Pompeii included small trees among the other plants. "Although trees in kitchen gardens are not mentioned by ancient writers, they may have been common, just as they are in kitchen gardens of modern Pompeii," garden archaeologist Wilhelmina Jashemski suggests.[6] The mid-first-century agricultural writer Columella mentions mulberries, plums, apricots, damsons, and peaches at the end of his "garden poem" (*On Agriculture* 10.400–418), strengthening Jashemski's suggestion. Let us assume, then, that Hilarion's "little garden" included "many fruit trees," though it may also have simply abutted an orchard (43). As the late fourth- or early fifth-century agricultural writer Palladius notes, such proximity was recommended: "Gardens and orchards ought to be very near the house" (*On Agriculture* 1.34).

Literary sources augment material remains to give some sense not only of where gardens were located and what plants they included but also of how the activity of gardening was both practiced and conceptualized in Roman antiquity. Columella's agricultural handbook innovates by devoting its tenth volume entirely to horticulture. Presented as a poetic supplement to Vergil's *Georgics*, which (by Vergil's own admission) neglected the topic of gardening, the poem's 436 hexameters serve as a supplement to Columella's own prosaic account of farming as well. As John Henderson has argued, Columella's verses emerge as a kind of vegetal efflorescence, "a flowery burst of hothouse enthusiasm," that complements and contrasts with "the world of canny, applied know-how of garden lovers everywhere" that supersedes it in Book 11.[7] There the matter-of-fact tone of the treatment of farming in Books 1–9 is resumed, in a calendrical recapitulation first of farming and then of gardening instruction directed to the *vilicus*, or farm manager. Book 12, directed to the *vilica*, the male manager's female counterpart, focuses on the intake of produce from the entire estate, weaving farm and garden products into one account. At the end of the agricultural process, the separate domains of field and garden no longer matter: domestic production is multicultural. But so too is gardening. Thus, despite its modest scope and marginal status, the garden is a microcosm of the entire farm.[8] "Horticulture is agriculture and arboriculture writ small—but it is a concentrated replica of the whole; an intense, intensive fraction."[9] To garden is to engage on a small scale with an intricate diversity of lavish and astonishing plants, each with its own special needs and timetable—flowers, vegetables, herbs, fruits. Ostensibly controlled and contained, the garden always exceeds its bounds; indeed, it reveals vegetal life itself—all life, perhaps—as uncontainable. From this perspective, as Henderson puts it (*pace* Marder), "What is *more* poetic than gardening?"[10] Which is also to say: What is more extravagant, more superfluous, or more pleasurable?[11]

Columella was a major source, though by no means the only one, for the agricultural writer Palladius, a contemporary of Jerome. Palladius reserves poetry for a volume on grafting and organizes his prose work on farming according to the flow of work across the seasons of the year. One volume is dedicated to each month's tasks, and each volume includes a chapter on gardening. But before he describes the annual cycle of gardening, Palladius must, like Columella, describe the garden itself. In the introduction to the work, he specifies that the garden should be located not only near the house (like the orchard) but also near the cattle barn, "the moisture of which may fertilize it spontaneously." There should be a river, well, or reservoir nearby. The soil should not be too claylike. Finally, the garden should be enclosed with a fence, whether made from brick, stones, or a hedge of thornbushes, and it should be divided internally into twelve-by-six-foot raised beds (Palladius, *On Agriculture* 1.34).

Columella's poem begins its celebration of horticulture with flowers—

snowdrops, marigolds, narcissus, snapdragons, lilies, hyacinths, violets, roses, all-heal, celandine, and poppies (Columella, *On Agriculture* 10.96–109)—and ends with fruits (10.400–418), as we have seen. Palladius omits such flourishes, focusing exclusively on the plants at the heart of the garden—vegetables and herbs. The sober work of vegetable gardening unfolds month by month, with the slow but inexorable turn of the seasons, each bringing its distinctive set of tasks, which must be folded into the larger context and workload of the farm. Tellingly, the garden's exuberant growth cannot be entirely ordered and contained even by the heavily imposed calendrical structure of Palladius's work. The art of horticulture rests in the details, and the timing of planting varies according to individual species, as well as climate and other environmental conditions; the sowing of a particular plant may also stretch across more than one month or occur in multiple growing seasons. January's volume introduces the versatile lettuce plant, to take merely the first example that occurs. But we immediately learn that lettuce can also be sown in December and transplanted in February or sown in February and transplanted in April. In fact, "it may be sown all the year, if the place is rich, well manured, and watered." Not only does January's volume lose its temporal focus with lettuce, but the account of lettuce loses focus on lettuce itself, since we also learn that the plant can benefit from being sown together with other seeds—cress, basil, rocket, radish—so long as they are all fertilized with goat dung. This leads Palladius to remark that cress and rocket can be sown not only in January but in any month, and the same is true for cabbage. Garlic does well when sown in January, but that is not the only time it can be planted (Palladius, *On Agriculture* 2.14). And so the months roll by, offering possibility as much as prescription with respect to timing and other aspects of horticulture. Familiar plants appear along with new ones in most of the volumes: February adds artichoke, coriander, poppy, savory, onions, dill, mustard, asparagus, mallow, mint, fennel, parsnip, chervil, beet, leek, chive, turnip, elecampane, Egyptian bean, and anise (3.24); March adds cardoons, marjoram, caper, endive, melon, cucumber, rue, gourd, spinach, thyme, and cumin (4.9); April adds parsley (in several varieties), orach, thyme, cat mint (5.3); July adds navew and turnip (8.2); and if for the rest of the year no *new* plants are added to the calendar of sowing, no month is without its planting possibilities (6.5, 7.4, 9.5, 10.13, 11.11, 12.6, 13.3).

From start to finish, Palladius attunes his readers to the best moments and methods for initiating and nurturing the life of each kind of plant, while requiring them to make constant judgments and adjustments. His chronologically ordered account suggests that it is not so much the needs of humans that regulate the life cycle of plants as the needs of plants that regulate the flow of human life and activities. Or perhaps better: plants, humans, and other participants in the garden, such as water and dung, co-produce the temporality and rhythms of gardening. To be sure, the traditional Roman techniques that Palladius transmits intend to control the conditions of plant growth so as to maximize and exploit vegetal productivity for human consumption; moreover, his text seeks to impose an order of its own on the bewildering variety of gardening tasks, in a mirroring of literary and vegetal domains. However, it is also evident at every turn that this control and order are unattainable for the farmer, least of all in the garden, with its proliferating and indeed poetic diversity of plant life, needs, and gifts.

When Hilarion visited Antony's dwelling place in Egypt, the famous hermit's disciples were eager to display the evidence of their master's horticultural labors. "These grape vines, these little trees he planted himself. This little plot he cultivated with his own hands. This pond for irrigating his little garden was constructed with much sweat. This hoe for digging the ground he had for many years." Antony's *hortulus*, also described as a *pomarium*, or orchard, is said to have been "planted with little trees and green with vegetables" (*Life of Hilarion* 31). Antony is the gardener in this jewel-like desert garden, small and tidy, meticulously cultivated to sustain the small community of disciples.[12] But Hilarion does not conform to this model; indeed, he departs from his mentor's example rather decisively. His garden, which includes fruit trees, like Antony's, and no doubt vegetables as well, was created and cared for by someone else. He comes to it belatedly, when its growth is already well under way, and his intentions do not seem to be the same as Antony's, or indeed those of most gardeners. He is pleased to dwell in the garden but is not described as tending it, and he is explicitly said not to eat its fruit (43).

Jerome's cryptic description, contrasting so notably with his characterization of Antony's garden as a site of diligent cultivation, raises a number of questions. What happens to a garden when humans cease to submit themselves to the temporalizing regime of traditional horticultural practice— when no one sows, fertilizes, weeds, prunes, or harvests anymore? What happens when the walls that separate garden from forest begin to crumble? What happens when maximized productivity and consumption no longer define the goals of life in the *hortulus*? What happens, in other words, in Hilarion's garden (fig. 3.8)?

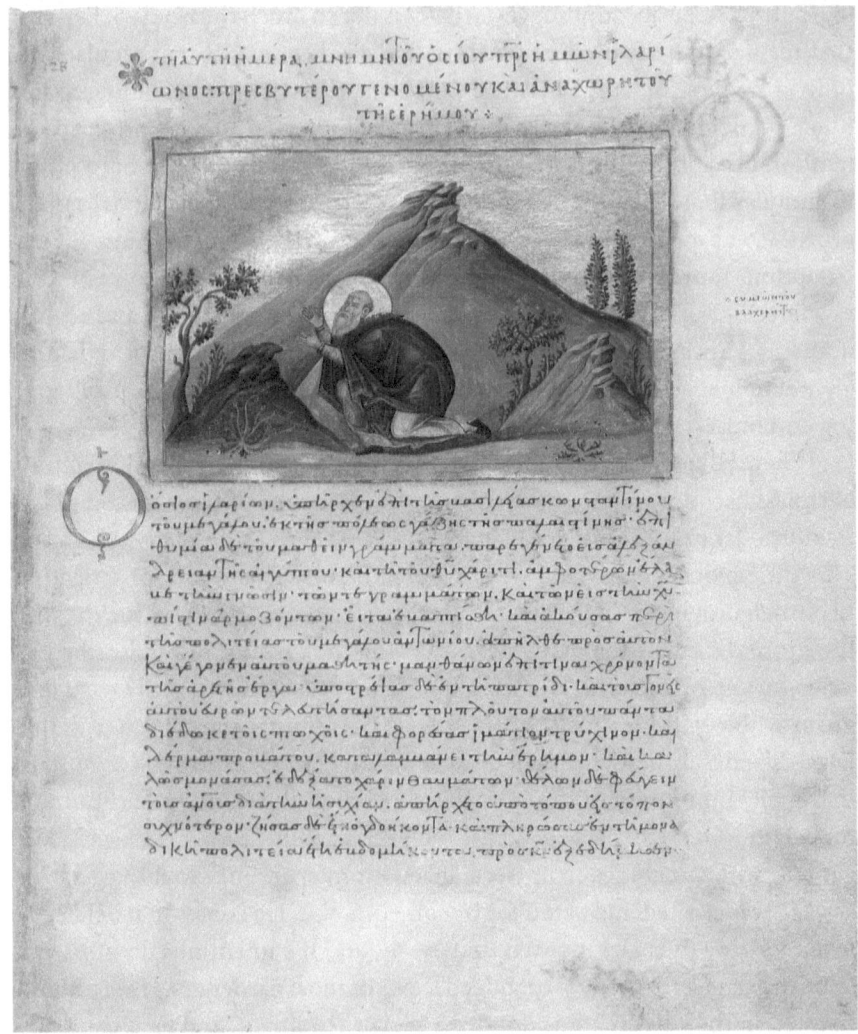

FIGURE 3.8 Miniature painting of Saint Hilarion, from the collection of brief Saints' Lives known as the *Menologion of Basil II*. Codex Vaticanus Graecus 1613, p. 128. Constantinople, ca. 1000 CE. © Biblioteca Apostolica Vaticana.

Japanese biologist-turned-farmer Masanobu Fukuoka founded an agricultural and philosophical movement that he called "natural farming" or, more whimsically, "do-nothing farming."[13] Slightly later, and partly influenced by Fukuoka, Australian environmentalists Bill Mollison and David Holmgren developed a similar method, which they dubbed "permaculture."[14] These converging movements share the goal of nurturing sustainable habitats designed to imitate—or perhaps better, cooperate with—synergies found in natural or uncultivated ecosystems. Fukuoka's particular approach centers on five apophatic principles—"no tillage, no fertilizer, no pesticides, no weeding, and no pruning." By minimizing "human meddling and intervention," his way of farming "strives to restore nature from the destruction wrought by human knowledge and action, and to resurrect a humanity divorced from God," as he puts it.[15]

Across decades of attentive practice, experimentation, and rumination, Fukuoka revived and promoted the simple lifestyle of the traditional Japanese "quarter-acre farmer," in which leisure for poetry-writing or other spiritual and recreational practices might be accommodated by the rhythms of agricultural work. In addition to planting alternating symbiotic crops of rice and winter grain in his fields, Fukuoka also planted fruit trees on the mountainside and grew vegetables and herbs "in a semi-wild way" between the trees. "The important thing is knowing the right time to plant," he writes, seeming to echo Palladius. The trick is to give the vegetables a head start with respect to the seasonal weeds. "For the spring vegetables the right time is when the winter weeds are dying back and just before the summer weeds have sprouted. For the fall sowing, seeds should be tossed out when the summer grasses are fading away, and the winter weeds have not yet appeared."[16] When plants are cut back, whether weeds or crops, they should be left to lie on the ground, returning nutrients to the soil. Moreover, if chickens are allowed to wander among the plants, they too will fertilize the soil while eating worms and insects that may be harmful to the vegetables. For their part, trees protect smaller plants from too much sun. "It is an amazing sight to see many unfamiliar vegetables thriving here and there on the mountain," notes Fukuoka. "In my orchard I grow burdock, cabbage, tomatoes, carrots, mustard, beans, turnips and many other kinds of herbs and vegetables in this semi-wild way."[17]

There is a difference between minimizing human "meddling" and simple human "abandonment" of the garden. Chickens, trees, and even weeds have their roles to play in the life of vegetables, and so do humans. Fukuoka learned the hard way that trees that had already been pruned could not simply be left to grow "naturally"; in this manner, he decimated an entire citrus orchard.[18] And permaculture gardens are typically highly designed spaces, reflecting concentrated human intentionality, directed toward correcting past mistakes. As the "Permaculture Designs Cyprus" website puts it, "Permaculture gives us the hope and tools to prove that the reversal and regeneration of degenerated living ecosystems is possible."[19] Even if reversal or restoral is not one's goal, a garden is a place where humans must discover their role in relation to nonhuman others; it is a place where plant, soil, water, animal, and human coincide.

Having exhibited an almost missionary zeal in his desire to convert others to natural farming and having drawn many disciples to study and imitate his practices, later in life Fukuoka withdrew from such striving. "I am retired now and live in a mountain hut in the orchard," he writes at age seventy-three. (He would live to be ninety-five.) "The best part of living a retired life on the mountain, isolated from news of the outside world, is that I have a different sense of time."[20] A day might be experienced as a year. Past and future recede, and only the present remains. "Put sincere effort into each day's work and leave no footprint here on earth," the old man advises.[21] In the end, each person has to find her own way, he suggests: the interdependence of all beings so vividly on display in gardens is seen most clearly in the context of human solitude. "We can only walk our paths alone."[22] (fig 3.9).

Perhaps we can imagine Hilarion as a do-nothing gardener like Fukuoka. Unhurried and attentive to his surroundings, he may have found ways to help the already-established plants in his little plot, while keeping his interventions to a minimum. (After all, he was not battling the effects of a history of agribusiness of modern scope.) He may have pulled a few weeds where they threatened to choke more beneficial vegetation. He may even have scattered some seeds from time to time. In return, the vegetables and herbs would have provided him with a nutritious diet. As for the fruits of the trees, perhaps he left these to attract birds, who would (like Fukuoka's chickens) eat insects and worms that might otherwise trouble the garden.[23] Living a retired life on his mountain, surely Hilarion would have enjoyed listening to their songs. And as he watched the birds flitting between fruit trees and forest, he may have reflected on the permeability of boundaries in his "semi-wild" garden, a microcosm of creation's vast diversity and complex relationality.

In 1985 the Thyssen ironworks in the Ruhr region of Germany closed. Less than a decade later, Duisburg-Nord Landschaftspark opened in the same place (figs. 3.10, 3.11). Designed by Peter Latz, the roughly 568-acre "landscape

FIGURE 3.9 Masanobu Fukuoka (1913–2008). Shikoku, Japan. Photograph courtesy of Chelsea Green Publishing and the Larry Korn Estate.

FIGURES 3.10 AND 3.11 Duisburg-Nord Landscape Park. Duisburg, Germany. © Blickwinkel/Alamy Stock Photos.

park" has garnered widespread attention and acclaim as a cultural heritage site that "accommodates an unprecedented openness to reuse and regeneration (both social and ecological)."[24] The site includes an industrial heritage trail that allows visitors to engage the workings and history of the Thyssen blast furnace plant through its traces and effects on the built and natural landscape. At the same time, the architectural remains of the factory have been opened to new developments and uses that build on and respond creatively to the distinctive features of the historic structures and landscape. In addition to walking and biking trails, flexible event spaces, a restaurant, a viewing platform, a light installation, a mural, a climbing wall, a high ropes course, and a diving basin have all emerged in the ruins. Yet much of the park has also been left to develop with minimal intervention from humans, remaining open to exploration and improvisation on the part of visitors.[25]

Landscape architect Joern Langhorst highlights the distinctive and compelling presence at Duisburg-Nord and other postindustrial sites of ruins that are simultaneously (and inextricably) "cultural" and "natural."[26] The decay of built structures is matched by, and entwined with, overgrown vegetation and the pollution of soil and water. However, the doubly ruined landscape tells a story of generativity as well as decline. As Langhorst emphasizes, humans and nonhumans "co-author" the park's open-ended processes and emergent ecologies, sharing agency in the production of what he calls an "aesthetics of ecological performance."[27] Langhorst explores the complex relationship of this performative aesthetics to artistic traditions of representing landscapes as either pastoral or sublime, tame or wild.[28] Although postindustrial ruins are commonly aligned with the dramatic and even terrifying landscapes associated with the sublime, the immersive and participatory character of the park partly collapses the distance between self and other that undergirds the traditions of both the sublime and the pastoral: nature is not "out there" (like a painting) but all around, and culture is folded into it.[29]

Elissa Rosenberg presses this point even more strongly, going on to argue for the crucial role played by gardens in a design that has the aim of "preserving this strange landscape while transforming its meaning,... absorbing it anew into our everyday lives."[30] She emphasizes the degree to which the park's gardens perform the temporal interweaving of human life with the lives of plants and other beings. "The garden articulates the theme of time, understood at Duisburg in terms of the cycles of destruction and cultivation, as well as through its resonance with history and cultural memory. As such, it represents the antithesis of the sublime, which exists outside time and represents both an escape from history and a retreat from physical nature into the realm of human spiritual values."³¹ Unlike both sublime and pastoral landscapes, the garden enfolds human making into the materiality of the site: human and botanical creativity are both at work in its processes. This is especially so in the case of "entropic gardening," as geographer Caitlin DeSilvey names it—in which a plot has been left to its own devices just long enough, or just far enough, for a genuinely collaborative process among humans, plants, architecture, and others to emerge.³²

An interpretive sign along the path to the main entrance identifies the entire park at Duisburg-Nord as a "sacred garden" of sorts.³³ Thus, gardens are not only incorporated into the park; the trope of gardening frames its interpretation as a whole. At the same time, gardens as such are used "expansively and eclectically" throughout the park, as Rosenberg notes, sometimes evoking conventional forms, whether civic or domestic, sometimes inventing "new forms that challenge accepted definitions of what a garden might be."³⁴ In the central part of the park, gardens have been created in the ruins of bunkers that formerly held iron ore and coal. Some of these are traditional in their forms and plantings (lavender, roses, hydrangea, boxwood),³⁵ highlighting the incongruity of their setting. Others express the toxicity of the site, populated by exotic species transplanted from contaminated soils elsewhere on the grounds. Still others appear to be self-seeded, such as one spotted by DeSilvey in which a "thicket of pear and alder rose over the concrete walls."³⁶ Moreover, even the more formal gardens are not tended closely or consistently; when DeSilvey visited, "the hydrangea was rangy and unkempt, flopping over the box hedge and obscuring the clean lines of the design."³⁷ And everywhere between the cracks of walks, walls, and buildings, as well as in open spaces on the site, vegetation springs forth, cut back and pruned only enough to keep it from overwhelming the landscape.

Farther from the center of the park, in an area marked "wilderness" on the Duisburg-Nord map, are the remains of a walled garden from a prior era. Fittingly, the discovery and reactivation of this garden was the first project in the making of the landscape park. As Latz and his colleagues were initially surveying the dense thicket of willow and birch that had overtaken this part of the industrial site, they came across a cluster of sweet mock-orange trees. Searching for other "garden fugitives," they found crab apples and hawthorn growing in parallel rows. Collaborating with local citizens, they began to clear out some of the overgrowth. Their goal was not to restore the garden as it had been but to enable it to reemerge as something new. They created planting boxes from materials available on the site and filled them with "everything that could pass for soil, even including fire bricks and screws," as Latz relates, adding, "all soils are habitats."[38] Plants sprouted in the midst of these strange objects, with their varied mineral compositions, some of them typical opportunistic waste-site species—dock bramble, willowherb, mullein, burdock—and others cultivated species—asters, daisies, ornamental grasses.[39] The interplay between vegetal exuberance, architectural decay, and human intervention is constantly at work in such a space and also ambiguous in its balances: agencies blur. Departing from the map's legend, Latz himself sees not a garden in the wilderness but rather a wilderness in the garden, reflecting a partial breakdown in the "dualism of exterior and interior, the wild and the tamed."[40] Here, as on an ancient farm, the garden serves as a microcosm of the whole.

Different as this postindustrial site is from Hilarion's Cypriot mountaintop, it nonetheless helps us think about the distinctive ecologies of gardens abandoned and then reoccupied, about the dynamic roles of plants and ruined buildings in such places, and finally about the aesthetic qualities that may accrue to them. Jerome's description of Hilarion's mountaintop dwelling—itself a literary curation of natural-cultural heritage—combines recognizable bucolic features of the classic literary "pleasant place" with those of what he declares to be a "terrifying place" (43). Within that larger context, Hilarion's garden mimics the pastoral beauty of its natural setting while incorporating sublime elements of the surrounding forest and temple ruins; however, it is finally neither the pastoral nor the sublime, but another aesthetic that characterizes the garden itself. Like the Duisburg-Nord park, Hilarion's *hortulus* constitutes what garden designer and theorist Gilles Clément's calls a "third landscape"—an intermediate or borderland space, emerging between fields and forests or on the edges of roads or banks of rivers, for example, and supporting unusually high levels of biodiversity and adaptation.[41] Its borderland status may even include a postindustrial aspect: on the opposite slope of the Troodos mountain range, perhaps fifty miles northeast of Hilarion's home, as the crow flies, barren slag heaps at Skouriotissa stand as reminders of the long history of copper mining and smelting in Cyprus, an industry still active in late antiquity. As Tassos Papacostas notes, "It has been estimated that the timber used during 3.5 millennia of copper production came from forests covering sixteen times the area of the whole island."[42] Jerome's contemporary, Ammianus Marcellinus, indicates that in his day Cyprus was still known as rich in timber for shipbuilding (14.8.14), another industry that placed major demands on the island's forests and thus affected its ecologies. The island must have gone through numerous cycles of deforestation and regeneration by late antiquity.

The highest peaks of the Troodos Mountains were once covered with Cyprus cedar (*Cedrus brevifolia*),[43] a tree endemic to Cyprus that grows up to one hundred feet high or more and can live more than five hundred years.[44] Pliny mentions the mast of a ship made of its wood, marveling that "it was one hundred and thirty feet in length and took three men to span its girth" (*N.H.* 16.76.40). Archaeological remains of cedar, as well as alder, pine, and cypress, have also been found in the Roman copper mines.[45] Today, however, the Cyprus cedar is found only in a restricted area in the most inaccessible part of the Troodos Mountains, near Mt. Tripylos.[46] The lower slopes of the mountains in the Paphos district where Hilarion likely lived are now mostly cleared or downgraded to scrub, but in the old man's time they would have been covered with the indigenous Cyprus oak (*quercus infectoria*), holly oak (*quercus calliprinos*), olive (*olea europea*), and Calabrian pine (*pinus brutia*).[47] Although most of the oak forests of Cyprus are now gone, a few massive trees survive, such as one outside the mountain village of Fyti in the Troodos, said to be eight hundred years old.[48] Calabrian pine is currently the dominant tree in Cypriot forests,[49] and even in Hilarion's day, this "high seeding, invading species"[50] might have been eager to breach the boundaries of the garden with its saplings, much as the willow and birch did in the walled garden at Duisburg-North. If the pines had begun to move in with the fruit trees and vegetables during Hilarion's sojourn, they did not overwhelm the terrain. The other plants held their own. The garden was still recognizably a garden.

We might, then, think of Hilarion not only as a gardener but also as a guardian of (horti)cultural heritage. The garden, to which he comes belatedly, belongs to a small country estate or farm (*villula*), as we have seen, likely derelict. It must have been walled or otherwise clearly bounded, because the saint is described as exiting its precinct. It is also said to be located near "the ruin of a very old temple" still populated by the ghosts of deities once worshipped on the site. Hilarion has chosen to live in a place with a history, then, a place haunted by its past, we might even say—architectural as well as vegetal, divine as well as human. He demonstrates no impulse either to repress or to appropriate this past. Instead, he pronounces himself glad to have "demons" and "shades" for neighbors. He is not interested in demolishing the temple or replacing it with a church; nor, as far as we can tell, does he desire to impose his own order on the garden. He lives content among built and botanical ruins. And by living among them, he makes something new of them, both materially and aesthetically. Becoming part of the place, he has an effect on its ecologies, even if we can only speculate about what that effect might be. Beyond that, his presence as a holy man imbues the site with a power of signification in excess of its material relations and properties. In Jerome's telling, living in this place becomes both an art and a performance, and Hilarion's mountaintop emerges as a kind of landscape park where cultivated garden and uncultivated wilderness meet and mingle.

Is Hilarion a do-nothing farmer? A curator of entropic horticulture? Or is he just another garden-variety holy man? Jerome dubs him "a rose among thorns" (2), a wild rose, perhaps, such as the *cistaceae*, or rock roses, that grow throughout the Mediterranean, sometimes spontaneously, sometimes cultivated in gardens.[51] Not native to the place, the saint is a pioneer species, moving into the ruins, putting down roots, unfurling leaves and petals—exploring possibilities, in short. Transplanted back to Palestine, he still remains in Cyprus. "It is nothing out of the ordinary for the plant to fall apart, to fall off with or from itself, without compromising its existence," as Marder notes. "The plant is not one."[52] It grows both here and there, now and then.

Hilarion's plant-being does not exclude human-being. Vegetal existence, or "plant soul," is enfolded in human existence, and the project of human ethical formation may be framed as a kind of becoming-plant. "If ethics… is the relation to the other, then it must be rooted in the ontology of vegetal life," writes Marder. Plants, even more fundamentally than other life forms, are exposed and oriented to their others—earth, water, air, and light, as well as fungi and other microbes. "The ethics of plants is therefore a kind of homecoming, a harkening of ethical discourse back to the domain of life where it originated."[53] A garden may be a place where humans fail to live into their own vegetal conviviality, choosing to dominate rather than grow-with the plants that are, as Emanuele Coccia puts it, "the constant genesis of our cosmos."[54] Alternatively, a garden may be a place where humans finally discover "what it means to be in the world."[55]

To be in the world is to be in the garden, rather than merely shaping and observing it from the outside. It is to recognize that there are no gardeners who are not also part of the garden, and conversely, that all the participants in the garden are also gardeners, in their own way—co-authors of the ever-emerging landscape. Nonetheless, humans have a particular role to play in this context. Indeed, a garden is the site of human encounter with other living creatures, an encounter marked by the privilege and burden of consciousness and the capacity to anticipate and plan. And yet humans may have more to learn than to teach. "I try to listen to plants and animals, insofar as I can," writes Clément, regarding his own role as gardener. "Beyond those silent masters, I owe everything to the messengers: teachers, scientists, philosophers, whose role is to astonish us by showing us the fragile diversity that the garden supports."[56] Environmental journalist Michael Pollan writes of his "education in the garden" as a process by which the garden of his imagination—"gnat-free and ever in bloom"—slowly draws closer to "the garden as an actual place"—a stage for struggle with insects, woodchucks, deer, and invasive grasses.[57] As the gap between the two gardens narrows, the fight to dominate gradually (and of necessity) gives way to compromise and collaboration with other creatures. At the same time, knowingness gives way to wonder.

Hilarion's garden remains a mystery to us, as does his role within it. Life in a garden is always a mystery, after all; so much of what goes on is invisible to the human eye. And never more so than in a thriving, intricately multicultural, partly entropic garden in which the human is as much cohabitant as director or designer. Slipping quietly among the trees, almost merging with their trunks, the old man on the mountain—"Hilarion of the Woodlands"— invites us to enter into the ever-emerging experiment of conviviality that is life on this planet.[58]

LITERARY CARTOGRAPHIES

... *in utrisque locis*	in both places
magna quotidie signa fiunt,	great miracles occur daily,
sed magis in hortulo Cypri,	but more in the garden of Cyprus,
forsitam quia plus illum locum dilexerit.	perhaps because he loved that place more.

JEROME OF STRIDON

READERS ARE ALSO TRAVELERS. To read is already to be on the move, starting with the eyes and the hands. Activating the imagination, reading transports us to other places and times, exposing us to novel sensations, experiences, and points of view. However, readers are not only travelers of the imagination. Physical travel often inspires literature, and literature inspires travel in turn. Jerome was a wanderer, just as Hilarion was: his nineteenth-century biographer goes so far as to say that his life "est tout entière dans ses voyages."[1] Would he have written his hagiography if he had not visited Cyprus himself? An unanswerable question, of course, but surely it would not have been the same text in that case. And although his *Life of Hilarion* is not a personal travelogue, it *is* a tale of travel. Does Jerome intend his text to inspire readers to visit Cyprus too? And what happens if and when they do? To frame the question more broadly: How does literature call to places, and how do places respond to the call of literature?

An ambivalence about place and travel runs through Jerome's text,[2] and it complicates the answers to these questions. Poets made Paphos famous, and Jerome seeks to make Hilarion's hermitage equally well known—a place loved by a holy man, a place where miracles still occur. But he pursues this goal paradoxically, by rendering the place obscure. Jerome describes Hilarion's final retreat not only as remote, as we have seen, but also as unmappable. Visitors following a "trackless path (*iter inuium*)" find it with difficulty, if at all (*Life of Hilarion* 43). The specification that the place is twelve miles from the sea gives a measure of its distance from the island's connective coastline (43). However, it does not allow us to identify the location of Hilarion's hermitage with any precision, even if we assume, based on Jerome's narrative, that it was in the general vicinity of Paphos.

Jerome follows Athanasius in celebrating the obscurity of a holy habitat. The *Life of Antony*, which Jerome always keeps in his sights, specifies that the great desert father commanded his companions to bury his remains in a secret place, lest any be tempted to keep his body as a relic—something the Egyptians were said to do with their martyrs (*Life of Antony* 90–92). The text thus introduces tension between the claims of hagiographical literature and the nascent cult of saints. Jerome leans into that tension. Palestine may boast possession of Hilarion's body. Cyprus, however, can lay claim to his spirit, as evidenced by the greater proliferation of miracles on the site, "perhaps because he loved that place more" (*Life of Hilarion* 47). Added almost as if an afterthought, these final words of Jerome's *Life*—*plus illum locum dilexerit*—privilege place over relic as the mediator of holy presence and power: a place can remember a missing saint better than a bit of bone can.[3] In addition, the *Life of Hilarion* seems implicitly to privilege texts as the vehicles that transport their readers to the holy places. If Hilarion's life journey ends in uncharted territory, how is one to find it other than through Jerome's hagiography?

We might even say that the narrated journey performatively breaks down cartographic space. As a youth, Hilarion set out on the well-traveled route from Gaza to Alexandria (2), then detoured into the unmapped desert (*eremus*) of Egypt where the great Antony lived (3). Returning to Gaza at age fifteen, he entered not the town of his birth but the desert some seven miles inland (3), refusing to complete the circle; thus, his homecoming ended in a space without name or identifiable coordinates. Fifty years later, he set out on a second, much longer journey. This time too he would almost, but not quite, return to his starting point by the time he was done. Initially retracing the steps of his prior trip in reverse, he headed to Antony's hermitage (30–32) and from there to the area around Alexandria (33). Then he once again took a detour: "Leaving Bruchium, through the trackless desert (*per inuiam solitudinem*), he entered the Oasis" (34), perhaps the "Great Oasis" of Libya (modern Siwa) or one of the monastic settlements in the Western Desert of Egypt—Nitria, Kellia, or Scetis.⁴ But by now Hilarion's fame preceded him, and even the uncharted desert provided no opportunity for him to lose himself; he therefore determined to travel further west. "He thought he would sail to desert islands (*ad solas insulas*), so that the one whom the land had made known, the sea would at least hide." Journeying by camel "through the vast desert (*per uastam solitudinem*)," he reached the Libyan port city of Paraetonium (34), where he boarded a ship for Sicily (35), landing at Pachynus, near Syracuse (36). Heading twenty miles inland, he lived on a deserted plot of land where he gathered wood to sell (37). However, there too fame pursued the old man (38), and he eventually sailed to Epidaurus in Dalmatia in order to escape the crowds of miracle-seekers who inevitably arrived (39). Only one more stage of his journey remained—the trip to Cyprus.

Jerome initially maps Hilarion's travels through the recitation of known toponyms, noting the number of days it took to get from one place to the next: starting from Betilium near Gaza, he journeyed five days to Pelusium, three days to Theubanum, three days to (Egyptian) Babylon, three days to Aphroditon, three days to Antony's mountain (30), and then back again to Aphroditon (32). This most basic form of literary cartography, known as the *periplous* ("sailing around"), goes back to the Phoenicians and ancient Greeks, consisting in lists of ports and other coastal landmarks that circle the Mediterranean Sea and describe its naval routes.⁵ As Jerome continues the list—Bruchium (33), the Oasis (34), Paraetonium (34), Pachynus (36), Epidaurus (39)—the traditional form begins to dissolve. Concise measures of distance are replaced by meandering narratives. At the same time, the well-mapped and -measured coastal routes give way first to the trackless desert and then to the trackless sea, where the old man hopes to hide: the passage from Libya to Sicily crosses the largest expanse of the Mediterranean, during which one might be as much as two hundred miles from the shore for short stretches, in a body of water in which a sailor is otherwise rarely out of sight of land.⁶ Along the way, the narrative reveals both desert and sea as ambivalent topographies: the desert is no longer completely deserted, having been colonized by monks, while the sea is as much connective as distancing, allowing others to track the old man. Even insular sites threaten to expose Hilarion once again, so long as he hugs the well-populated coastlines; thus, upon reaching Sicily, he immediately "fled to the places inland (*ad mediterranea fugit loca*)" (37). Ultimately it is in the interior of Cyprus that he finds his refuge. There the shifting, undefined space of the sea is matched not by the desert but by the unmappable "middle land" of Cyprus's densely forested mountains.

Hilarion is a late ancient Odysseus, restless and elusive. It is no accident that Jerome opens by audaciously comparing himself positively to the famous poet: "If Homer were present, he would either envy or be overwhelmed by my subject" (1). He directs our attention to Achilles, protagonist of the *Iliad*, but arguably it is the wandering hero of the *Odyssey* whom Hilarion most closely resembles. He is no warrior or martyr but a resourceful survivor. The holy man's sea journey from the Dalmatian coast to Cyprus is the most vividly described stage of his travels; it is also the place where his route overlaps with that of Odysseus, albeit in reverse. Returning from Troy, Odysseus sailed south through the Aegean Sea along the east coast of Greece, passing through the Cyclades and rounding the treacherous Cape Maleas, intending to turn north toward Ithaca on the other side of the Peloponnese. There a storm blew him off course, sending him nine days' west of the cape into uncharted waters (*Odyssey* 9.80–84); it would take him ten years to get home, seven of which he spent stalled on the island of Ogygia with the seductive goddess Calypso. Hilarion traveled in the opposite direction, sailing south along the west coast of Greece, past Ithaca and around Cape Maleas, where pirates attempted—and miraculously failed—to attack the boat that carried him (*Life of Hilarion* 41). From there it was smooth sailing through the Cyclades, where the saint "heard the voices of unclean spirits clamoring from the cities and villages and running down to the shore," like so many Sirens, before he finally reached Paphos in Cyprus, the goddess's island (42). Diverted by the charms of his haunted garden, he only returned home to Gaza some seven years later, after his death and seemingly against his own will (46).

Burkhard Wolf comments on "the deterritorialized structure of the *Odyssey*," with its wily hero whose wanderings take place "on undescribed and even indescribable terrain." He concludes, "If one wants to understand it as a 'topographic' text, the *Odyssey* seems to present a paradox: the endeavor of tracing and describing the places of a nonplace."[7] We might say something similar about the *Life of Hilarion*. Beginning with the poetic-cartographic recitation of known place names that launches the saint on his looping journey, Jerome's text subsequently opens onto fluid and unstable spaces that exceed representation. Cape Maleas sent Odysseus on his wandering path, and it does the same for Hilarion. Cyprus is not so much a sought-after destination as the spot where he is cast ashore, its mountain a place that remains to be traced and described—a place that ultimately evades cartographic capture. The journey there is an *iter inuium*, a way that is no way (43). The Latin phrase echoes Apuleius's *Metamorphoses* and before that Virgil's *Aeneid*,[8] but perhaps it captures best the twists and turns of the Greek epics that stand at the beginning of all of these tales of wandering heroes—not only the Homeric *Odyssey* but also the ancient *Kypria* or *Cypriot Tales*, whose heroes circumnavigated the eastern Mediterranean on an errant clockwise path, "wandering through Cyprus, Phoenicia, and the Egyptians" (Odyssey 4.83).[9]

Surprisingly, perhaps, the deterritorialized structure of the *Odyssey* has not prevented its readers from attempting to reconstruct the hero's itinerary, whether this is understood to conform to a "real" or an "imaginary" geography. If anything, the unlocatability of an island like Ogygia has increased the desire to identify it with some known place—Malta or Ireland, say. Already in antiquity, the possibilities were much discussed, with Strabo famously arguing against Polybius that Ogygia was not in the western Mediterranean but rather "appears manifestly [φανερῶς] to have been imagined [πλαττόμενα] as in the Atlantic ocean" (*Geographies* 1.2.18). Scholars continue to debate the topic: if the work of Victor Bérard,[10] which confines Odysseus's journeys to the Mediterranean, remains influential, more (literally) outlandish theories also abound.[11]

A similar desire to locate arises with respect to the *Life of Hilarion*. Carefully mapping the saint's travels based on her own cartographic knowledge, Ilona Opelt identifies Hilarion's Sicilian abode with the Cava of Ispica. Some of the clues that guide her are text-based: the location fits Jerome's description of the place as twenty miles inland from Pachynus (thus well off the coastal roads that connect the port with both Syracuse and Agrigentum) and as having access to rural, agricultural economies where a hermit might support himself by selling wood. Other clues have to do with the place itself: not only does the cave-pocked canyon present a geography that might be especially attractive to a hermit familiar with the cave-dwelling ascetics of Egypt, she argues, but it also bears traces of ascetic habitation that are still visible to the archaeologist's eye.[12] We thus have the satisfaction of connecting Hilarion's time with our own, through apparent continuity of place. Following a similar logic, Opelt places the saint's Cypriot hermitage near an ancient sanctuary of Hera in the Troodos Mountains, where the monastery of Agia Moni is currently located. The location fits Jerome's description of a site in the mountains in the vicinity of Paphos, twelve miles from the coast (in fact, it is closer to twenty miles) and in close proximity to a pagan temple. Moreover, because the remains of a sixth-century basilica are incorporated into the church of Agia Moni, the place satisfies the criterion of "survival of the ancient significance" (*Fortlebens der antiken Bedeutung*) that Opelt apparently understands to be indicated by Jerome's closing mention of the miracles that continue to be performed at the site in his own day.[13] Tradition attributes the monastic foundation not to Hilarion circa 366 but to Saints Nicolaus and Eutychius circa 300 CE, but this is not a problem for Opelt: what matters, it seems, is that the site remains marked and remembered as holy. As we shall see, others map the terrain differently, but like her, they respond to cues that are at once textual, geographical, and archaeological.

In fact, travelers have been looking for the site of Hilarion's final home for centuries. Multiple places have offered themselves in response to the call of Jerome's small and ambiguous bit of text, from a dramatic mountain perch near Kyrenia on the north coast of Cyprus, to a cave near the remote village of Episkopi ten miles east of Paphos, to the site of Aphrodite's famous temple in Palaipaphos (Kouklia), and a cave just inside the walls of ancient Paphos. All these places are marked by suggestive topographies and archaeological remains, including, in Episkopi, a boulder that the saint is said to have thrown while battling demons. None, however, simply prevails in its claims. This is not only because the text resists mapping. It is also because places never cooperate fully with literary fantasy. They are shaped and affected by writing, but they push back too, in their complex and ever-changing materialities. In short, ambiguity persists. And because it does, reading and traveling continue to incite one another, sometimes confirming, sometimes disrupting, in the impossible drive to produce a perfect correspondence of textual and physical place. In the process, it becomes clear that literature is much more than a mimetic representation of place, place much more than a passive referent. Yet the two connect nonetheless, however fleetingly, through the mobile, sensate bodies of reading humans.

Let us look at this history a bit more closely. Jerome's reference to the miracles that continued to occur in Hilarion's garden suggests that the saint's hermitage was still attracting pilgrims when he composed his hagiography some two decades after Hilarion's death in 371. However, there is no evidence of a lasting cult at the site. When the church historian Sozomen, writing in Constantinople in the early 440s, gives us a name for the locale (or alternately, for Hilarion's first Cypriot dwelling), his interests seem strictly biographical:[14] "He practiced philosophy at a place called Charbyris" (*Church History* 5.10). He reports that Hilarion was celebrated with an annual festival in Palestine (3.14) but makes no reference to ongoing cultic activity at Charbyris, and his source for this name is probably Palestinian rather than Cypriot; he was proud of the fact that his grandfather, who was from the town of Bethelia, near Gaza, had been converted to Christianity by Hilarion, along with other members of his family (5.15). Aside from a few such personal embellishments, Sozomen's account of the saint is largely dependent on Jerome's *Life*, which had been translated into Greek by the early fifth century.[15] Jerome's work is also likely to have been the inspiration for Gennadios, the former patriarch of Constantinople, who sailed to Paphos in 471 in order to visit "the mountain where long ago the great Hilarion established a peaceful and ascetic combat [παλαίστραν] against the demons." Tragically, the old man never reached the hermitage; he lost his way and died in a late November snowstorm on the outskirts of Paphos in a village called Kissoptera.[16]

The unseasonable whiteout is suggestive: although late seventeenth-century mapmakers inserted one "Cachibris" near Paphos, in a possible attempt to map the holy man's dwelling,[17] as we shall see, Charbyris remains an "unlocated toponym" for current cartographers.[18] The twelfth-century Cypriot hermit Neophytos is our source for the story of Gennadios's visit and death, but when he composed an encomium for Hilarion intended for liturgical use, he borrowed from earlier abbreviations of Jerome's *Life* and made no mention of a Cypriot shrine or any native traditions.[19] Perhaps no such traditions existed at that point. The earliest saints' cults and hagiographical literature produced in Cyprus centered almost exclusively on local leaders. From the fifth through seventh centuries, "the only hagiography developed in Cyprus would be devoted to Cypriot saints, all of them bishops."[20] Jerome's *Life of Hilarion* remained the work of an outsider, written about an outsider, and by the end of antiquity, Hilarion's mountaintop garden seems to have disappeared from sight, except as an artifact of Jerome's mobile text.

When the hermitage reappeared, it was translated to the north coast of Cyprus, through the creative misapprehension of Western Christians, for whom Jerome was a revered teacher of the church and Hilarion a most relatable saint, precisely because he was an outsider to Cyprus. The French Crusader Guy of Lusignan, a contemporary of the Greek monk Neophytos, was installed as king of Cyprus in 1192 by Richard the Lionhearted, who had wrested control of the island from its Byzantine ruler, the usurper Isaac Komnenos, in the prior year. "The state of our country now is no better than that of the raging sea under a great storm and tempest," Neophytos lamented.[21] Guy and his successors would reign (at least nominally) in Cyprus for almost three centuries. They would also be strong patrons

FIGURE 3.12 Saint Hilarion's Castle. Kyrenia, Cyprus. © Zoonar GmbH/Alamy Stock Photo.

of the cult of Hilarion, whose remains were thought to be preserved in a Byzantine fortress in the Kyrenian mountains, far from Paphos. The early fifteenth-century Cypriot historian Leontios Makhairas indicates that "the castle of Saint Hilarion" (fig. 3.12) was in fact named after a more recent Saint Hilarion, one of three hundred Christians said to have fled to Cyprus when "the Saracens seized the Land of Promise" (1.31–32), whether in the seventh century or the twelfth.[22] However, for the Lusignans and most others since, this was the castle of *Jerome's* Hilarion.

As the twentieth-century British writer Lawrence Durrell put it much later, "The site demands a saint with a biography."[23] We might add that the biography demands a saint with a site as well. And the dramatic mountain-top, rising some 2,375 feet above the nearby sea, has answered the call of Jerome's text very eloquently for centuries. I myself have felt the lure of the place, with its dramatic perch, crumbling ruins, and sweeping vistas, even imagining that I glimpsed the perfect setting for a garden. An errant etymology also lends a hand in cementing the identification: originally known in Greek as "Didymos," or "twin," for its double peaks, the mountain became "*dieu d'amour*," or "god of love," in French. Visiting Cyprus in 1333, Wilhelm von Boldensele observes, "Also in Cyprus is the body of the blessed Hilarion under the royal care in the castle which is called Gedamors." A slightly later fourteenth-century travel narrative attributed to John de Mandeville reports, "And in the castle of Amours lyeth the body of saint Hilarion and men keep it right worshipfully."[24] Writing in the sixteenth century, Estienne de Lusignan implicitly identifies the love god's ruined palace with the temple ruins near which Jerome's Hilarion dwells, suggesting that Hilarion's battles with the demons resulted in a transfer of the castle's name from Cupid to Hilarion. Responding to de Lusignan's narrative, Durrell notes drily, "I prefer the Crusader name of Dieudamor."[25]

Hilarion's presence on the island was conjured through the power not only of text and landscape but also of the Cypriot liturgy. Living reclusively on the margins of Paphos, much as Hilarion had, in the twelfth century, Neophytos had incorporated an abbreviated version of Jerome's *Life* into his own monastic calendar of devotional readings, and Hilarion's feast day must have been part of the local Cypriot liturgy before him as well. The French Crusaders addressed themselves to a more international audience, supplementing rather than distilling Jerome's account. A sumptuous, early fifteenth-century liturgical manuscript transmitting the music of the Lusignan court of Nicosia opens with an office and a mass for Hilarion; a flyleaf has been added to the codex containing a synopsis of a bull issued by Pope John XXIII sanctioning the text of the office and indicating that King Janus of Cyprus (1398–1432) commissioned the text.[26] The manuscript also includes a motet for Hilarion that "emphasizes the propriety of the cult of Hilarion instituted by the Lusignan and closes with a prayer for King Janus and the Dominicans."[27] Likely copied circa 1435 by Jean Hanelle, the chapel master to the king of Cyprus, the codex was destined for Brescia in northern Italy, where the ambitious Pietro Avogadro found it advantageous to align himself with the liturgical culture of Lusignan court and even to adopt "the exotic Hilarion" as his "protector-saint."[28] Would the music of the codex have incited Avogadro to travel, even in his imagination, to the distant castle on the northern coast of Cyprus where the saint's body was thought to rest?

As Tassos Papacostas points out, there has often been a divergence "between views originating within the island and those originating outside it." In the modern period, while Hilarion's Castle has continued to attract foreign tourists, Cypriot tradition has identified a cave in the Ezousa valley as the site of the saint's hermitage, a more geographically plausible, if still unverifiable, claim.[29] The cave is just outside the village of Episkopi, about ten miles inland from Paphos (not to be confused with the Episkopi of the Limmasol district, near Kourion). Although the village itself is only 617

FIGURE 3.13 Episkopi Rock with Saint Hilarion's Church. Episkopi Village, Paphos, Cyprus. © Ian Rutherford/Alamy Stock Photo.

feet above sea level, a rocky cliff rises dramatically another 230 feet above it to the west. We may imagine Hilarion settled on top of this impressive monolith, where a small church dedicated to the saint currently perches (fig. 3.13). However, that church was not built until 1953, following a devastating earthquake in which part of the monolith itself collapsed, and the ruins of the medieval church associated with Hilarion's hermitage are in the village at the foot of the cliff, not on top of it. The cave itself is about a mile outside the village on a low hill facing the Ezousa valley.[30] Nearby in the river bed is the "stone of Atsupa," said to have been hurled by Hilarion during his battles with the demons.[31] In the mid-twentieth century the cave still functioned as a shrine where local people lit candles or oil lamps and prayed to the saint. Writing in 1977, scholars visiting the site reported, "The entrance to the cave is marked by a wild pear-tree. Nobody is allowed by the Saint to cut a branch of the tree." They added, "St. Hilarion also appears to be helpful to the girls who have trouble with their lovers. They light their candle and ask him 'to tame their lovers' [ὁ ἅγιος Ἰλαρίων νὰ ἱλαρώση τοὺς ἀγαπητικούς]."[32] Sacred trees understood to be under the protection of a saint, such that "any kind of damage done to the tree, or even the attempt to break its twigs or branches was believed to bring great harm," are not uncommon in Cyprus.³³ The role of fruit tree protector is also consistent with Jerome's *Life*, and indeed the wild pear, which lives eighty to a hundred years and flourishes on the edges of forests, is currently a rare species, in need of protection.³⁴ At the same time, the saint seems to have taken on distinctly aphroditic functions in Episkopi. Or perhaps the girls merely understood from his name—deriving from *hilaros*, cheerful, merry, bright—that he embodied the power to make their loved ones happy. In recent decades, the area around Hilarion's cave and church has become a destination for knowing ecotourists: Episkopi is currently touted for its striking geological formations, rich biodiversity, and botanical gardens.³⁵

Nor are Hilarion's Castle and the cave at Episkopi the only candidates for Hilarion's hermitage. Other places have also offered themselves to more historically minded readers of Jerome's text. Some have wanted to identify the ruined temple near Hilarion's hermitage with Aphrodite's famous sanctuary, despite the flatness of the terrain and its proximity to the coast. One recent scholar pronounces the identification "almost certain."³⁶ And indeed, this is an alluring possibility, given the iconic status of the goddess's sacred precinct, whether one discovers in it evidence of "fiercely competitive religious attitudes" in late fourth-century Cyprus³⁷ or simply a satisfying irony.³⁸ Yet another candidate has emerged at Toumballos, or Garrison's Camp, just inside the north gate of ancient Nea Paphos. There archaeologists excavating in the 1990s discovered a small, two-apsed ancient Christian basilica adjoining a subterranean pagan sanctuary. The antiquity of the church, together with its unusual north–south orientation, was suggestive. They hypothesized that the church memorialized the place where Hilarion heard the voices of demons echoing in the ruins of a temple, speculating that these voices might actually have been the cries of wild animals reverberating spookily in the underground chambers.³⁹ Curiously, this hypothesis requires ignoring most of Jerome's locational cues while taking a rather literal approach to one of the more fanciful elements of the text—the resounding of demonic voices in the place.

What other places might yet offer themselves? As we have seen, Ilona Opelt suggests the site of the monastery of Agia Moni, on the southwestern slope of the Troodos Mountains. I myself have found it pleasurable to imagine Hilarion living in the sacred grove of Apollo of the Woodlands at Kourion, where (according to the third-century rhetorician Aelian) deer took refuge from hunters and hounds (*On the Nature of Animals* 11.7). Archaeologists have imagined that they detect signs of a tree cult at Kourion, anticipating more recent Cypriot attitudes of reverence toward sacred trees, such as that found at Episkopi.[40] Could Hilarion of the Woodlands provide a link between these histories? Here the dialogue between text and archaeological landscape leads us into the realm of free-floating imagination. And why not? Hilarion's hermitage has always been sliding off the map.

At age sixty-three, Hilarion suffered a crisis; by the time he reached sixty-five, the crisis had sent him on a journey (*Life of Hilarion* 29). "Journeys, like artists, are born and not made. A thousand differing circumstances contribute to them, few of them willed or determined by the will—whatever we may think," writes Lawrence Durrell as he begins his account of his own journey to Cyprus.[41] No two journeys are the same, then, and yet travel often inspires imitation—especially the kind of travel we call "pilgrimage." Maps are, among other things, a medium for rendering journeys repeatable.

In 1597, Abraham Ortelius was the first to produce a map of *The Wanderings of Ulysses* (fig. 3.14). The exquisite engraving locates Calypso's Ogygia just off the coast of the "heel" of the Italian peninsula; not so very far away, Ithaca is tucked between the island of Samos and the mainland of Greece, more or less where we would expect it. A series of tiny ships, some of them sinking, indicate the route (and the challenges) of Odysseus's journey home from Troy.[42] About a century later, in 1693, Hilarion's hermitage makes its first appearance on an even more remarkable map, titled (in French) *The Deserts of Egypt, the Thebaid, Arabia, Syria, &c: where the places inhabited by the Holy Fathers of the Deserts are marked*, and published in Paris by Estienne Michalet (fig. 3.15).[43] The arrow of a compass in the lower right corner of the page indicates that north is toward the upper right corner; it also references the instrument of geographic orientation that enabled even the seas to be mapped and navigated by early modernity. The eastern end of the Mediterranean Sea extends down from the top center of the map at a forty-five-degree angle to the right, with the Red Sea rising up from the bottom, also angling slightly right, toward the larger body of water. Among the first things to catch the eye is a large island tucked into the northeast corner of the Mediterranean, shaped vaguely like a hand with a pointing finger, as well as two small ships aligned horizontally below it and to the left, framed by the coasts of Palestine and Egypt. The island, of course, is Cyprus—part of the "et cetera" of the map's title. In the southwest, running west to east,

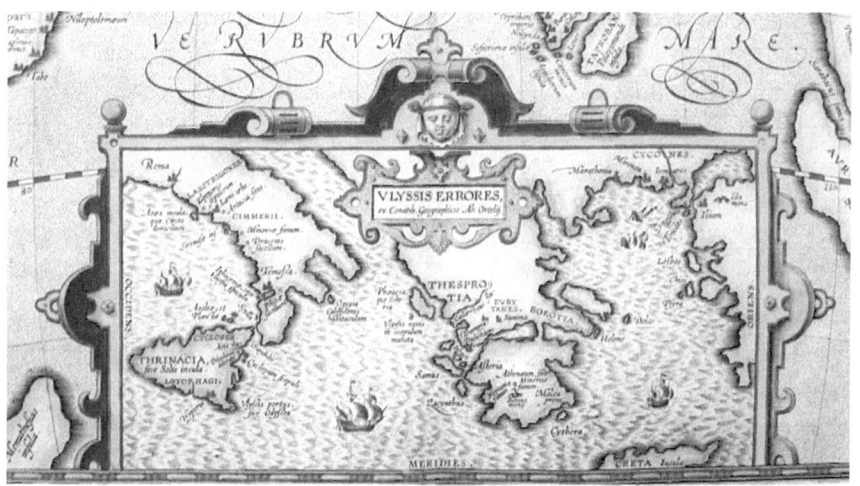

FIGURE 3.14 Abraham Ortelius. *Wanderings of Ulysses*. Map inset, engraved in 1597, printed by Balthasar Moretus in 1624. Source: Wikimedia Commons.

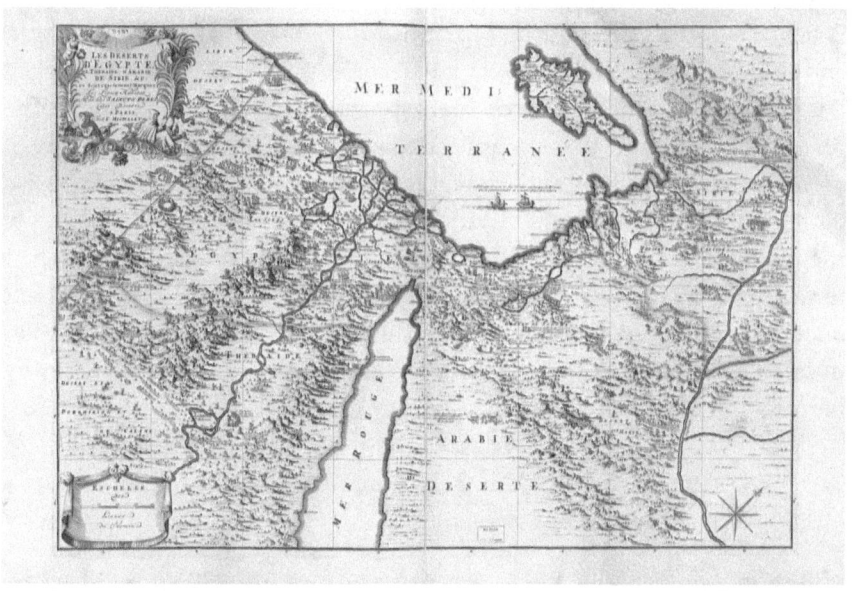

FIGURE 3.15 Estienne Michalet. *The Deserts of Egypt, the Thebaid, Arabia, Syria, etc.: Where the places inhabited by the holy fathers of the deserts are exactly marked*. Map, published in Paris, 1693. Photograph courtesy of the Library of Congress, Geography and Map Division.

are sites labeled the "desert where Saint Hilarion retired," "New Paphos," and "Old Paphos." North of the "desert" is the city "Arsinoe" and just under it "Cachibris"; Andreas and Judith Stylianou argue that the latter is a corruption of Sozomen's "Charbyris."[44] Perhaps the desert and Cachibris point respectively to Hilarion's first and second dwelling places on Cyprus (or vice versa); perhaps they indicate the same place; or perhaps Cachibris has nothing to do with Hilarion after all. The boats, intriguingly reminiscent of the sailing vessels on the Odyssey map, are less ambiguous. "Saint Hilarion stops a ship of pirates who pursue and are about to engage him and forces it to retreat," the caption reads. In Jerome's *Life*, the event takes place off the coast of Greece (thus, off this map), but here it has been brought into the orbit of the desert dwellers of the east.

If Hilarion is an isolated figure on the Mediterranean Sea and its only depicted island, the lands encircling that sea are teeming with ascetic life: there he moves not alone but among others like him. A richly illustrated and annotated topography, its miniaturized scale significantly smaller than that of the ships, reveals the saint founding monasteries and performing miracles in Gaza, leaving his native land behind, tarrying in the desert near Bruchium outside Alexandria, departing for the Oasis in the Libyan desert, and embarking on a ship for Sicily at Paraetonium. At that point, his journey takes him beyond the bounds of this map, until he reappears in Cyprus. The final stop is his burial place near Majuma, the port of Gaza. He is the most mobile saint on the map, and through the map we may follow his clockwise path around the sea, whether in imagination or in the flesh. We might say that the map in this way more fully embodies an invitation merely implicit in the text—to visit the holy habitats ourselves, much as Hilarion himself once visited Antony's mountain cell. Through its distinctive combination of cartography, image, and text, it shows us a world of places made holy by hermits and offers to navigate our journey to those places.

In his memoir, *An Odyssey*, classicist Daniel Mendelsohn tells the story of a journey that he took with his father, first on the page, then on a ship. The elder Mendelsohn, a somewhat cantankerous retired mathematician, unexpectedly decided to audit his son's college seminar on Homer's *Odyssey* one spring. At the younger Mendelsohn's suggestion, the two embarked immediately following the course on a cruise designed to retrace the route of the legendary hero's wanderings. "But in the end, as the result of a string of irritating events beyond the control of the captain or his crew, ... we were unable to make the last stop on the itinerary," relates Mendelsohn. "And so we never saw Ithaca, the place to which Odysseus strove so famously to return; never reached what may be the best-known destination in literature." He adds, "But then, the *Odyssey* itself, ... schools its hero in disappointment, and teaches its audience to expect the unexpected."[45] Moreover, reaching one's destination may not be the point. As Constantine Cavafy puts it, in a well-known poem that Mendelsohn has translated and was asked to discuss with his fellow passengers in the course of the cruise,[46] "Ithaca gave you the beautiful journey; / Without her you wouldn't have set upon the road. / But now she has nothing left to give you."[47] At any rate, Mendelsohn and his father never did make it to Ithaca together, for a few months after the trip his father suffered a fall that eventually resulted in his death. Before that, however, the cruise had brought him to the satisfying and surprising conclusion that "the poem is actually more real than the place!"[48]

Seen through the lens of Mendelsohn's memoir, Cyprus is my own Ithaca. It is a destination that has kept me moving throughout a year of disappointment and grief, and it is also a destination that has eluded me. The year was framed by two planned trips to the Mediterranean island, each one canceled, as we all suffered the shocking effects of a global pandemic that left us confined to our homes, cut off even from family and friends—like Odysseus stalled on Calypso's Ogygia. (I think too of Hilarion in his early sixties, as I am, restless and stuck in his monastic leadership role, beset with an "incredible desire" to leave Gaza.) In between those successively canceled trips, my mother died a death that was as expected as such a shattering event can be, while my father (like Mendelsohn's, a mathematician) died unexpectedly: he too fell, and we read Cavafy's "Ithaca" at his memorial service. A year and a half prior, my brother, partner, and I had fulfilled one of my father's desires by taking him on a trip to the Caucasus, and only weeks before his fall, he had still hoped to travel again. "You know, I can go pretty much anywhere with this walker," he assured me, with a twinkle in his eye. "Maybe you can come with me to Cyprus," I said. "Maybe I can," he grinned.

"Always in your mind keep Ithaca. / To arrive there is your destiny," Cavafy writes.[49] I have already booked my room in Nicosia for next year. For places are as real as poems, if differently so: one does not simply ratify the reality of the other. In the meantime, I have traveled this past year by reading and writing, obsessing on an island far away and long ago, without always knowing or even needing to know why. I have also traveled by paying attention to the places I was in. Oddly, Hilarion's Cyprus, in its very inaccessibility, has taught me to be more fully present and attentive in upstate New York, western Massachusetts, and southern Vermont. And those places have helped me come to know Hilarion's Cyprus. They too have answered the call of Jerome's text, offering mountain, forest, garden, bird, deer, even bear and fox, but also works of art and music. And always literature. This was not the travelogue I thought I was going to write, but it is a kind of travelogue nonetheless, I now see.

According to Jerome, Hilarion made one more trip following his sojourn in Cyprus, returning posthumously to the Palestinian monastery that he had founded near his birthplace—a place that is now even more scarred by tragedy and violence than the politically divided island of Cyprus. From this perspective, he did after all return to his starting point, like Odysseus before him. It is possible, of course, that I will never travel to Cyprus again, except in my imagination, and likely that even if I do, I will not be able to move easily across the border between north and south, as I have done in the past. But I will surely never be able to visit the Gaza Strip, where two million Palestinians live in siege-like conditions, exacerbated by the repercussions of a recent flare-up of violence between Hamas and Israel, even as I write. And yet the place calls out to me. It has stories to tell, stories that stretch back for millennia and at the same time extend into our own present. One such story is directly implicated in Jerome's narrative, and it implicates us too, as readers of Jerome.

In 1990, local construction workers came upon fragments of mosaic at Tell Umm el-'Amr, a site located on a sandy ridge near the Mediterranean coast about six miles south of the city of Gaza. These fragments turned out to be part of the remains of a large monastic complex. Arguing on stylistic grounds, Palestinian and French archaeologists have determined that the church that was part of this complex was built in the late fourth or early fifth century,[50] making this possibly the oldest monastery in the Middle East for which we have archaeological evidence.[51] The building was entirely reconstructed three times before an earthquake destroyed it in the seventh century; intermediate stages between reconstructions can be identified. But there is more. A mosaicked inscription in the pavement of the oldest layer of the church invokes "our holy father Hilarion," and under that pavement lies a small, vaulted chamber. Archaeologists speculate that this chamber was both Hilarion's original monastic cell and the place of his final burial.[52]

How to map desire of and for places, between text and travel? Hilarion is said to have loved Cyprus, but he left no traces there, or at least his traces are so very fragmentary as to be no longer legible. Yet still we search for them, and in so doing we come to know and love the place too. I will finally reach the island again next summer, I do hope.

Hilarion is said to have loved Cyprus, but it is Palestine that called him back home and wrote his name on its sandy shores. I long to visit Gaza as well, to touch the stones and walk the paths that others have touched and walked, remembering Hilarion. But those stones, those paths, those fragments of matter and memory, excavated and protected by hard-working, under-funded archaeologists, visited by local school children, are beyond my reach. They are also shockingly vulnerable.[53] For that reason, among so many others, we must hold Gaza too in our memories and desires.

IV
CODA

Reading begins only once one consents to cross the ocean of the expanse of tropic possibility, within which the literal has to be understood as one *figurative* position among others; the ocean of the contextual inexhaustiveness that results; and the ocean of an interminable labor of interpretation that is required. Reading begins only once one has left the home soil of the original text, and it drifts thereafter, buoyed by what is never anything more than the lure of a return to that soil, to identifiable, definitive, literal meaning. There is no line in the sand for it, but rather an ocean of possibility.

DAVID WILLS

AN OCEAN OF POSSIBILITY

THE PASSAGE COMES TO ME as a fragment, cited out of context.[1] As such, it invites reflection on the journey just taken. Jerome's *Life of Hilarion—the home soil of the original text*, in David Wills's phrasing—has provided my point of departure, again and again. But I have not pursued *a return to that soil* with the aim of producing a definitive or authoritative interpretation of the text, or even of its rendering of Hilarion's Cyprus. Readers hoping for that kind of study will long since have set this book aside, and rightly so. Whatever training or expertise I might claim, here I have pursued an amateur's reading, in the sense invoked by Carolyn Dinshaw—meandering, inquisitive, eclectic. "Amateurism is bricolage, bringing whatever can be found, whatever works, to the activity."[2] Images sit alongside words, and places and times mingle. Seismology and archaeology commune with poetry and sculpture, gardening handbooks with traveling tips. This book has followed the *drift* of reading, as Wills puts it. It has launched itself onto *an ocean of possibility*. There the literal and the figurative are no longer clearly distinct, any more than are map and territory. And if we imagine ourselves, with Wills, as interpretive adventurers, we should also attend to the agency and mobility of texts themselves. Have I been reading the *Life of Hilarion* or has it been reading me? Have I broken the text into pieces or has it cracked along its own fault lines? Have I staged its encounters with other artifacts, or have the fragments found each other? These are not mutually exclusive options. Have I sought this text, this place, or have they reached out to me?

In the course of this experiment in open and amateurish reading, I have found myself circling around two themes or topoi. Earthquakes and gardens give the book its title and its structure, even (one might say) its argument. Paphos is fallen, the temple is in ruins, the trees untended. Our world has been shaken: *we* have been shaken. We are waiting to see what might yet emerge—or rather, we are waiting to see what we can do with what is already sprouting through the cracks. As I suggested at the outset, this book, like Jerome's text itself, may be thought of as a kind of seismogram, registering intensities known in the body at the most intimate scale of human feeling, and also known in the earth at scales too vast for human comprehension. Through the mediation of art—a Saint's Life, a poem, a performance, a sculpture, a painting, a park—we may hope to bring those scales closer together, so that humans can begin to know and feel with the planet too. The intensities registered are the intensities of earth's terrifying quaking, ripping through our carefully constructed habitats, exposing the radical precarity of all things. They are also the intensities of earth's still-persistent flourishing, of life amidst the ruins, at once unbearably fragile and astonishingly tenacious. Earthquakes and gardens: *the literal has to be understood as one* figurative *position among others.*

We apprehend the intensities of our shared vulnerability and resilience through memory, and we remember by coming apart and reassembling ourselves. This is happening all the time, but occasionally the process is dramatic enough that we cannot but attend to it. A parent dies, an ice cap melts. A child is born, a sapling sprouts. Perhaps we even begin to lean into the process—to cultivate the skill of falling to pieces as a necessary aspect of living and growing, as we also become increasingly aware of all the ways that our dying-and-living is woven into the dying-and-living of other beings. The beings with whom we are interwoven include human-made ones, like buildings and gardens and texts, which have lives and deaths of their own, of course. The things we help make, help make us in turn. Those things include religion too.

Jerome's Hilarion is partly a creature of religion; so is Hilarion's Cyprus. To be more specific, Hilarion's Cyprus is shaped by a version of Christianity that was flourishing in the mid-fourth-century Mediterranean, in the midst of, influenced by, and sometimes competing with other religious traditions, not least the worship of Aphrodite. Basilicas and monasteries would soon transform the terrain of town and village. But Hilarion's Cyprus, as Jerome represents it, existed betwixt and between such well-defined times and spaces. It comes to us as an open and fluid place, an emergent place, haunted and expectant—less *topos* than *chora*. There life thrived in the ruins of monuments and at the blurred boundaries of cultivation and wilderness, where humans came into relation with their mineral, vegetal, and animal others and in so doing encountered divinity. Or so I have imagined it.

Throughout this book, I have gestured toward histories of religion that have been told and might be told again—the histories of Christianization, of asceticism, of pilgrimage, or of literary Lives of Saints, say—but I have not followed those narrative paths, or at least not very far. Here at the end, I am more interested in asking what this densely mediated encounter with Hilarion's Cyprus might contribute to how we understand *religion as such*, from a perspective at once humanistic and more-than-human. Is religion one way that humans engage the unsettling transience of material existence? its wondrousness and mystery? its unfathomable interconnectedness and vibrant intensities? Turning the question around, is there something about such engagements that is usefully named "religious" even when they are no longer securely attached to cultural institutions or practices generally recognized as such? Might we also describe them in other ways, and what difference would it make if we did? Would something be lost? I reckon it would. But what?

Wary of dogmatic assertions, I have addressed the question of religion's "what" implicitly rather than explicitly, leaning into the rich ambiguities of the figurative, the poetic, the artistic. *Earthquakes and gardens*: perhaps we can think religion through these tropes, these topoi, these sites of imaginative unfurling. Is religion a technique for producing being-quakes, for unsettling certainties, for breaking open human subjects and the closed, static worlds that we build out of a futile desire to keep ourselves safe? Is it *also* a kind of gardening, a set of practices by which we collectively cultivate the arts of mutual flourishing, of living-with our others, all the others—as best we can? And if religion is something that humans cannot pursue alone, how do we understand religious agency with respect to the category of the human? The question is not whether nonhuman beings also have (their own kind of) religion, but what kind of subjectivity religion makes. Do earthquakes and gardens invite us to think all religious subjects as "more-than-human" (or perhaps better, as "more-than*")? Put otherwise, is religion a way for humans (and others) to confront and overcome the limits of their own identity—even to learn to think like the earth?

What, finally, might we say about the particular importance of *place* with respect to religion? It might have seemed at times that I was inviting us to understand Hilarion's Cypriot garden, which I have called a "holy habitat," as a kind of "sacred" space, as the modern study of religion has conceived it, in opposition to worldly or "profane" space.[3] In this case, the book could have been read as a contribution to the study of the sacralization of space in Christian late antiquity—the shift of Christianity from a "utopian" to a "locative" religion. Such a contribution would have taken the form of an intervention, complicating the narrative, highlighting the incongruity of sacred places that, unlike monumental sanctuaries, refuse to be mapped.[4] But a stronger intervention seems to me to be required: I have chosen instead to emphasize a nondualistic, choric understanding of place as a matrix of relational becoming—*place as possibility*, to put it simply.

Here I find the Platonic figuration of *chora* as winnowing basket especially suggestive. It must be said, however, that it is an odd kind of winnowing basket that Plato describes. No external agent wields it; rather, it is buffeted by the disordered potencies with which it is filled, while also being possessed of its own agency, as a consequence of that buffeting. "It is itself shaken by these and, in turn, being moved, shakes them," Plato's Timaeus notes succinctly (Timaeus 52e). Moreover, this shaking is generative: it produces a kind of order or form, through a process similar to that of separating wheat from chaff, he further explains (53a). At this point, the distinction between shaker and shaken is thoroughly blurred. *Chora* manifests as the cumulative and collective effect of all the agencies at work within it and on it. Being shaken, it shakes. Indeed, it quakes! And out of this unsettling movement, prior orders are disrupted and new orders emerge—the flow of becoming.[5] Places are not, then, empty spaces waiting to receive their contents, but neither are they pre-existing structures that impose their order on those who enter. They are not even simply the sum total of all their parts. Places are the movements of all of us who inhabit them, and they are the effects that we have on one another, and they are also something else—a resonance, an amplification, or alternately a dissonance, a dispersal of forces that arise from us all and return us all to ourselves, changed. Places are always shaping us, but only because of the ways we and all the others are always shaping them at the same time.

From this perspective, we might say not only that all places are potentially sacred, but that *place as such* is sacred, in and as the creative potential that resides in its distinctive resonances and dissonances. It is in place, shaking and shaken, that we become. It is true that particular landscapes seem to call to one another—mountain to mountain, desert to desert, stream to stream. But the deeper connection between and among places lies perhaps in their relational generativity, their choric possibility, and their irreducible particularity. To learn to know and love one place is not to know and love all places, but it is to be capable of knowing and loving other places. It is to be able to glimpse something wondrous in the situatedness of all that becomes. So it is that Hilarion's Cyprus could teach me to know and love the places I was in, and the places I was in could teach me to know and love Hilarion's Cyprus.

In making such a suggestion about the sacredness of place, does this book speak not only *about* religion but also *from within* religion—speak religiously, that is, even theologically? If so, what does this say about the relation between religion and its study? The academic discipline of religion has worked hard to extricate itself from the suspiciously authoritarian and often partisan assertions of theology. It has also had reason to be wary of what Steve Wasserstrom calls "religion after religion"—the secularized mysticism enshrined by some twentieth-century historians of religion.[6] But do we need to fear a style of scholarship for which the methodological starting point is sympathy rather than alienation, curiosity rather than judgment, a sense of affinity rather than suspicion, with regard to the religious? Obviously, I think not. Indeed, I would suggest that we have too much to lose if we do *not* risk what Tyler Roberts calls "criticism as spiritual exercise."[7] Is this not a powerful way to begin to recover our attunement to the places that both hold us close and open us wide to the surrounding world?

I raise such existential and disciplinary questions reflectively, here at the end, standing in for so many other questions that have also been posed along the way, or that might still be posed. To end with more questions than we started with is not a bad thing. It means that we are still engaged, still curious, still open—that Hilarion's Cyprus has more to teach us. And *why Hilarion's Cyprus*? Perhaps you are still wondering. Could it have been *another* place? Could it have been *any* place? Could it have been *any other* place?

"Only *in place* does singularity ever arise, and only *as singular* do places themselves appear," writes Jeff Malpas.[8] I have tried to stage an encounter with *this* place, long ago and far away—Hilarion's Cyprus. Jerome's *Life of Hilarion* was the postcard on my desk, one that meant different things to me at different times, one that finally drew me and held me for reasons that exceed my knowing. In hagiography, suggests de Certeau, "a particular place is made relative through a composition of many places."[9] In the *Life of Hilarion*, the multiplicity and relativity of place is emphasized in the final suspension of the saint between Gaza and Cyprus—the one place laying claim to the saint's body, the other to his greater love. The singularity of the beloved Cyprus is placed in relation to the singularity of Gaza as Hilarion's point of departure and return. My own encounter with Hilarion's Cyprus in this book has opened me to other, closer places, equally singular. And the drift of reading continues. A place is not defined by its limits, any more than a text is. It has no limits. It is an ocean of possibility.

ACKNOWLEDGMENTS

THIS BOOK IS A PANDEMIC BABY, written between March of 2020, when quarantine was a novel and shocking reality, and January of 2022, when the latest wave of the virus (this one dubbed "omicron") was peaking, and masking, distancing, and isolating had long since become familiar techniques. The book is also a sabbatical baby, and for the great gift of a full year's research leave in academic year 2020–21, I owe gratitude first to the Clark Art Institute's Research and Academic Program and its director, Caroline Fowler, and second to Syracuse University's College of Arts and Sciences and its dean, Karin Ruhlandt. The Clark, an exquisite museum and research center set in the equally exquisite landscape of the Northern Berkshires, was a peaceful and meditative place to spend a year of great loss as well as joy, and it offered itself to me *as a place* in ways I could not have anticipated. At the same time, I kept myself always also oriented to that *other* place, Cyprus, and for the sustaining hope of a return to that Mediterranean island, I am grateful to the Cyprus American Archaeological Research Institute in Nicosia and its director, Lindy Crewe, who gave me the support of a summer fellowship and was willing to defer my residency not once but twice.

A seed for this project was planted as early as May of 2018, when my partner Glenn and I saw the fabulous show *Hyperobjects*, co-curated by Laura Copelin and Timothy Morton, at Ballroom Marfa in West Texas. If I had not experienced Sissel Marie Tonn's *Intimate Earthquake Archive* as part of that exhibit, I don't think this book (or anything like it) would have been written. Laura has been welcoming and supportive of this project from the start.

A year later, in May of 2019, the notion of a work centered on Hilarion's Cyprus began to crystallize as I was writing grant applications, with crucial help from Derek Krueger, who helped me lick my proposal into shape. Derek is one of the smartest readers I know and also one of the most generous. He usually seems to see what I am doing more clearly than I can, and he always helps me make it better. Eventually he read the whole manuscript. I should mention too that it was Derek who first brought me to Cyprus in March of 2016, along with Glenn Peers, Gene Rogers, and Warren Woodfin, wonderful traveling companions, all.

In March of 2020, at almost the last moment in which it was still possible to enjoy a live event, Mike Chin visited Syracuse, hosted by the incomparable group of Central New York late antiquity scholars known as LARCeNY. His genre-bending performance incorporated a puppet show, a lecture, and an art installation. On that occasion and others, Mike's work and his conversation have given me permission to think very differently about what it means to do history. Mike also intuited at an early point that writing a book about earthquakes would not leave me unshaken.

At the Clark, I enjoyed the company of the other residential fellows, especially Amy Freund, Timothy Hyde, Jennifer Nelson, Robert Schindler, and Saundra Weddle. Timothy helped me think about remote places and the unpredictable afterlives of buildings. Jennifer asked challenging questions about violence and the temporality of spoliation, among other things. Those conversations and many others were only possible because RAP administrator Jessie Sentivan took such good care of us, and librarian Karen Bucky kept us supplied with books, even under the most challenging circumstances. Kathy Morris, director of Collections and Exhibitions, also generously shared with me her knowledge of Thomas Schütte's sculpture *Crystal*. And I am grateful for the outside guests who took the time to attend my (videotaped) lecture and (virtual) seminar in September of 2020 and offered such helpful and stimulating responses, including Denise Buell, Mike Chin, Jennifer Glancy, Michael Ann Holly, Herbert Kessler, Derek Krueger, Patricia Cox Miller, and Keith Moxey. Michael and Keith also read and commented on one of my chapters, and Michael lent me books on ruins.

Timothy Hyde put me in touch with Tessa Kelly, and Tessa responded with extraordinary warmth. She took the time to read and discuss my chapter on remoteness and to talk to me about *The Mastheads* studios in Pittsfield (about half an hour south of the Clark), and she also gave me a tour of the studios on one of the coldest, snowiest days of winter. I was pleased to be able to spend a day in one of the studios the following June.

I'd like to give a shout out to MASS MoCA too, just down the road in North Adams, to the east of the Clark. I was able to spend countless happy hours in its safely cavernous spaces, many of those in the company of Ledelle Moe's marvelous sculptures.

ACKNOWLEDGMENTS

In a time of relative isolation, it meant a lot to me that people were willing to answer emails from a stranger. Bahriye Kemal read part of my chapter on poetry and responded warmly to my queries about Fikret Demirag. Miguel Neves wrote to me of his love for historic earthquakes. Sissel Marie Tonn responded kindly to my emailed queries about her earthquake-related works. Tom Davis generously shared his memories, his unpublished writings, and his photographs of excavations at Kourion, and David Soren also responded helpfully to my emails. When I requested photographs of her sculptures, Ledelle Moe asked for a copy of my manuscript and actually read some of it. Ryan Dewey supplied me with copies of his articles and answered readily when I wrote with questions about *Copper Boulder* and others of his works.

Not everyone who helped me was a stranger, needless to say. My dear friend Sharon Betcher talked to me patiently about gardening and recommended the writings of Masanobu Fukuoka. Marco Formisano and Cristiana Sogno kindly invited me to share some of my work in a Zoom presentation in the spring of 2021, as did my colleagues in the Syracuse University Religion Department in the fall of that year. And at a crucial stage near the very end of my writing process, Patricia Cox Miller and William Robert read the entire manuscript and met with me to discuss it, offering invaluable advice and encouragement. I could not ask for better colleagues and friends.

Jerry Singerman has been my editor at the University of Pennsylvania Press for twenty years, and his support and friendship have sustained me throughout that time. When his unexpected retirement forced me to look elsewhere for a publishing venue, Kyle Wagner, Katie Lofton, and John Modern gave this book a home in their Class 200 series at the University of Chicago Press. I am grateful to them for believing in the project and for pushing me to make it better.

I lost both of my parents while working on this book. Sometimes the grief, resonating with other griefs, both personal and collective, has felt bottomless. Writing is good therapy (for me, anyway), but it is the support of friends and family that has carried me. I am especially grateful for the steadfast care of my children James Burrus Kelly and Mary Burrus Kelly, my brother Charlie Burrus, and my beloved Glenn Peers. Glenn has accompanied me every step on this journey from Marfa and Austin to Syracuse and Williamstown and now Bennington. He was with me in Cyprus in 2016 and will be with me again if we ever make it back. Because of his love, I am shaken but not shattered, ready to seek new beginnings for life amidst the ruins.

NOTES

MEMORIES

1. "The Loma Prieta Earthquake of October 17, 1989: A Brief Geologic View of What Caused the Loma Prieta Earthquake and Implications for Future California Earthquakes," US Geological Survey pamphlet (November 1989), 2, https://pubs.usgs.gov/unnumbered/70039527/report.pdf.
2. "M 6.9 - Loma Prieta, California Earthquake," online at https://earthquake.usgs.gov/earthquakes/eventpage/nc216859/impact.
3. Michel Serres, *Biogea*, trans. Randolph Burks (Minneapolis, MN: Univocal, 2012), 28.
4. "Hayes Valley Farm," online at http://www.hayesvalleyfarm.org/. I owe my awareness and appreciation of Hayes Valley Farm to a lecture by Margaretha Haughwout, delivered in Syracuse University's Visiting Artist Lecture Series on 16 January 2020.
5. Emanuela Guidoboni, "Historical Seismology: The Long Memory of the Inhabited World," in *International Handbook of Earthquake and Engineering Seismology, Part A*, ed. W. H. K. Lee, et al. (Amsterdam: Academic Press, 2002), 775.
6. Guidoboni, "Historical Seismology," 781.
7. Guidoboni, "Historical Seismology," 786.
8. Guidoboni, "Historical Seismology," 787.

THREE NOTES ON METHOD

1. The term is Bertrand Westphal's; see his "Elements of Geocriticism," in *Geocriticism: Real and Fictional Spaces*, trans. Robert T. Talley (New York: Palgrave Macmillan, 2011), 111–47.
2. As Eric Prieto notes, Westphal's geocriticism has blind spots from an ecological perspective, omitting entirely "the role of direct experience in shaping our understanding of the spaces and places we inhabit. At no time does Westphal consider the role that direct observation and fieldwork might contribute to the geocritical enterprise" ("Geocriticism Meets Ecocriticism: Bertrand Westphal and Environmental Thinking,"

in *Ecocriticism and Geocriticism: Overlapping Territories in Environmental and Spatial Studies*, ed. Robert T. Tally Jr. and Christine M. Battista [New York: Palgrave Macmillan, 2016], 26).

3. On the concept of hyperobject, see Timothy Morton, *Hyperobjects: Philosophy and Ecology after the End of the World* (Minneapolis: University of Minnesota Press, 2013). On pandemic as hyperobject, see Morgan Meis, "Timothy Morton's Hyper-pandemic," *New Yorker*, 8 June 2021.

4. Morton, *Hyperobjects*, 19.

5. Catherine Michael Chin, "Four Notes on Memory Theatre," *Ancient Jew Review*, 6 January 2020, n.p.

SETTING OUT, WITH JEROME

1. Paul B. Harvey, "Jerome Dedicates his 'Vita Hilarionis,'" *Vigiliae Christianae* 59, no. 3 (2005): 286–97.

2. As Andrew Jacobs notes, "Epiphanius's biography shares several details" with that of Jerome's Hilarion: "origin in Palestine; study (and then monastic conversion) in Egypt; return to Palestine; emigration to Cyprus." He adds, "Whether Hilarion was an influence on Epiphanius during his career, or later their biographies became blurred, must remain unclear" (*Epiphanius of Cyprus: A Cultural Biography of Late Antiquity* [Berkeley: University of California Press, 2016], 9 n. 19).

3. As per ORBIS: The Stanford Geospatial Network Model of the Roman World (http://orbis.stanford.edu/).

4. Susan Weingarten develops the possible connection with a local serpent cult of Cadmus (*The Saint's Saints: Hagiography and Geography in Jerome* [Leiden: Brill, 2005], 142–44).

5. Gavin Kelly, "Ammianus and the Great Tsunami," *Journal of Roman Studies* 94 (2004): 148–55.

6. This is my own inference, building on Gavin Kelly's source theory. The placement of the tsunami in the Adriatic, together with the image of boats stranded in high places, suggest that Jerome is familiar with the source that Kelly has posited for Ammianus. As far as I know, scholars have missed the link between Jerome's account of a tsunami in the Adriatic and that of the Byzantine chroniclers. Emanuela Guidoboni and John Ebel note, "For the Dalmatian coast, this cryptic reference is the only one known that might refer to this tsunami"—i.e., the 365 tsunami mentioned by Ammianus (*Earthquakes and Tsunamis in the Past: A Guide to Techniques in Historical Seismology* [Cambridge: Cambridge University Press, 2009], 54).

7. This reading of Ammianus Marcellinus closely follows the interpretation of Kelly, "Ammianus and the Great Tsunami." Lionel Mary makes a similar argument in "Reconnaissance par les gouffres: Métaphysique des séismes et poétique de l'histoire chez Ammien Marcellin," in *Connaissance et représentations des volcans dans l'antiquité*, ed. Éric Foulon (Clermont-Ferrand: Presses Universitaires Blaise Pascal, 2004), 171–90.

8. Antony died in 356 (Jerome, *Chronicle* 322 [Ol. 283.4]). According to Jerome, Hilarion

was sixty-five at the time (*Life of Hilarion* 29), which puts his birth in 291. Jerome asserts that he died at age eighty (44–45), which puts his death in 371. He lived in Cyprus for seven years before his death (43), which suggests that he arrived in 364, soon after the tsunami in Epidaurus.

9. Kelly, "Ammianus and the Great Tsunami," 146.

10. Kelly, "Ammianus and the Great Tsunami," 158, 161. Kelly notes that the fifth-century church historian Socrates similarly associates the earthquake and tsunami with Procopius's usurpation (*Church History* 4.3). Jerome had also placed the earthquake and tsunami in the same year as Procopius's death (366), in his *Chronicle*, completed ca. 380 (*Chronicle* 326 [Ol.286.2]). Might either the *Consularia Constantinopolitana* or another source shared with Ammianus underlie this common narrative alignment of the earthquake with Procopius's usurpation and the attending civil war? See R. W. Burgess, "A Common Source for Jerome, Eutropius, Festus, Ammianus, and the Epitome de Caesaribus between 358 and 378, along with Further Thoughts on the Date and Nature of the Kaisergeschichte," *Classical Philology* 100, no. 2 (2005): 166–92.

11. Again, for estimates of distances and travel times, see ORBIS: The Stanford Geospatial Network Model of the Roman World (http://orbis.stanford.edu/).

12. On the trope of the city as a (ruined) woman, see Susan Stewart, *The Ruins Lesson: Meaning and Material in Western Culture* (Chicago: University of Chicago Press, 2020), 102–7.

13. François Jacques and Bernard Bousquet catalogue some twenty-seven ancient and medieval writers who appear to refer to the 365 earthquake, yet their details vary considerably ("Le cataclysme du 21 Juillet 365: Phenomene regional ou catastrophe cosmique?" in *Tremblements de terre, histoire et archéologie: IVèmes Rencontres internationales d'archéologie et d'histoire d'Antibes* [Association pour la promotion et la diffusion des connaissances archéologiques, 1984], 183–98).

14. Jerome, *Chronicle* 326 (Ol.286.2) (ca. 380); *Life of Hilarion* 40 (ca. 390); *Commentary on Isaiah* 5.15.1 (410). Note that Jerome's Areopolis is generally assumed to be present Rabba in Jordan, which fits the passage in Isaiah that he is exegeting, but might it be the Greek Areopolis on the Mani Peninsula of the Peloponnese, which better suits the context of a tsunami? Regarding the possibility that Jerome, likely born in 347, could refer to himself as *infans* in his adolescence, see R. C. Jensen, "The Kourion Earthquake: Some Possible Literary Evidence," *Report of the Department of Antiquities, Cyprus* (1985): 311.

15. Guidoboni, "Historical Seismology," 787.

16. Guidoboni, "Historical Seismology," 787–88.

17. P. A. Pirazzoli, J. Laborel, and S. C. Stiros, "Earthquake Clustering in the Eastern Mediterranean During Historical Times," *Journal of Geophysical Research* 101, no. B3 (10 March 1996): 6084. See also Stathis C. Stiros, "The AD 365 Crete Earthquake and Possible Seismic Clustering During the Fourth to Sixth Centuries AD in the Eastern Mediterranean: A Review of Historical and Archaeological Data," *Journal of Structural Geology* 23 (2001): 545–62.

18. Paolo Antonio Pirazzoli, "The Early Byzantine Tectonic Paroxysm," *Zeitschrift für Geomorphologie* Supp. 62 (December 1986): 31–49.

19. Stathis C. Stiros, "The 8.5+ Magnitude, AD365 Earthquake in Crete: Coastal Uplift, Topography Changes, Archaeological and Historical Signature," *Quaternary International* 216 (2010): 54.
20. Pirazzoli, Laborel, and Stiros, "Earthquake Clustering," 6085.
21. Stiros, "The 8.5+ Magnitude, AD365 Earthquake," 55, 58, table 3.
22. Stiros, "The 8.5+ Magnitude, AD365 Earthquake," 59–62.
23. David Soren, "An Earthquake on Cyprus: New Discoveries from Kourion," *Archaeology* 38, no. 2 (1985): 55. See also David Soren and Thomas Davis, "Seismic Archaeology at Kourion: The 1984 Campaign," *Report of the Department of Antiquities, Cyprus* (1985): 299; Jensen, "Kourion Earthquake"; David Soren, "The Day the World Ended at Kourion: Reconstructing an Ancient Earthquake," *National Geographic* 174 (July 1988): 30–53; David Soren and Jamie James, *Kourion: The Search for a Lost Roman City* (New York: Doubleday, 1988).
24. Stiros, "The 8.5+ Magnitude, AD365 Earthquake," 61. Note that others have dated the Cyprus earthquake later. Emanuele Guidoboni, for example, dates it to ca. 370, based largely on Jerome's evidence, which she interprets as indicating that Paphos was in ruins in Jerome's day, but not Hilarion's (Emanuela Guidoboni, et al., *Catalogue of Ancient Earthquakes in the Mediterranean up to the 10th Century* [Rome: Instituto Nazionale di Geofisica, 1994], 277–78). Nicholas Ambraseys dates it to ca. 375, primarily on the grounds that Libanius in *Oration* 2 (380/381) could not be referring to an earthquake as distant as ca. 365. However, he also mistakenly dates Hilarion's arrival in Paphos to 370 (assuming, unlike Guidoboni, that Paphos was already in ruins when Hilarion arrived) and identifies the latest coins found at Kourion as dating to the second rather than the first consulships of Valentinian and Valens (374/375), contra Soren (Nicholas N. Ambraseys, *Earthquakes in the Mediterranean and Middle East: A Multidisciplinary Study of Seismicity up to 1900* [Cambridge: Cambridge University Press, 2009], 157; cf. Nicholas N. Ambraseys, "The Seismic History of Cyprus," *Revue de l'Union Internationale de Secours* 3 [March 1965]: 28).
25. On the importance of collaboration between archaeologists, scientists, and historians, see Antonino Di Vita, "Archaeologists and Earthquakes: The Case of 365 AD," *Annali Di Geofisica* 38, no. 5-6 (1995): 971–76.
26. "We are not Cypriots, nor, heaven forbid, have we seen our city destroyed by earthquake, but still you could hear many people moaning and lamenting, 'Alas, poor cities! Where are you now?' and no one has reproved us for thinking that we shared in the disaster, though separated from the island by such a stretch of sea" (Libanius, *Oration* 2.52 [380/381]).
27. Only one instance of uplift in northern Cyprus is noted in Pirazzoli, Laborel, and Stiros, "Earthquake Clustering," 6085, table 1.
28. Soren and Davis, "Seismic Archaeology at Kourion," 296. See also Soren and James, *Kourion*, 59, 85–87.
29. Soren, "An Earthquake on Cyprus," 57–58 See also Soren and James, *Kourion*, 88–90.
30. Soren and James, *Kourion*, 119, 131–33.
31. Soren and Davis, "Seismic Archaeology at Kourion," 299–300 See also Soren and James, *Kourion*, 57–58.

32. See Jensen, "The Kourion Earthquake," 307, n. 5.
33. Noel Lenski, *Constantine and the Cities: Imperial Authority and Civic Politics* (Philadelphia: University of Pennsylvania Press, 2016), 158–59.
34. Eugène Bernard, *Les voyages de Saint Jérome* (Paris: Charles Douniol, 1864), 324.
35. I borrow this detail from David Soren's description of the east side of an excavated room at Kourion as "disturbed by a stately carob tree" (Soren, "An Earthquake on Cyprus," 56; cf. Soren and Davis, "Seismic Archaeology at Kourion," 296).
36. Francesca Ceci, "The House of the Goddess: Coins Tell the Cypriot Aphrodite Myth," in *Archaeometry and Aphrodite: Proceedings of the Seminar 13th June 2013 CNR Rome*, ed. Maria Rosaria Belgiomo (Rome: De Strobel, 2013), 184–88.
37. Terence Bruce Mitford, "The Cults of Roman Cyprus," *Aufstieg und Niedergang der römischen Welt* 18, no. 3 (1990): 2179–80.
38. Marcus Rautman, "From Polytheism to Christianity in the Temples of Cyprus," in *Ancient Journeys: A Festschrift in Honour of Eugene Numa Lane* (Stoa Consortium. http://www.stoa.org/texts/2001/01/0014/section_1/, 2001). Georgios Deligiannakis places "the end of public paganism" slightly later, following the earthquake in the 360s that destroyed Paphos and Kourion ("From Aphrodite[s] to Saintly Bishops in Late Antique Cyprus," in *Authority and Identity in Emerging Christianities in Asia Minor and Greece*, ed. Cilliers Breytenbach and Julien M. Ogerau [Leiden: Brill, 2018], 326–46; "The Last Pagans of Cyprus: Prolegomena to a History of Transition from Polytheism to Christianity," in *Church Building in Cyprus [Fourth to Seventh Centuries]: A Mirror of Intercultural Contacts in the Eastern Mediterranean*, ed. Marietta Horster, Doria Nicolaou, and Sabine Rogge [Münster: Waxmann Verlag, 2018], 23–44). On the transition of Cyprus's sacred landscape from pagan to Christian, see also Giorgos Papantoniou and Athanasios K. Vionis, "Landscape Archaeology and Sacred Space in the Eastern Mediterranean: A Glimpse from Cyprus," *Land* 6, no. 40 (2017): 1–18.
39. For an account of excavations of post-earthquake Byzantine Kourion, with emphasis on the usefulness of "resilience theory," see Thomas W. Davis, "A New Window on Byzantine Kourion," *Cahiers du Centre d'Etudes Chypriotes* 43 (2013): 103–15.
40. Gwynneth der Parthog, *Byzantine and Medieval Cyprus: A Guide to the Monuments* (New Barnet, UK: Interworld Publications, 1994), 63.
41. Philip Young, "The Cypriot Aphrodite Cult: Paphos, Rantidi, and Saint Barnabas," *Journal of Near Eastern Studies* 64, no. 1 (2005): 26.
42. Rita C. Severis, *Travelling Artists in Cyprus, 1700–1960* (London: Philip Wilson, 2000), 33.
43. Stewart, *Ruins Lesson*, 2.
44. Stewart, *Ruins Lesson*, 11.
45. Stewart, *Ruins Lesson*, xiv.
46. Tonnes Bekker-Nielsen, *The Roads of Ancient Cyprus* (Copenhagen: Museum Tusculanum Press, 2004), 114–40.
47. Michel de Certeau, "Walking in the City," in *The Practice of Everyday Life*, trans. Steven Randall (Berkeley: University of California Press, 1984), 91–110.
48. Certeau, "Walking in the City," 92.
49. Certeau, "Walking in the City," 96.

50. Certeau, "Walking in the City," 97.
51. John Ladouceur goes so far as to state that the ruined temple near Hilarion's abode "is almost certainly the Paphian Temple of Aphrodite" ("Christians and Pagans in Roman Nea Paphos: Contextualizing the 'House of Aion' Mosaic," *UCLA Historical Journal* 29, no. 1 [2018]: 59). He is not the only one to make this assumption. See, for example, Weingarten, *Saint's Saints*, 142, 148.
52. *Eyewitness Travel: Cyprus* (New York: DK Publishing, 2014), 50.
53. Patrick Bowe, "The Sacred Groves of Ancient Greece," *Studies in the History of Gardens and Designed Landscapes* 29, no. 4 (2009): 238–39. Note that Sappho refers to a sacred grove of apple trees dedicated to Aphrodite (Pierre Bonnechere, "The Place of the Sacred Grove [*Alsos*] in the Mantic Rituals of Greece: The Example of the *Alsos* of Trophonios at Lebadeia [Boetia]," in *Sacred Gardens and Landscapes: Ritual and Agency*, ed. Michel Conan [Cambridge, MA: Harvard University Press, 2007], 20–21). Regarding archaeological evidence for a sacred grove at the temple of Venus at Pompeii, see Maureen Carroll, "Temple Gardens and Sacred Groves," in *The Gardens of the Roman Empire*, ed. Wilhelmina F. Jashemski, et al. (Cambridge: Cambridge University Press, 2018), 160–62.
54. While citrons and lemons reached the Mediterranean by the Roman period, as elite products, sour oranges, limes, and pummelos did not arrive until the tenth century, sweet oranges until the fifteenth, mandarins until the early nineteenth (Dafna Langgut, "The Citrus Route Revealed: From Southeast Asia Into the Mediterranean," *Horticultural Science* 52, no. 6 [2017]: 814–22).
55. On dendrites, see, e.g., Thomas Arentzen, Virginia Burrus, and Glenn Peers, *Byzantine Tree Life: Christianity and the Arboreal Imagination* (London: Palgrave Macmillan, 2021), 107–62.
56. Catherine Kearns, "Cyprus in the Surging Sea: Spatial Imaginations of the Eastern Mediterranean," *Transactions of the American Philological Association* 148, no. 1 (2018): 56.
57. Kearns, "Cyprus in the Surging Sea," 55.
58. In its liminality, Hilarion's garden is not unlike a sacred grove, which often "hints at a blending of nature and culture" (Bonnechere, "Place of the Sacred Grove," 26).
59. Certeau, "Walking in the City," 108.
60. Caitlin DeSilvey, *Curated Decay: Heritage Beyond Saving* (Minneapolis: University of Minnesota Press, 2017), 13.
61. DeSilvey, *Curated Decay*, 14–15.
62. DeSilvey, *Curated Decay*, 26–31.
63. DeSilvey, *Curated Decay*, 41–42.
64. DeSilvey, *Curated Decay*, 32–33.
65. See the edition of the "Samos translation" in Ruth Strout, "The Greek Versions of Jerome's *Vita Sancti Hilarionis*," in *Studies in the Text Tradition of Jerome's "Vitae Patrum*," ed. William A. Oldfather (Urbana: University of Illinois Press, 1943), 416–41.
66. Päivi Kymäläinen and Ari A. Lehtinen, "Chora in Current Geographical Thought: Places of Co-Design and Re-Membering," *Geografiska Annaler: Series B, Human Geography* 92, no. 3 (2010): 252.

67. See Virginia Burrus, *Ancient Christian Ecopoetics: Cosmologies, Saints, Things* (Philadelphia: University of Pennsylvania Press, 2019), 11–25.
68. Kymäläinen and Lehtinen, "Chora in Current Geographical Thought," 252.
69. Kymäläinen and Lehtinen, "Chora in Current Geographical Thought," 253.
70. Kymäläinen and Lehtinen, "Chora in Current Geographical Thought," 252.
71. Kymäläinen and Lehtinen, "Chora in Current Geographical Thought," 258.
72. Stewart, *Ruins Lesson*, 5.
73. Soren and James, *Kourion*, 5.
74. Soren and James, *Kourion*, 167.
75. Thomas W. Davis, "Earthquakes and the Crisis of Faith: Social Transformation in Late Antique Cyprus," *Buried History* 46 (2010): 13.
76. The latter has been argued by Young, "Cypriot Aphrodite Cult," 34–43.
77. Catherine Keller argues this point eloquently in *The Face of the Deep: A Theology of Becoming* (London: Routledge, 2003).
78. DeSilvey, *Curated Decay*, 11.
79. DeSilvey, *Curated Decay*, 153.
80. Soren and James, *Kourion*, 200; see also color plate between pp. 130–31.
81. Westphal, "Elements of Geocriticism," 113–14.
82. Prieto, "Geocriticism Meets Ecocriticism," 27.
83. DeSilvey, *Curated Decay*, 188.

POETRY AND PLACE

1. Bertrand Westphal, "Elements of Geocriticism," in *Geocriticism: Real and Fictional Spaces*, trans. Robert T. Talley (New York: Palgrave Macmillan, 2011), 113.
2. Whether the process of composition that resulted in the epics in something like their presently preserved form was oral, literary, or (most likely) a mixture of both remains hotly contested; see, e.g., Rainer Friedrich, *Postoral Homer: Orality and Literacy in the Homeric Epic* (Stuttgart: Franz Steiner Verlag, 2019).
3. Anne Carson, trans., *If Not, Winter: Fragments of Sappho* (New York: Vintage Books, 2002), 71.
4. Judith Schalansky, *An Inventory of Losses*, trans. Jackie Smith (New York: New Directions Books, 2020), 17.
5. Carson, *If Not, Winter*.
6. Schalansky, *Inventory of Losses*, 126.
7. This reading is the result of the emendation of the third ἢ (or) to ἡ (the).
8. Strabo 1.2.33, in H. C. Hamilton and W. Falconer, trans., *The Geography of Strabo* (London: George Bell & Sons, 1903), 65.
9. Strabo 1.2.33, in Horace Leonard Jones, trans. and ed., *Strabo. Geography. Books 1–2*, Loeb Classical Library (Cambridge, MA: Harvard University Press, 1917), 148–49. Jones likewise emends the Greek text.
10. Carson, *If Not, Winter*, 5, 7.

11. Carson, *If Not, Winter*, 3.
12. See the discussion of E. R. Dodds, ed., *Euripides. Bacchae*, 2nd ed. (Oxford: Clarendon Press, 1960), 124–26.
13. K. O'Nolan, "A Note on the *Bacchae*," *Classical Review* 8, nos. 3/4 (1958): 204–6.
14. As Rebecca Armstrong notes, "Garlands or floral offerings themselves are mentioned in religious and semi-religious contexts quite frequently" in Virgil's poetic corpus (*Vergil's Green Thoughts: Plants, Humans, and the Divine* [Oxford: Oxford University Press, 2019], 22).
15. F. G. Maier and V. Karageorghis, *Paphos: History and Archaeology* (Nicosia: A. G. Leventis Foundation, 1984), 13–22.
16. On Jerome's knowledge of at least one work by Claudian, see Alan Cameron, "St. Jerome and Claudian," *Vigiliae Christianae* 19, no. 2 (1965): 111–13.
17. Udo Frings, *Claudius Claudianus: Epithalamium de nuptiis Honorii Augusti: Einleitung und Kommentar* (Meisenheim am Glen: Verlag Anton Hain, 1975), 131–32.
18. Michael Roberts, "The Use of Myth in Latin Epithalamia from Statius to Venantius Fortunatus," *Transactions of the American Philological Association* 119 (1989): 330.
19. Roberts, "Use of Myth," 330.
20. See Frings, *Claudius Claudianus*, 131–57.
21. Alan Cameron, *Claudian: Poetry and Propaganda at the Court of Honorius* (Oxford: Clarendon Press, 1970), 100.
22. On allusion in late ancient poetry, see Aaron Pelttari, *The Space That Remains: Reading Latin Poetry in Late Antiquity* (Ithaca, NY: Cornell University Press, 2014), 115–60.
23. Michael Roberts, *The Jeweled Style: Poetry and Poetics in Late Antiquity* (Ithaca, NY: Cornell University Press, 1989), 55.
24. Roberts, *Jeweled Style*, 55.
25. Jaś Elsner and Jesús Hernández Lobato, "Introduction: Notes Towards a Poetics of Late Ancient Literature," in *The Poetics of Late Latin Literature*, ed. Jaś Elsner and Jesús Hernández Lobato (Oxford: Oxford University Press, 2017), 11.
26. See Leslie Hill's account of Maurice Blanchot's "distinction between an art of the fragment that is nostalgic for the work and content to remain within established horizons, and one that reaches beyond the horizon and beckons to an unforeseeable future without present" (*Maurice Blanchot and Fragmentary Writing: A Change of Epoch* [London: Continuum, 2012], 29).
27. See Steven D. Smith, *Greek Epigram and Byzantine Culture: Gender, Desire, and Denial in the Age of Justinian* (Cambridge: Cambridge University Press, 2019), 118–26, 221–39.
28. Fikret Demirag, *Limnidi Atesinden Bugune Kitap 1* (Lefkosa: Galeri Kultur Yayinlar, 1992), 29, cited and translated in Bahriye Kemal, *Writing Cyprus: Postcolonial and Partitioned Literatures of Place and Space* (New York: Routledge, 2020), 196.
29. Demirag, *Limnidi*, 28, cited and translated in Kemal, *Writing Cyprus*, 194.
30. Demirag, *Limnidi*, 63, cited and translated in Kemal, *Writing Cyprus*, 196.
31. Demirag, *Limnidi*, 85, cited and translated in Kemal, *Writing Cyprus*, 197.
32. Kemal, *Writing Cyprus*, 191.
33. Demirag, *Limnidi*, 29, cited and translated in Kemal, *Writing Cyprus*, 196.
34. The reference is to Melina Mercouri in the 1955 film *Stella*.

35. Stephanos Stephanides, *The Wind Under My Lips* (Athens: To Rodakio, 2018), 86.
36. Stephanides, *Wind Under My Lips*, 122.
37. In fact, two limestone statues of the Cypriot goddess were discovered near Trikomo—the torso from the sixth century BCE to which I have referred, as well as a fourth-century BCE turreted figure (Jacqueline Karageorghis, *Kypris: The Aphrodite of Cyprus* [Nicosia: A. G. Leventis Foundation, 2005], 220–22).
38. Stephanides, *Wind Under My Lips*, 290.
39. Stephanides, *Wind Under My Lips*, 294.
40. Stephanides, *Wind Under My Lips*, 302, 290.
41. Stephanides, *Wind Under My Lips*, 294.
42. Stephanides, *Wind Under My Lips*, 293.
43. Christine E. Morris and Giorgos Papantoniou, "Cypriot-Born Aphrodite: The Social Biography of a Modern Cultural Icon," in *Il trono variopinto: Figure e forme della Dea dell'Amore*, ed. Luca Bombardieri, Tommaso Braccini, and Silvia Romani (Alessandria: Edizione dell-Orso, 2014), 187.
44. Stephanides, *Wind Under My Lips*, 293.
45. "Whether talking of Cyprus as the island of Venus or of Aphrodite, both sides are joined in silent collusion over forms of exploitation linked to gender" (Yiannis Papadakis, "Aphrodite Delights," *Postcolonial Studies* 9, no. 3 [2006]: 245).
46. Stephanides, *Wind Under My Lips*, 296–98.
47. Papadakis, "Aphrodite Delights," 237–38.
48. Stephanides, *Wind Under My Lips*, 296, 298.
49. Theopisti Stylianou-Lambert, "Rock of Aphrodite: In 5 Photographic Acts," in *Re-Envisioning Cyprus*, ed. Peter Loizos, Nicos Philippou, and Theopisti Stylianou-Lambert (Nicosia: University of Nicosia Press, 2010), 73–87; Theopisti Stylianou-Lambert, "En-Gendering a Landscape: The Construction, Promotion and Consumption of the Rock of Aphrodite," in *Photography and Cyprus: Time, Place and Identity*, ed. Liz Wells, Theopisti Stylianou-Lambert, and Nicos Philippou (London: I. B. Tauris, 2014), 143–66.
50. Stephanides, *Wind Under My Lips*, 86.
51. Demirag, *Limnidi*, 29, cited and translated in Kemal, *Writing Cyprus*, 196.
52. Hilarion's desire was the focus of my reading in *The Sex Lives of Saints: An Erotics of Ancient Hagiography*, Divinations: Rereading Late Ancient Religion (Philadelphia: University of Pennsylvania Press, 2004), 39–45.

CURATING EARTHQUAKES

1. Shimon Wdowinski, et al., "Seismotectonics of the Cyprian Arc," *Geophysical Journal International* 164, no. 1 (2006): 176–81.
2. Soteris Kramwis and Efstathios Kyriacou, "Larnaca, Cyprus: Geotechnical map and microseismicity study," *Engineering Geology and the Environment*, vol. 2 (Rotterdam: Balkema, 1997), 1323 [1321–36].
3. Manetti's catalog is preceded by an account of the causes of earthquakes and followed

by a detailed description of an earthquake on December 5, 1456, in the Kingdom of Naples that he himself had witnessed. See Emanuela Guidoboni and John E. Ebel, *Earthquakes and Tsunamis in the Past: A Guide to Techniques in Historical Seismology*. Cambridge: Cambridge University Press, 2009, 158–60.

4. US Geological Survey, Earthquake Catalog: https://earthquake.usgs.gov/earthquakes/search/.

5. Lou Stoppard, "Everyone's a Curator Now," *New York Times*, 5 March 2020. https://www.nytimes.com/2020/03/03/style/curate-buzzword.html.

6. For example, Emanuela Guidoboni associates Jerome's passage with an earthquake dated around 370, distinct from the 365 Crete earthquake mentioned by Ammianus Marcellinus (Emanuela Guidoboni, with Alberto Comastri and Giusto Traina, *Catalogue of Ancient Earthquakes in the Mediterranean up to the 10th Century* [Rome: Instituto Nazionale di Geofisica, 1994], 277). Nicholas Ambraseys associates it first with "a series of earthquakes which shook Cyprus between 365 and 378" (Nicholas Ambraseys, "The Seismic History of Cyprus," *Revue de l'Union Internationale de Secours* 3 [March 1965]: 28) and subsequently more specifically with an earthquake around 375 (Nicholas Ambraseys, *Earthquakes in the Mediterranean and Middle East: A Multidisciplinary Study of Seismicity up to 1900* [Cambridge: Cambridge University Press, 2009], 157). Stathis Stiros associates it first with the 365 Crete earthquake mentioned by Ammianus Marcellinus (Stathis Stiros, "The AD 365 Crete Earthquake and Possible Seismic Clustering During the Fourth to Sixth Centuries AD in the Eastern Mediterranean: A Review of Historical and Archaeological Data." *Journal of Structural Geology* 23 (2001): 550, 557, 560) and subsequently with a separate earthquake taking place around the same time (see Stathis Stiros, "The 8.5+ Magnitude, AD365 Earthquake in Crete: Coastal Uplift, Topography Changes, Archaeological and Historical Signature." *Quaternary International* 216 (2010): 61).

7. Ambraseys, "Seismic History of Cyprus," 35.

8. Ambraseys, "Seismic History of Cyprus," 37–38.

9. Ambraseys, "Seismic History of Cyprus," 39–40.

10. Ambraseys, "Seismic History of Cyprus," 39.

11. David Soren and Jamie James, *Kourion: The Search for a Lost Roman City* (New York: Doubleday, 1988), 56–57.

12. Soren and James, *Kourion*, 88.

13. Guidoboni, et al., *Catalogue of Ancient Earthquakes*, 411.

14. Soren and James, *Kourion*, 118.

15. Michel Serres, *Biogea*, trans. Randolph Burks (Minneapolis, MN: Univocal, 2012), 29.

16. Serres, *Biogea*, 29.

17. Valerie Trouet, *Tree Story: The History of the World Written in Rings* (Baltimore: Johns Hopkins University Press, 2020), 113–16.

18. Serres, *Biogea*, 28.

19. In a subsequent work, Ambraseys locates a 341 earthquake at Salamis, which had also suffered from a significant earthquake in 332. Yet some confusion persists, as he goes on to say that "Paphos was so badly damaged by the earthquakes of AD 332 and 341 that it was not rebuilt for some time" (*Earthquakes*, 142).

20. Ambraseys here lists a 367 earthquake centered at Kourion but does not list Paphos as one of the places affected. In a subsequent work, he proposes ca. 375 as the date of the earthquake that left Paphos in ruins and also destroyed Kourion; however, he also cites Jerome's *Life of Hilarion* as evidence for the damage to Paphos, placing the date of Hilarion's arrival at 370 (rather than 364), which suggests an earlier date (*Earthquakes*, 157).
21. Excerpted from Ambraseys, "Seismic History of Cyprus," 39.
22. American Museum of Natural History, "Earthquakes," https://www.amnh.org/exhibitions/permanent/planet-earth/why-are-there-ocean-basins-continents-and-mountains/earthquakes.
23. Republic of Cyprus, Department of Antiquities, http://www.mcw.gov.cy/mcw/da/da.nsf/All/21E14D80F55D8539C22571990020DC5C?OpenDocument.
24. On the earthquake house "family," see Soren and James, *Kourion*, 131–34.
25. Soren and James, *Kourion*, 119.
26. Soren and James, *Kourion*, 88–92.
27. Caitlin DeSilvey, *Curated Decay: Heritage Beyond Saving* (Minneapolis: University of Minnesota Press, 2017), 5.
28. Thomas Davis, "An Amateur's Dream: George McFadden at Kourion," in *The Archaeology of Ancient Kourion*, ed. Ellen Hersher and Joanna Smith (Philadelphia: University of Pennsylvania Press, forthcoming). I thank Professor Davis for his conversation and for sharing this essay with me prior to publication.
29. On new museum foundations under the Republic of Cyprus, see Alexandra Bounia and Theopisti Stylianou-Lambert, "National Museums in Cyprus: A Story of Heritage and Conflict," in *Building National Museums in Europe 1750–2010*, ed. Peter Aronsson and Gabriella Elgenius (Linköping, Sweden: Linköping University Electronic Press, 2011), 179: "After 1960, the years that followed saw the increase of funds available for the cultural affairs of the island and the Antiquities Department's needs: excavation, repairs and restoration of ancient monuments, in collaboration mainly with the Church authorities and the Evkaf, were among the activities that were encouraged during this period; the encouragement was most probably part of an effort to ground the new Republic into its cultural past, but also to encourage new economic developments, such as tourism and modernisation."
30. Thomas Davis, "Amateur's Dream."
31. Thomas Davis, "Amateur's Dream."
32. See Soren and James, *Kourion*.
33. Soren, "The Day the World Ended at Kourion." A brief documentary film was also produced during the second season.
34. See the object catalog on the Penn Museum's "Digital Kourion" website at https://www.penn.museum/sites/kourion/objects.php.
35. Thomas Davis, "Amateur's Dream."
36. Part 1 of Soren's co-authored, popularizing account of the excavation is titled "The Earthquake That Ended Antiquity" (*Kourion*). Note that Soren had also hoped to work with Star Wars film set designer Harry Lange on a reconstruction of the Temple of Apollo at Kourion, but this proposal too was rejected by the Department of Antiquities (personal correspondence with David Soren, 25 November 2020).

37. Morton develops this concept across a number of works, including *The Ecological Thought* (Cambridge, MA: Harvard University Press, 2010) and *Hyperobjects*.
38. *Hyperobjects* (exhibition), https://www.ballroommarfa.org/program/hyperobjects/.
39. Regine, "A Bodily Experience of Man-Made Earthquakes," *We Make Money Not Art*, 9 April 2018, https://we-make-money-not-art.com/a-bodily-experience-of-man-made-earthquakes/.
40. Regine, "Bodily Experience of Man-Made Earthquakes."
41. Michelle Geraerts and Jarl Schulp, "Intimate Mapping—In Conversation with Jonathan Ruess & Sissel Marie Tonn," *Fiber*, 2 June 2020, https://www.fiber-space.nl/news/intimate-mapping-in-conversation-with-jonathon-reus-sissel-marie-tonn/.
42. Nance Klehm, "To Dig a Hole (You Create a Heap)," *Learned Pig*, 20 April 2020, https://www.thelearnedpig.org/to-dig-a-hole-you-create-a-heap/7877.
43. "M5.0 Earthquake Hits West Texas, New Mexico Border," https://www.usgs.gov/news/m50-earthquake-hits-west-texas-new-mexico-border#:~:text=On%20March%2026%2C%202020%2C%20a,near%20the%20New%20Mexico%20border.&text=This%20earthquake%20occurred%20in%20an,the%20region%20is%20under%20examination.
44. The Long Now Foundation website, https://longnow.org/.
45. On other recent works of art that use performative techniques to move beyond representations of earthquakes as spectacles, see Ella Mudie, "The Spectacle of Seismicity: Making Art from Earthquakes," *Leonardo* 43, no. 2 (2010): 133–39.
46. "Shell and Exxon's €5bn Problem: Gas Drilling That Sets Off Earthquakes and Wrecks Homes," *Guardian*, 10 October 2015.
47. Sissel Marie Tonn, *An Education of Attention* (exhibition), https://sisselmarietonn.com/project/an-education-of-attention.
48. See Mark Roosien, *The Liturgical Commemoration of Earthquakes in Late Antique Constantinople: At the Intersection of Ritual, Environment, and Empire* (PhD diss., Notre Dame University, 2018). On the two fifth-century earthquakes that led to the initial creation of the earthquake liturgies of Constantinople, see also Brian Croke, "Two Early Byzantine Earthquakes and their Liturgical Commemoration," *Byzantion* 51, no. 1 (1981): 122–47.
49. Catherine Michael Chin, "Four Notes on Memory Theatre," *Ancient Jew Review*, 6 January 2020, n.p.
50. Robin George Andrews, "Life's Pulsating Beat Is Now a Murmur on the World's Seismographs," *New York Times*, 10 April 2020, B3.
51. Cf. Caitlin DeSilvey, *Curated Decay: Heritage Beyond Saving* (Minneapolis: University of Minnesota Press, 2017).
52. Caitlin DeSilvey, Simon Naylor, and Colin Sackett, *Anticipatory History* (Axminster, Devon: Uniformbooks, 2011), 10.

LIFE IN RUINS

1. Susan Stewart, *The Ruins Lesson: Meaning and Material in Western Culture* (Chicago: University of Chicago Press, 2020), 5.
2. Alois Riegl, "The Modern Cult of Monuments: Its Character and Origin," *Oppositions: A Journal for Ideas and Criticism in Architecture* 25 (1982): 33.
3. Riegl, "Modern Cult of Monuments," 32.
4. The range of motivations and meanings that may be ascribed to *spolia* are well explored and interrogated in Richard Brilliant and Dale Kinney, eds., *Reuse Value*: Spolia *and Appropriation in Art and Architecture from Constantine to Sherrie Levine* (Farnham, UK: Ashgate, 2011). Here I am not primarily concerned with how late ancient viewers experienced and interpreted *spolia* but with what we might make of them.
5. Stewart, *Ruins Lesson*, 64.
6. W. A. Daszewski and D. Michaelides, *Guide to the Paphos Mosaics* (Nicosia: Bank of Cyprus Cultural Foundation, 1988), 11.
7. F. G. Maier and V. Karageorghis, *Paphos: History and Archaeology* (Nicosia: A. G. Leventis Foundation, 1984), 285.
8. Maier and Karageorghis, *Paphos*, 288.
9. Demetrios Michaelides, "Mosaic Decoration in Early Christian Cyprus," in *Church Building in Cyprus (Fourth to Seventh Centuries): A Mirror of Intercultural Contacts in the Eastern Mediterranean*, ed. Marietta Horster, Doria Nicolaou, and Sabine Rogge (Münster: Waxmann, 2018), 216.
10. Maier and Karageorghis, *Paphos*, 288.
11. Demetrios Michaelides, "Mosaic Workshops in Cyprus from the Fourth to the Seventh Centuries CE: Two Parallel Lives?" in *From Roman to Early Christian Cyprus*, ed. Laura Nasrallah, AnneMarie Luijendijk, and Charalambos Bakirtzis (Tübingen: Mohr Siebeck, 2020), 97. See also Daszewski and Michaelides, *Guide to the Paphos Mosaics*, 57–60.
12. Maier and Karageorghis, *Paphos*, 291.
13. Cf. Daszewski and Michaelides, *Guide to the Paphos Mosaics*, 62–63. At least one medieval painting of the nativity and first bath of Christ appears on Cyprus, in the Church of St. Nicholas on the Roof in Katopetria (Andreas Stylianou and Judith A. Stylianou, *The Painted Churches of Cyprus: Treasures of Byzantine Art*, 2nd ed. [Nicosia: A. G. Leventis Foundation, 1997], 68–71). The painting is from the fourteenth century, but the iconography goes back to late antiquity. The earliest surviving version may be a Coptic stone relief from the second half of the fourth century, assuming it was originally a Christian representation and not a later Christian appropriation of a representation of the bath of Dionysos (Gertrud Schiller, *Iconography of Christian Art*, vol. 1, trans. Janet Seligman [London: Lund Humphries, 1971], 64–65).
14. Craig Barker, "Twenty Years of the University of Sydney Excavations of the Theatre Precinct in Nea Paphos in Cyprus," *Ancient History: Resources for Teachers* 45 (2015): 47. See also Craig Barker, "From Performance to Quarry: The Evidence of Architectural

Change in the Theatre Precinct of Nea Paphos in Cyprus Over Seven Centuries," in *Continuity and Destruction in the Greek East: The Transformation of Monumental Space from the Hellenistic Period to Late Antiquity*, ed. Sujatha Chandrasekaran and Anna Kouremenos (Oxford: British Archaeological Reports, 2015), 33–48.

15. On the "perdurance" of buildings, see Nicola Camerlenghi, "How Long Are the Lives of Medieval Buildings? Framing Spatio-Temporalities in the Study of the Built World," in *The Long Lives of Medieval Art and Architecture*, ed. Jennifer M. Feltman and Sarah Thompson (London: Routledge, 2019), 20–26.
16. Barker, "Twenty Years," 48.
17. A. H. S. Megaw notes that the Paphos basilica was "in size surpassed in Cyprus only by St. Epiphanius' basilica at Salamis/Constantia" ("Reflections on Byzantine Paphos," in ΚΑΘΗΓΗΤΡΙΑ: *Essays Presented to Joan Hussey for Her 80th Birthday* [Camberley, Surrey, UK: Porphyrogenitus, 1988], 136–39).
18. On relics as *spolia*, see Paolo Liverani, "Reading *Spolia* in Late Antiquity and Contemporary Perception," in Brilliant and Kinney, *Reuse Value*, 45–46.
19. Gwynneth der Parthog, *Byzantine and Medieval Cyprus: A Guide to the Monuments* (New Barnet, UK: Interworld Publications, 1994), 41–43.
20. Camerlenghi, "Lives of Medieval Buildings," 28.
21. der Parthog, *Byzantine and Medieval Cyprus*, 43.
22. Robert Harding website, https://www.robertharding.com/preview/526-343/st-paulamps-pillars-paphos-cyprus-europe/.
23. I am following Daniela Summa's tentative suggestion to read Εὐστόργιε (vocative) rather than Εὐστόργις (nominative) ("The Christian Epigraphy of Cyprus: A Preliminary Study," in *Early Christianity in Asia Minor and Cyprus: From the Margins to the Mainstream*, ed. Stephen Mitchell and Philipp Pilhofer [Leiden: Brill, 2019], 239, n. 50).
24. J. R. Green and E. W. Handley, "Eustorgis in Paphos," in *Philathenaios: Studies in Honour of Michael J. Osborne*, ed. A. M. Tamis, C. J. Mackie, and S. G. Byrne (Athens: Greek Epigraphic Society, 2010), 203–4, 207–8.
25. Michaelides, "Mosaic Decoration," 224–28; Michaelides, "Mosaic Workshops in Cyprus," 99.
26. Note, however, that Green and Handley leave open the possibility that it was inscribed while still in the theater (Green and Handley, "Eustorgis in Paphos," 203–5). Both chronology and the apparent Christian content of the inscription seem to me to make it far more likely that the column was inscribed after it was moved to the church.
27. Green and Handley, "Eustorgis in Paphos," 197–203, 205–7.
28. Summa, "The Christian Epigraphy of Cyprus," 232–34, 238–41.
29. Green and Handley, "Eustorgis in Paphos," 210–11.
30. Barker, "Twenty Years," 48.
31. Summa, "Christian Epigraphy of Cyprus," 241.
32. Camerlenghi, "Lives of Medieval Buildings," 18.
33. Martin Devecka, *Broken Cities: A Historical Sociology of Ruins* (Baltimore: Johns Hopkins University Press, 2020), 37, 44.
34. Stewart, *Ruins Lesson*, 122–23.
35. Stewart, *Ruins Lesson*, 127.

36. Stewart, *Ruins Lesson*, 132–33.
37. The painting is housed in the Lichtenstein Museum in Vienna. Images of the painting are reproduced in Arthur J. DiFuria, *Maarten Van Heemskerck's Rome: Antiquity, Memory, and the Cult of Ruins* (Leiden: Brill, 2019), 210, and Tatjana Bartsch, *Maarten Van Heemskerck: Römische Studien zwischen Sachlichkeit und Imagination* (Munich: Hirmer, 2019), 117.
38. Tatjana Bartsch identifies the following monuments in van Heemskerck's painting: "das Kolosseum, das Pantheon, der Saturn-Tempel vom Forum Romanum, die Trajanssäule, die Statue des Tiber vom Kapitol and die Hercules-und-Antaeus-Gruppe" (*Maarten Van Heemskerck*, 117). Arthur DiFuria suggests that the allusions are less exact: "A veritable overgrowth of imagined temples, orphaned columns, piers, and arches reminds us of specific Roman buildings without quoting them verbatim" (DiFuria, *Maarten Van Heemskerck's Rome*, 209).
39. DiFuria suggests that "Jerome is nearly as diminutive as the figures exploring the ruins"; in fact, he is much closer to the scale of the monumental statues, even taking into account that he is foregrounded relative to the other figures.
40. Stewart, *Ruins Lesson*, 136.
41. See Eugene F. Rice, *Saint Jerome in the Renaissance* (Baltimore: Johns Hopkins University Press, 1985), 99–115.
42. See Hilmar M. Pabel, *Herculean Labors: Erasmus and the Editing of St. Jerome's Letters in the Renaissance* (Leiden: Brill, 2008). Holbein's portrait is reproduced in fig. 1 on p. 3. See also Lisa Jardine, *Erasmus, Man of Letters: The Construction of Charisma in Print* (Princeton, NJ: Princeton University Press, 1993), 55–82.
43. DiFuria, *Maarten Van Heemskerck's Rome*, 211.
44. Alexander Nagel and Christopher S. Wood, *Anachronic Renaissance* (New York: Zone Books, 2010).
45. The print is housed in the National Gallery of Art, Washington, DC. (https://www.nga.gov/collection/art-object-page.91354.html). Stewart includes the image and a description (*Ruins Lesson*, 134).
46. Stewart, *Ruins Lesson*, 132.
47. DiFuria, *Maarten Van Heemskerck's Rome*, 232.
48. Stewart, *Ruins Lesson*, 132.
49. See Stewart, *Ruins Lesson*, 133–34.
50. Indeed, the fascination with photographs of urban ruins in our own moment is so strong and so ambivalent as to have earned it the name "ruin porn." The case of Detroit is taken up in John Patrick Leary's influential critique ("Detroitism: What Does 'Ruin Porn' Tell Us about the Motor City?," *Guernica/15 Years of Global Arts & Politics* [15 January 2011]).
51. Riegl, "Modern Cult of Monuments," 31.
52. Michael Ann Holly, *The Melancholy Art* (Princeton, NJ: Princeton University Press, 2013), 22–24.
53. Susan Cross, "Ledelle Moe: When," in *Ledelle Moe: When* (North Adams, MA: MASS MoCA, 2019), 13.
54. Cross, "Ledelle Moe: When," 16.

55. Cross, "Ledelle Moe: When," 21. As Jennifer Nelson points out to me, the figure has special affinities with the so-called Madonna of Humility in particular.
56. Cross, "Ledelle Moe: When," 21.
57. Riegl, "Modern Cult of Monuments," 32.
58. Maier and Karageorghis, *Paphos*, 103, fig. 86.
59. Jacqueline Karageorghis, *Kypris: The Aphrodite of Cyprus* (Nicosia: A. G. Leventis Foundation, 2005), 30.
60. Milette Gaifman, *Aniconism in Greek Antiquity* (Oxford: Oxford University Press, 2012), 180.
61. Riegl, "Modern Cult of Monuments," 33.
62. Judith Schalansky, *An Inventory of Losses*, trans. Jackie Smith (New York: New Directions Books, 2020), 17.
63. Andrew Hui, *The Poetics of Ruins in Renaissance Literature* (New York: Fordham University Press, 2016), 24.

GEOGRAPHIES OF THE REMOTE

1. For evidence that the late ancient desert imaginary continues to move readers in surprising new ways, see the innovative queer Chicanx reading of Peter Anthony Mena, *Place and Identity in the Lives of Antony, Paul, and Mary of Egypt: Desert as Borderland* (London: Palgrave Macmillan, 2019).
2. Gerardo Bocco, "Remoteness and Remote Places: A Geographic Perspective," *Geoforum* 77 (2016): 178.
3. Bocco, "Remoteness," 179.
4. Bocco, "Remoteness," 180.
5. Judith Schalansky, *Pocket Atlas of Remote Islands: Fifty Islands I Have Not Visited and Never Will*, trans. Christine Lo (New York City: Penguin Books, 2010), 8–9.
6. Schalansky, *Pocket Atlas of Remote Islands*, 7.
7. Henry George Liddell, Robert Scott, Henry Stuart Jones, *A Greek-English Lexicon* (Oxford: Clarendon, 1940), s.v. "ὅρος."; is it relevant that a similar word, ὄρος, means "boundary"?
8. Hermann Kees, *Ancient Egypt: A Cultural Topography*, trans. Ian F. D. Morrow (Chicago: University of Chicago Press, 1961), 96–106.
9. We learn that he was about thirty-five when he left the tombs (*Life of Antony* 10) and that he lived in the fortress for about twenty years (14).
10. Antony's departure is said to take place after the persecution of 311 in which Peter, bishop of Alexandria, was martyred (46–47). His death is dated to 356, and he is said to have reached the age of 105, which would make him about 60 when he left for the inner mountain, roughly five years after emerging from the fortress.
11. For references to the "outer mountain," see *Life of Antony* 61, 72, 73, 84, 89, 91. For references to the "inner mountain," see *Life of Antony* 51, 82, 91.
12. As Hermann Kees writes, "In spite of the fact that the valley of the Nile is hedged on

both sides by deserts, man has in all ages broken through these barriers to reach countries that were not accessible to him by water" (Kees, *Ancient Egypt*, 116).
13. These figures are thanks to Google maps.
14. Schalansky, *Pocket Atlas of Remote Islands*, 24.
15. I also discuss this correspondence in Thomas Arentzen, Virginia Burrus, and Glenn Peers, *Byzantine Tree Life: Christianity and the Arboreal Imagination* (London: Palgrave Macmillan, 2021).
16. Daniel Viviroli, et al., "Mountains of the World, Water Towers for Humanity: Typology, Mapping, and Global Significance," *Water Resources Research* 43 (2007): 1–13, doi:W07447.
17. The danger represented by the river was real. Basil's younger brother, another Gregory, would later report that a third brother, Naucratius, had lived for five years in "a remote spot [ἐσχατιάν τινα] near the Iris," thickly wooded and tucked into the hollow of a mountain, when he died tragically while hunting for food (Gregory of Nyssa, *Life of Macrina* 3). In three poetic epigrams, Gregory of Nazianzus laments Naucratius's death while fishing "in the roaring whirlpools of the river" (*Epigram* 156; cf. 157, 158).
18. Anna M. Silvas, "In Quest of Basil's Retreat: An Expedition to Ancient Pontus," *Antichthon* 41 (2007): 73–95.
19. Jody Michael Gordon, "Insularity and Identity in Roman Cyprus: Connectivity, Complexity, and Cultural Change," in *Insularity and Identity in the Roman Mediterranean*, ed. Anna Kouremenos (Oxford: Oxbow Books, 2018), 23.
20. Catherine Kearns, "Cyprus in the Surging Sea: Spatial Imaginations of the Eastern Mediterranean," *Transactions of the American Philological Association* 148, no. 1 (2018): 46.
21. Schalansky, *Pocket Atlas of Remote Islands*, 25.
22. Ryan Dewey, "Creating Experiences of Remoteness in Landscapes and Geographies," blog (2014), https://www.ryandewey.org/blog/2014/5/29/creating-experiences-of-remoteness-in-landscapes-geographies.
23. Michael Marder, *Dump Philosophy: A Phenomenology of Devastation* (London: Bloomsbury, 2021), 5.
24. Dewey, "Creating Experiences of Remoteness."
25. Dewey, "Creating Experiences of Remoteness."
26. Ryan Dewey, "Hacking Remoteness Through Viewpoint and Cognition," *Kerb* 22 (2014): 26.
27. Ryan Dewey, *Copper Boulder*, https://www.ryandewey.org/copper-boulder-1.
28. "La Val Stussavgia ha carmalà ils artists" (video), https://www.rtr.ch/novitads/grischun/surselva/la-val-stussavgia-ha-carmala-ils-artists.
29. Ryan Dewey, "Project Proposal: Alps Art Academy," 2018.
30. Dewey, "Project Proposal," 2018.
31. Miljana Radivojević, et. al., "The Provenance, Use, and Circulation of Metals in the European Bronze Age: The State of Debate," *Journal of Archaeological Research* 27 (2019): 166.
32. Dewey suggests that the oscillation between immersive disorientation and open sight lines intensifies our experience of remoteness ("Hacking Remoteness," 26–30). For a

focus on urban geographies, see also Ryan Dewey, "Agency and the Multifaceted Stories of Hybrid Places," *MONU* 20 (2014): 80.

33. Michael Conforti and Michael Cassins, *The Clark: The Institute and Its Collections* (London: Scala Arts, 2014), 130–34.

34. "Thomas Schütte: *Crystal*," https://www.clarkart.edu/exhibition/detail/thomas-schutte-crystal.

35. Kevin Bicknell, "*Crystal*: An Installation Comes to Life," *Journal of The Clark* 17 (2016): 34.

36. Dewey, "Hacking Remoteness," 27–29; Dewey, "Agency and the Multifaceted Stories," 82–83.

37. Bicknell, "*Crystal*," 30.

38. In this it is somewhat different from some of Schütte's other permanent installations, e.g., "Blockhaus" (2018, Vitra Campus, Weil am Rhein, Germany), "Teehaus" (2012, Neuss, Germany), or "One Man House II" (2007–2009, Roanne, France), all of which are more decisively architectural (http://www.thomas-schuette.de/).

39. *The Mastheads*, https://www.themastheads.org/studios-1.

40. Tessa Kelley, personal communication, 26 February 2021.

41. Herman Melville, *Moby Dick; or, The Whale* (New York: Harper Brothers, 1851), 171.

42. Melville, *Moby Dick*, 171–72.

43. Melville, *Moby Dick*, 175–76.

44. Kelly, personal communication.

45. Melville, *Moby Dick*, 169–71.

46. Rebecca Solnit, *A Field Guide to Getting Lost* (New York: Penguin, 2005), 27–28.

47. Michael Ann Holly, "Back of the Painted Beyond," *Art History* 42, no. 5 (2019): 902, 900.

48. Solnit, *Field Guide to Getting Lost*, 27.

49. Dewey, "Creating Experiences of Remoteness."

50. Estelle Zhong Mengual, "The Point of View of the Mountain," in *Critical Zones: The Science and Politics of Landing on Earth*, ed. Bruno Latour and Peter Weibel (Karlsruhe, Germany: ZKM/Center for Art and Media, 2020), 253.

ENTROPIC GARDENS

1. Marcus Rautman, "The Busy Countryside of Late Roman Cyprus," *Report of the Department of Antiquities, Cyprus* (2000): 317.

2. Michael Marder, "The Garden as Form," *The Learned Pig*, 21 November 2018.

3. Michael Marder, *Plant-Thinking: A Philosophy of Vegetal Life* (New York: Columbia University Press, 2013), 12.

4. Marder, "Garden as Form."

5. Elizabeth Macaulay-Lewis, "The Archaeology of Gardens in the Roman Villa," in *Gardens of the Roman Empire*, Wilhelmina F. Jashemski, et al. (Cambridge: Cambridge University Press, 2018), 119.

6. Wilhelmina F. Jashemski, "Produce Gardens," in *Gardens of the Roman Empire*, Wilhelmina F. Jashemski, et al. (Cambridge: Cambridge University Press, 2018), 123.
7. John Henderson, *The Roman Book of Gardening* (London: Routledge, 2004), 6, 10.
8. If not also of the cosmos itself: on the garden as microcosm that reveals the mysteries of nature and the order of the cosmos via the mediation of poetry in Columella, see Silke Diederich, *Römische Agrarhandbücher zwischen Fachwissenschaft, Literatur und Ideologie* (Berlin: De Gruyter, 2007), 247–51.
9. Henderson, *Roman Book of Gardening*, 10.
10. Henderson, *Roman Book of Gardening*, 18.
11. On the marginality, separateness, and superfluity of the garden in Columella, see Marco Formisano, "Beyond the Fence: Columella's Garden," in *Antike Erzähl- und Deutungsmuster: Zwischen Exemplarität und Transformation*, ed. Simone Finkmann, Anja Behrendt, and Anke Walter (Berlin: De Gruyter, 2019), 501–14.
12. Here Masanobu Fukuoka, *Sowing Seeds in the Desert: Natural Farming, Global Restoration, and Ultimate Food Security* (White River Junction, VT: Chelsea Green, 2012), is suggestive.
13. Although he began his practice decades earlier, Fukuoka's ground-breaking *The One-Straw Revolution* was first published in English translation in 1978 (Masanobu Fukuoka, *The One-Straw Revolution: An Introduction to Natural Farming*, trans. Larry Korn [New York: New York Review Books, 2009]).
14. Bill Mollison and David Holmgren's inaugural work was *Permaculture One: A Perennial Agricultural System for Human Settlements* (Ealing, London: Transworld, 1978).
15. Masanobu Fukuoka, *The Natural Way of Farming: The Theory and Practice of Green Philosophy* (Mapusa, Goa: Other India Press, 1985), 5.
16. Fukuoka, *One-Straw Revolution*, 66.
17. Fukuoka, *One-Straw Revolution*, 67, 69.
18. Fukuoka, *One-Straw Revolution*, 13.
19. "What Is Permaculture?" https://www.permaculturedesignscyprus.com/what-is-permaculture.
20. Fukuoka, *One-Straw Revolution*, 183.
21. Fukuoka, *One-Straw Revolution*, 183–84.
22. Fukuoka, *One-Straw Revolution*, 184.
23. I thank theologian and gardener Sharon Betcher for this suggestion.
24. Caitlin DeSilvey, *Curated Decay: Heritage Beyond Saving* (Minneapolis: University of Minnesota Press, 2017), 99.
25. For a description of the park from the viewpoint of its designer, see Peter Latz, *Rust Red: Landscape Park Duisburg-Nord* (Munich: Hirmer, 2016). See also the park website at landschaftspark.de/en/.
26. Joern Langhorst, "Re-Presenting Transgressive Ecologies: Post-Industrial Sites as Contested Terrains," *Local Environment: The International Journal of Justice and Sustainability* 19, no. 10 (2014): 1111.
27. Langhorst, "Re-Presenting Transgressive Ecologies," 1117, 1111, 1114.
28. Langhorst, "Re-Presenting Transgressive Ecologies," 1114.

29. Langhorst, "Re-Presenting Transgressive Ecologies," 1120–21.
30. Elissa Rosenberg, "Gardens, Landscape, Nature: Duisburg-Nord, Germany," in *The Hand and the Soul: Aesthetics and Ethics in Architecture and Art*, ed. Sanda Iliescu (Charlottesville, VA: University of Virginia Press, 2009), 212.
31. Rosenberg, "Gardens, Landscape, Nature," 212.
32. DeSilvey, *Curated Decay*, 113.
33. DeSilvey, *Curated Decay*, 104.
34. Rosenberg, "Gardens, Landscape, Nature," 223.
35. DeSilvey, *Curated Decay*, 107.
36. DeSilvey, *Curated Decay*, 107.
37. DeSilvey, *Curated Decay*, 107.
38. Latz, *Rust Red*, 22.
39. DeSilvey, *Curated Decay*, 108.
40. Latz, *Rust Red*, 25.
41. Gilles A. Tiberghien, "Forward," in *The Planetary Garden and Other Writings*, Gilles Clément (Philadelphia: University of Pennsylvania Press, 2006), viii–ix.
42. Tassos Papacostas, "The Economy of Late Antique Cyprus," in *Economy and Exchange in the East Mediterranean During Late Antiquity*, ed. Sean Kingsley and Michael Decker (Oxford: Oxbow Books, 2015), 111.
43. J. V. Thirgood, *Cyprus: A Chronicle of Its Forests, Land, and People* (Vancouver: University of British Columbia Press, 1987), 32.
44. Takis C. Tsintides, Georgios N. Hadjikyriakou, and Charalambos S. Christodoulou, *Trees and Shrubs in Cyprus* (Nicosia: Leventis Foundation—Cyprus Forest Association, 2002), 74.
45. Thirgood, *Cyprus*, 72.
46. Tsintides, Hadjikyriakou, and Christodoulou, *Trees and Shrubs*, 35–36.
47. Thirgood, *Cyprus*, 32–33.
48. Tsintides, Hadjikyriakou, and Christodoulou, *Trees and Shrubs*, 118–19.
49. Tsintides, Hadjikyriakou, and Christodoulou, *Trees and Shrubs*, 77.
50. Thirgood, *Cyprus*, 32.
51. For wild roses currently found in Cyprus, see the "Cyprus Wild Flowers Searchable Database": http://cypruswildflowers.com/cgi-bin/site/main.pl?action=list&sort=english_name&flower=rose.
52. Marder, *Plant-Thinking*, 80, 132.
53. Marder, *Plant-Thinking*, 182.
54. Emanuele Coccia, *The Life of Plants: A Metaphysics of Mixture*, trans. Dylan J. Montanari (Cambridge: Polity, 2019), 10.
55. Coccia, *Life of Plants*, 5.
56. Gilles Clément, "The Wisdom of the Gardener," in *The Planetary Garden and Other Writings*, Gilles Clément (Philadelphia: University of Pennsylvania Press, 2006), 106.
57. Michael Pollan, *Second Nature: A Gardener's Education* (New York: Grove Press, 1991), 1.
58. For use of the term *conviviality* to describe the interdependence of humans and non-

humans in an ancient Cypriot context, see Michael Given, "Flowing Rock, Dancing around Trees: Conviviality and the Landscape of Cyprus," *Near Eastern Archaeology* 85, no. 1 (2022): 4–11.

LITERARY CARTOGRAPHIES

1. Eugène Bernard, *Les voyages de Saint Jérôme* (Paris: Charles Douniol, 1864), ii–iii.
2. This is part of a larger ambivalence in Jerome's work regarding pilgrimage and holy places; see Brouria Bitton-Ashkelony, *Encountering the Sacred: The Debate on Christian Pilgrimage in Late Antiquity* (Berkeley: University of California Press, 2005), 65–105.
3. Elsewhere Jerome defends the cult of relics as well; see Bitton-Ashkelony, *Encountering the Sacred*.
4. Ilona Opelt, "Des Hieronymus Heiligenbiographien als Quellen der historischen Topographie des östlichen Mittelmeerraums," *Römische Quartalschrift für Christliche Altertumskunde und Kirchengeschichte* 74, no. 3/4 (1979): 169.
5. Nicholas Purcell, "Periploi," in *Oxford Classical Dictionary, 4th Ed.*, ed. Simon Hornblower, Antony Spawforth, and Esther Eidinow (Oxford: Oxford University Press, 2012). For the use of *periploi* in the description of Paul's journey in the book of Acts, see M. Wilson, "The Lukan Periplus of Paul's Third Journey with a Textual Conundrum in Acts 20:15," *Acta Theologica* 36, no. 1 (2016): 229–54.
6. Duane W. Roller, *Ancient Geography: The Discovery of the World in Classical Greece and Rome* (London: I. B. Tauris, 2015), 8.
7. Burkhardt Wolf, "Muses of Cartography: Charting Odysseus from Homer to Joyce," in *Literature and Cartography: Theories, Histories, Genres*, ed. Anders Engberg-Pedersen (Cambridge, MA: MIT Press, 2017), 145.
8. Apuleius, *Metamorphoses* 6.18.2. Cf. Vergil, *Aeneid* 3.383, *inuia . . . uia*.
9. John Franklin argues with respect to the lost *Kypria* that "one or more versions of the poem must also have contained wandering adventures set in the eastern Mediterranean," including those of Helen, Paris, and Menelaus preceding the Trojan War, and that the title derives from the fact that the travels concentrated around Cyprus ("Lady Come Down: The Eastern Wandering of Helen, Paris, and Menelaus," *Classical Inquiries*, 5 May 2016, 1).
10. Victor Bérard, *Les navigations d'Ulysse* (Paris: A. Colin, 1971).
11. Among the most surprising, perhaps, is Henriette Mertz's suggestion that Odysseus travels as far as North America (Henriette Mertz, *The Wine Dark Sea: Homer's Heroic Epic of the North Atlantic* [Chicago: Self-published, 1964]).
12. Opelt suggests that the caves would have been abandoned in Hilarion's time but reoccupied by fugitives fleeing the Vandal invasions of the fifth century; she even suggests that Hilarion's cell may have formed the nucleus of the later monastic communities (Ilona Opelt, "Note al viaggio in Italia di S. Ilarione siro," *Augustinianum* 24, no. 1/2 [1984]: 305–14).
13. Opelt, "Des Hieronymus Heiligenbiographien," 174–75.

14. Eugen Oberhummer, "Charbyris," in *Paulys Realencyclopädie der classischen Altertumswissenschaft* 3.2 (1899), 2124.
15. Two early Greek translations of Jerome's work (one literal, one free), as well as a Coptic rendering of a third (also literal), survive. Sozomen appears to have been familiar with a version of the free translation (Ruth Strout, "The Greek Versions of Jerome's *Vita Sancti Hilarionis*," in *Studies in the Text Tradition of Jerome's "Vitae Patrum*," ed. William A. Oldfather [Urbana: University of Illinois, 1943], 308–11). Jerome indicates that the *Life of Hilarion* was translated almost immediately: in the penultimate entry of his *On Famous Men* (which was written not long after *Life of Hilarion*), he records that one Sophronius, "a highly learned man," had translated his work into an "elegant" Greek (*On Famous Men* 134). Sophronius's translation may be the one known by Sozomen (Elizabeth Fisher, "Greek Translations of Latin Literature," *Yale Classical Studies* 27 [1982], 193–200).
16. Neophytos, *Panegyric for Saint Gennadios* 5 (Hippolyte Delehaye, "Saints de Chypre," *Analecta Bollandiana* 26 [1907]: 224–25). As Catia Galatariotou notes, Neophytos's account of Gennadios's death seems to draw on "local popular legends" (Catia Galatariotou, *The Making of a Saint: The Life, Times and Sanctification of Neophytos the Recluse* [Cambridge: Cambridge University Press, 1991], 37).
17. Andreas Stylianou and Judith A. Stylianou, "St. Hilarion the Great in Paphos, Cyprus," *Kypriakai Spoudai* 41 (1977): 1–2.
18. D. Rupp, et al., "Charbyris: A Pleiades Place Resource," *Pleiades: A Gazetteer of Past Places* (2012), https://pleiades.stoa.org/places/711223.
19. Galatariotou, *Making of a Saint*, 26; Delehaye, "Saints de Chypre," 286.
20. Claudia Rapp, "Christianity in Cyprus in the Fourth to Seventh Centuries," in *Cyprus and the Balance of Empires: Art and Archaeology from Justinian I to the Coeur de Lion*, ed. Charles Anthony Stewart, Thomas W. Davis, and Annemarie Weyl Carr (Boston: American Schools of Oriental Research, 2014), 35.
21. Claude Delaval Cobham, *Excerpta Cypria: Materials for a History of Cyprus* (Cambridge: Cambridge University Press, 1908), 12.
22. Leontios Makhairas, *Recital Concerning the Sweet Land of Cyprus Entitled "Chronicle,"* trans. R. M. Dawkins (Oxford: Clarendon Press, 1932), vol. 1, 31. On the question of the date of the three hundred saints, see vol. 2, 56–57.
23. Lawrence Durrell, *Bitter Lemons* (London: Faber and Faber, 1957), 105.
24. Von Boldensele and de Mandeville are excerpted in Cobham, *Excerpta Cypria*, 16, 21.
25. Durrell, *Bitter Lemons*, 106. On Estienne de Lusignan's account, see also Dawkins, in Makhairas, *Chronicle*, vol. 2, 59.
26. Karl Kügle, "Glorious Sounds for a Holy Warrior: New Light on Codex Turin J.II.9," *Journal of the American Musicological Society* 65, no. 3 (2012): 638–39.
27. Kügle, "Glorious Sounds," 656, n. 48.
28. Kügle, "Glorious Sounds," 662, 669–80.
29. Tassos Papacostas, "Decoding Cyprus from Late Antiquity to the Renaissance: Discordant Visions, Saints, and Sacred Topography," in *Cyprus and the Balance of Empires: Art and Archaeology from Justinian I to the Coeur de Lion*, ed. Charles Anthony Stewart, Thomas W. Davis, and Annemarie Weyl Carr (Boston: American Schools of Oriental

Research, 2014), 187, 193. On Episkopi, see also Gwynneth der Parthog, *Byzantine and Medieval Cyprus: A Guide to the Monuments* (New Barnet, UK: Interworld Publications, 1994), 73–74.
30. Stylianou and Stylianou, "St. Hilarion the Great," 3.
31. https://cyprus.terrabook.com/cyprus/page/episkopi-paphou/.
32. Stylianou and Stylianou, "St. Hilarion the Great," 3.
33. Irene Dietzel, *The Ecology of Coexistence and Conflict in Cyprus: Exploring the Religion, Nature, and Culture of a Mediterranean Island* (Berlin: De Gruyter, 2014), 126. Dietzel here draws on the 1979 publication of Cypriot folklorist Anthimos Panaretou.
34. B. Richard Stephan, Iris Wagner, and Jochen Kleinschmit, *Technical Guidelines for Genetic Conservation and Use for Wild Apple and Pear* (Rome: International Plant Genetic Resources Institute, 2003).
35. Episkopi Paphos Environmental Information Centre, http://epeicentre.com/.
36. John Ladouceur, "Christians and Pagans in Roman Nea Paphos: Contextualizing the 'House of Aion' Mosaic," *UCLA Historical Journal* 29, no. 1 (2018): 59. See also Manfred Fuhrmann, "Die Mönchsgeschichten des Hieronymus: Formexperimente in erzählender Literatur," in *Christianisme et formes littéraires de l'antiquité tardive en occident*, ed. Manfred Fuhrmann, Entretiens sur l'Antiquité Classique (Geneva: Fondation Hardt, 1977), 48, n. 1; and Susan Weingarten, *The Saint's Saints: Hagiography and Geography in Jerome* (Leiden: Brill, 2005), 142, 148.
37. Ladouceur, "Christians and Pagans," 59.
38. See Virginia Burrus, *The Sex Lives of Saints: An Erotics of Ancient Hagiography*, Divinations: Rereading Late Ancient Religion (Philadelphia: University of Pennsylvania Press, 2004), 45.
39. Filippo Giudice and Giada Giudice, "La 'memoria' paleocristiana da Garrison's Camp a Nea Paphos (Cipro): Recenti scavi e nuovi risultati," *Corso di Cultura sull'Arte Ravennate e Bizantina* 44 (1998): 155.
40. David Soren and Jamie James, *Kourion: The Search for a Lost Roman City* (New York: Doubleday, 1988), 41–46.
41. Durrell, *Bitter Lemons*, 15.
42. "Ulyssis Errores," from the *Theatrum Orbis Terrarum* of Abraham Ortelius (1527–1598), engraved 1597, printed 1624; http://www.columbia.edu/itc/mealac/pritchett/00maplinks/early/arrian/arrian.html.
43. Estienne Michalet, *Les Deserts d'Egypte, de Thabaide D'Arabie, de Sirie, &c.: ou sont exactement marques les lieux habitez par les Saincts Peres des Deserts* (Paris: E. Michalet, 1693), https://www.loc.gov/item/2009580106/. See also Andreas Stylianou and Judith Stylianou, *The History of the Cartography of Cyprus* (Nicosia: Cyprus Research Center, 1980), 353.
44. Stylianou and Stylianou, "St. Hilarion the Great," 2.
45. Daniel Mendelsohn, *An Odyssey: A Father, a Son, and an Epic* (New York: Vintage, 2017), 7.
46. Mendelsohn, *An Odyssey*, 191–95.
47. C. P. Cavafy, "Ithaca," in *Complete Poems*, trans. Daniel Mendelsohn (New York: Knopf, 2009), 13.

48. Mendelsohn, *An Odyssey*, 199.
49. Cavafy, "Ithaca," 13.
50. Véronique Blanc-Bijon, "Les pavements en mosaïque de la basilique d'Hilarion (Nuseirat, Gaza): Nouveautés sur les ateliers de mosaïstes gaziotes," in *Estudios sobre mosaicos antiguos y medievales*, ed. Luz Neira Jiménez (Rome: "L'Erma" di Bretschneider, 2016), 392.
51. René Elter, "Gaza: Le plus ancien monastère de Terra Sainte," *Archéologia* 505 (2012): 34–51.
52. René Elter and Ayman Hassoune, "Le monastère de Saint-Hilarion à Umm-el-'Amr (bande de Gaza)," *Comptes rendus des séances de l'Académie des Inscriptions et Belles-Lettres* 148, no. 1 (2004): 365–69. See also René Elter and Ahmad Abd el-Rhadan, "Le monastère de Saint-Hilarion: évolution et développement architectural d'un sanctuaire de pèlerinage dans le sud de Gaza (Palestine)," *Les Cahiers de Saint-Michel de Cuxa* 38 (2007): 121–36.
53. Abdalhadi Alijia, "The Melancholy of the Palestinians: A Heritage Destroyed," *Open Democracy*, 26 October 2017.

AN OCEAN OF POSSIBILITY

1. David Wills, *Dorsality: Thinking Back through Technology and Politics*, Posthumanities (Minneapolis: University of Minnesota Press, 2008), 126–27. I thank William Robert for sharing this rich bit of text with me.
2. Carolyn Dinshaw, *How Soon Is Now? Medieval Texts, Amateur Readers, and the Queerness of Time* (Durham, NC: Duke University Press, 2012), 23.
3. Famously, by Mircea Eliade in *The Sacred and the Profane: The Nature of Religion*, trans. Willard R. Trask (New York: Harper Torchbooks, 1961).
4. The typology of locative and utopian religion is J. Z. Smith's, as is emphasis on the element of incongruity in religious traditions; see his "Map Is Not Territory," in *Map Is Not Territory: Studies in the History of Religions* (Leiden: Brill, 1978), 308–9.
5. I have more to say about the Platonic *chora* in *Ancient Christian Ecopoetics: Cosmologies, Saints, Things* (Philadelphia: University of Pennsylvania Press, 2019), 11–27.
6. Steven M. Wasserstrom, *Religion after Religion: Gershom Sholem, Mircea Eliade, and Henry Corbin at Eranos* (Princeton, NJ: Princeton University Press, 1999).
7. Tyler Roberts, *Encountering Religion: Responsibility and Criticism after Secularism* (New York: Columbia University Press, 2013), 143.
8. Jeff Malpas, "Place and Singularity," in *The Intelligence of Place: Topographies and Poetics*, edited by Jeff Malpas (London: Bloomsbury, 2015), 87.
9. Michel de Certeau, "A Variant: Hagio-Graphical Edification," in *The Writing of History*, translated by Tom Conley (New York: Columbia University Press, 1988), 282.

BIBLIOGRAPHY

Alijia, Abdalhadi. "The Melancholy of the Palestinians: A Heritage Destroyed." *Open Democracy*, 26 October 2017.

Ambraseys, Nicholas N. *Earthquakes in the Mediterranean and Middle East: A Multidisciplinary Study of Seismicity up to 1900*. Cambridge: Cambridge University Press, 2009.

———. "The Seismic History of Cyprus." *Revue de l'Union Internationale de Secours* 3 (March 1965): 25–48.

Andrews, Robin George. "Life's Pulsating Beat Is Now a Murmur on the World's Seismographs." *New York Times*, 10 April 2020, B3.

Arentzen, Thomas, Virginia Burrus, and Glenn Peers. *Byzantine Tree Life: Christianity and the Arboreal Imagination*. London: Palgrave Macmillan, 2021.

Armstrong, Rebecca. *Vergil's Green Thoughts: Plants, Humans, and the Divine*. Oxford: Oxford University Press, 2019.

Barker, Craig. "From Performance to Quarry: The Evidence of Architectural Change in the Theatre Precinct of Nea Paphos in Cyprus Over Seven Centuries." In *Continuity and Destruction in the Greek East: The Transformation of Monumental Space from the Hellenistic Period to Late Antiquity*, edited by Sujatha Chandrasekaran and Anna Kouremenos, 33–48. Oxford: British Archaeological Reports, 2015.

———. "Twenty Years of the University of Sydney Excavations of the Theatre Precinct in Nea Paphos in Cyprus." *Ancient History: Resources for Teachers* 45 (2015): 26–63.

Bartsch, Tatjana. *Maarten Van Heemskerck: Römische Studien zwischen Sachlichkeit und Imagination*. Munich: Hirmer, 2019.

Bekker-Nielsen, Tonnes. *The Roads of Ancient Cyprus*. Copenhagen: Museum Tusculanum Press, 2004.

Bérard, Victor. *Les navigations d'Ulysse*. Paris: A. Colin, 1971.

Bernard, Eugène. *Les voyages de Saint Jérôme*. Paris: Charles Douniol, 1864.

Bicknell, Kevin. "*Crystal*: An Installation Comes to Life." *Journal of The Clark* 17 (2016): 28–37.

Bitton-Ashkelony, Brouria. *Encountering the Sacred: The Debate on Christian Pilgrimage in Late Antiquity*. Berkeley: University of California Press, 2005.

Blanc-Bijon, Véronique. "Les pavements en mosaïque de la basilique d'Hilarion (Nuseirat, Gaza): Nouveautés sur les ateliers de mosaïstes gaziotes." In *Estudios sobre mosaicos antiguos y medievales*, edited by Luz Neira Jiménez, 390–98. Rome: "L'Erma" di Bretschneider, 2016.

Bocco, Gerardo. "Remoteness and Remote Places: A Geographic Perspective." *Geoforum* 77 (2016): 178–81.

Bonnechere, Pierre. "The Place of the Sacred Grove (*Alsos*) in the Mantic Rituals of Greece: The Example of the *Alsos* of Trophonios at Lebadeia (Boetia)." In *Sacred Gardens and Landscapes: Ritual and Agency*, edited by Michel Conan, 17–41. Cambridge, MA: Harvard University Press, 2007.

Bounia, Alexandra, and Theopisti Stylianou-Lambert. "National Museums in Cyprus: A Story of Heritage and Conflict." In *Building National Museums in Europe, 1750–2010*, edited by Peter Aronsson and Gabriella Elgenius, 165–201. Linköping, Sweden: Linköping University Electronic Press, 2011.

Bowe, Patrick. "The Sacred Groves of Ancient Greece." *Studies in the History of Gardens and Designed Landscapes* 29, no. 4 (2009): 235–45.

Brilliant, Richard, and Dale Kinney, eds. *Reuse Value*: Spolia *and Appropriation in Art and Architecture from Constantine to Sherrie Levine*. Farnham, UK: Ashgate, 2011.

Burgess, R. W. "A Common Source for Jerome, Eutropius, Festus, Ammianus, and the Epitome de Caesaribus between 358 and 378, along with Further Thoughts on the Date and Nature of the Kaisergeschichte." *Classical Philology* 100, no. 2 (2005): 166–92.

Burrus, Virginia. *Ancient Christian Ecopoetics: Cosmologies, Saints, Things*. Divinations: Rereading Late Ancient Religion. Philadelphia: University of Pennsylvania Press, 2019.

———. *The Sex Lives of Saints: An Erotics of Ancient Hagiography*. Divinations: Rereading Late Ancient Religion. Philadelphia: University of Pennsylvania Press, 2004.

Camerlenghi, Nicola. "How Long Are the Lives of Medieval Buildings? Framing Spatio-Temporalities in the Study of the Built World." In *The Long Lives of Medieval Art and Architecture*, edited by Jennifer M. Feltman and Sarah Thompson, 17–30. London: Routledge, 2019.

Cameron, Alan. *Claudian: Poetry and Propaganda at the Court of Honorius*. Oxford: Clarendon Press, 1970.

———. "St. Jerome and Claudian." *Vigiliae Christianae* 19, no. 2 (1965): 111–13.

Carroll, Maureen. "Temple Gardens and Sacred Groves." In *Gardens of the Roman Empire*, edited by Wilhelmina F. Jashemski, Kathryn L. Gleason, Kim J. Hartswick, and Amina-Aïcha Malek, 152–64. Cambridge: Cambridge University Press, 2018.

Carson, Anne, trans. *If Not, Winter: Fragments of Sappho*. New York: Vintage Books, 2002.

Cavafy, C. P. "Ithaca." In *Complete Poems*, translated by Daniel Mendelsohn. New York: Knopf, 2009.

Ceci, Francesca. "The House of the Goddess: Coins Tell the Cypriot Aphrodite Myth." In *Archaeometry and Aphrodite: Proceedings of the Seminar 13th June 2013 CNR Rome*, edited by Maria Rosaria Belgiomo, 181–90. Rome: De Strobel, 2013.

Certeau, Michel de. "A Variant: Hagio-Graphical Edification." In *The Writing of History*, translated by Tom Conley, 269–83. New York: Columbia University Press, 1988.

———. "Walking in the City." In *The Practice of Everyday Life*, translated by Steven Randall, 91–110. Berkeley: University of California Press, 1984.

Chin, Catherine Michael. "Four Notes on Memory Theatre." *Ancient Jew Review*, 6 January 2020.

Clément, Gilles. "The Wisdom of the Gardener." In *The Planetary Garden and Other Writings*, vii–ix. Philadelphia: University of Pennsylvania Press, 2006.

Cobham, Claude Delaval. *Excerpta Cypria: Materials for a History of Cyprus*. Cambridge: Cambridge University Press, 1908.

Coccia, Emanuele. *The Life of Plants: A Metaphysics of Mixture*, translated by Dylan J. Montanari. Cambridge, UK: Polity, 2019.

Conforti, Michael, and Michael Cassins. *The Clark: The Institute and Its Collections*. London: Scala Arts, 2014.

Croke, Brian. "Two Early Byzantine Earthquakes and Their Liturgical Commemoration." *Byzantion* 51, no. 1 (1981): 122–47.

Cross, Susan. "Ledelle Moe: When." In *Ledelle Moe: When*, 13–25. North Adams, MA: MASS MoCA, 2019.

Daszewski, W. A., and D. Michaelides. *Guide to the Paphos Mosaics*. Nicosia: Bank of Cyprus Cultural Foundation, 1988.

Davis, Thomas W. "An Amateur's Dream: George McFadden at Kourion." In *The Archaeology of Ancient Kourion*, edited by Ellen Hersher and Joanna Smith. Philadelphia: University of Pennsylvania Press, forthcoming.

———."Earthquakes and the Crisis of Faith: Social Transformation in Late Antique Cyprus." *Buried History* 46 (2010): 5–16.

———. "A New Window on Byzantine Kourion." *Cahiers Du Centre d'Etudes Chypriotes* 43 (2013): 103–15.

Delehaye, Hippolyte. "Saints de Chypre." *Analecta Bollandiana* 26 (1907): 161–297.

Deligiannakis, Georgios. "From Aphrodite(s) to Saintly Bishops in Late Antique Cyprus." In *Authority and Identity in Emerging Christianities in Asia Minor and Greece*, edited by Cilliers Breytenbach and Julien M. Ogerau, 326–46. Leiden: Brill, 2018.

———. "The Last Pagans of Cyprus: Prolegomena to a History of Transition from Polytheism to Christianity." In *Church Building in Cyprus (Fourth to Seventh Centuries): A Mirror of Intercultural Contacts in the Eastern Mediterranean*, edited by Marietta Horster, Doria Nicolaou, and Sabine Rogge, 23–44. Münster: Waxmann Verlag, 2018.

Demirag, Fikret. *Limnidi Atesinden Bugune Kitap 1*. Lefkosa: Galeri Kultur Yayinlar, 1992.

DeSilvey, Caitlin. *Curated Decay: Heritage Beyond Saving*. Minneapolis: University of Minnesota Press, 2017.

DeSilvey, Caitlin, Simon Naylor, and Colin Sackett. *Anticipatory History*. Axminster, Devon, UK: Uniformbooks, 2011.

Devecka, Martin. *Broken Cities: A Historical Sociology of Ruins*. Baltimore, MD: Johns Hopkins University Press, 2020.

Dewey, Ryan. "Agency and the Multifaceted Stories of Hybrid Places." *MONU* 20 (2014): 78–83.

———. "Creating Experiences of Remoteness in Landscapes and Geographies."

Blog, 2014. https://www.ryandewey.org/blog/2014/5/29/creating-experiences-of-remoteness-in-landscapes-geographies.

———. "Hacking Remoteness Through Viewpoint and Cognition." *Kerb* 22 (2014): 26–33.

Diederich, Silke. *Römische Agrarhandbücher zwischen Fachwissenschaft, Literature und Ideologie*. Berlin: De Gruyter, 2007.

Dietzel, Irene. *The Ecology of Coexistence and Conflict in Cyprus: Exploring the Religion, Nature, and Culture of a Mediterranean Island*. Berlin: De Gruyter, 2014.

DiFuria, Arthur J. *Maarten Van Heemskerck's Rome: Antiquity, Memory, and the Cult of Ruins*. Leiden: Brill, 2019.

Dinshaw, Carolyn. *How Soon Is Now? Medieval Texts, Amateur Readers, and the Queerness of Time*. Durham, NC: Duke University Press, 2012.

Di Vita, Antonino. "Archaeologists and Earthquakes: The Case of 365 AD." *Annali Di Geofisica* 38, no. 5–6 (1995): 971–76.

Dodds, E. R., ed. *Euripides. Bacchae*. 2nd ed. Oxford: Clarendon Press, 1960.

Durrell, Lawrence. *Bitter Lemons*. London: Faber and Faber, 1957.

Eliade, Mircea. *The Sacred and the Profane: The Nature of Religion*, translated by Willard R. Trask. New York: Harper Torchbooks, 1961.

Elsner, Jaś, and Jesús Hernández Lobato. "Introduction: Notes Towards a Poetics of Late Ancient Literature." In *The Poetics of Late Latin Literature*, edited by Jaś Elsner and Jesús Hernández Lobato, 1–22. Oxford: Oxford University Press, 2017.

Elter, René. "Gaza. Le plus ancien monastère de Terra Sainte." *Archéologia* 505 (2012): 34–51.

Elter, René, and Ahmad Abd el-Rhadan. "Le monastère de Saint-Hilarion: Evolution et développement architectural d'un sanctuaire de pèlerinage dans le sud de Gaza (Palestine)." *Les Cahiers de Saint-Michel de Cuxa* 38 (2007): 121–36.

Elter, René, and Ayman Hassoune. "Le monastère de Saint-Hilarion à Umm-el-'Amr (bande de Gaza)." *Comptes rendus des séances de l'Académie des Inscriptions et Belles-Lettres* 148, no. 1 (2004): 359–82.

Fisher, Elizabeth. "Greek Translations of Latin Literature." *Yale Classical Studies* 27 (1982): 173–215.

Formisano, Marco. "Beyond the Fence: Columella's Garden." In *Antike Erzähl- und Deutungsmuster: Zwischen Exemplarität und Transformation*, edited by Simone Finkmann, Anja Behrendt, and Anke Walter, 501–14. Berlin: De Gruyter, 2019.

Franklin, John C. "Lady Come Down: The Eastern Wandering of Helen, Paris, and Menelaus." *Classical Inquiries*, 5 May 2016, 1–11.

Friedrich, Rainer. *Postoral Homer: Orality and Literacy in the Homeric Epic*. Stuttgart: Franz Steiner Verlag, 2019.

Frings, Udo. *Claudius Claudianus: Epithalamium de nuptiis Honorii Augusti: Einleitung und Kommentar*. Meisenheim am Glen: Verlag Anton Hain, 1975.

Fuhrmann, Manfred. "Die Mönchsgeschichten des Hieronymus: Formexperimente in erzählender Literatur." In *Christianisme et formes littéraires de l'antiquité tardive en occident*, edited by Manfred Fuhrmann, 41–99. Entretiens sur l'Antiquité Classique. Geneva: Fondation Hardt, 1977.

Fukuoka, Masanobu. *The Natural Way of Farming: The Theory and Practice of Green Philosophy*. Mapusa, Goa: Other India Press, 1985.

———. *The One-Straw Revolution: An Introduction to Natural Farming*, translated by Larry Korn. New York: New York Review Books, 2009.

———. *Sowing Seeds in the Desert: Natural Farming, Global Restoration, and Ultimate Food Security*. White River Junction, VT: Chelsea Green, 2012.

Gaifman, Milette. *Aniconism in Greek Antiquity*. Oxford: Oxford University Press, 2012.

Galatariotou, Catia. *The Making of a Saint: The Life, Times and Sanctification of Neophytos the Recluse*. Cambridge: Cambridge University Press, 1991.

Geraerts, Michelle, and Jarl Schulp. "Intimate Mapping—In Conversation with Jonathan Ruess & Sissel Marie Tonn." *Fiber*, 2 June 2020. https://www.fiber-space.nl/news/intimate-mapping-in-conversation-with-jonathon-reus-sissel-marie-tonn/.

Giudice, Filippo, and Giada Giudice. "La 'memoria' paleocristiana da Garrison's Camp a Nea Paphos (Cipro): Recenti scavi e nuovi risultati." *Corso di Cultura sull'Arte Ravennate e Bizantina* 44 (1998): 143–64.

Given, Michael. "Flowing Rock, Dancing around Trees: Conviviality and the Landscape of Cyprus." *Near Eastern Archaeology* 85, no. 1 (2022): 4–11.

Gordon, Jody Michael. "Insularity and Identity in Roman Cyprus: Connectivity, Complexity, and Cultural Change." In *Insularity and Identity in the Roman Mediterranean*, edited by Anna Kouremenos, 4–40. Oxford: Oxbow Books, 2018.

Green, J. R., and E. W. Handley. "Eustorgis in Paphos." In *Philathenaios: Studies in Honour of Michael J. Osborne*, edited by A. M. Tamis, C. J. Mackie, and S. G. Byrne, 197–211. Athens: Greek Epigraphic Society, 2010.

Guidoboni, Emanuela, with Alberto Comastri and Giusto Traina. *Catalogue of Ancient Earthquakes in the Mediterranean up to the 10th Century*. Rome: Instituto Nazionale di Geofisica, 1994.

———. "Historical Seismology: The Long Memory of the Inhabited World." In *International Handbook of Earthquake and Engineering Seismology, Part A*, edited by W. H. K. Lee, H. Kanamori, P. C. Jennings, and C. Kisslinger, 775–90. Amsterdam: Academic Press, 2002.

Guidoboni, Emanuela, and John E. Ebel. *Earthquakes and Tsunamis in the Past: A Guide to Techniques in Historical Seismology*. Cambridge: Cambridge University Press, 2009.

Hamilton, H. C., and W. Falconer, trans. *The Geography of Strabo*. London: George Bell & Sons, 1903.

Harvey, Paul. B. "Jerome Dedicates his 'Vita Hilarionis.'" *Vigiliae Christianae* 59, no. 3 (2005): 286–97.

Henderson, John. *The Roman Book of Gardening*. London: Routledge, 2004.

Hill, Leslie. *Maurice Blanchot and Fragmentary Writing: A Change of Epoch*. London: Continuum, 2012.

Holly, Michael Ann. "Back of the Painted Beyond." *Art History* 42, no. 5 (2019): 892–913.

———. *The Melancholy Art*. Princeton, NJ: Princeton University Press, 2013.

Hui, Andrew. *The Poetics of Ruins in Renaissance Literature*. New York: Fordham University Press, 2016.

Jacobs, Andrew S. *Epiphanius of Cyprus: A Cultural Biography of Late Antiquity*. Berkeley: University of California Press, 2016.

Jacques, François, and Bernard Bousquet. "Le cataclysme du 21 Juillet 365: Phenomene regional ou catastrophe cosmique?" In *Tremblements de terre, histoire et archéologie: IVèmes Rencontres internationales d'archéologie et d'histoire d'Antibes*, 183–98. Association pour la promotion et la diffusion des connaissances archéologiques, 1984.

Jardine, Lisa. *Erasmus, Man of Letters: The Construction of Charisma in Print*. Princeton, NJ: Princeton University Press, 1993.

Jashemski, Wilhelmina F. "Produce Gardens." In *Gardens of the Roman Empire*, edited by Wilhelmina F. Jashemski, Kathryn L. Gleason, Kim J. Hartswick, and Amina-Aïcha Malek, 121–51. Cambridge: Cambridge University Press, 2018.

Jensen, R. C. "The Kourion Earthquake: Some Possible Literary Evidence." *Report of the Department of Antiquities, Cyprus* (1985), 307–11.

Jones, Horace Leonard, trans. and ed. *Strabo. Geography. Books 1–2*. Loeb Classical Library. Cambridge, MA: Harvard University Press, 1917.

Karageorghis, Jacqueline. *Kypris: The Aphrodite of Cyprus*. Nicosia: A. G. Leventis Foundation, 2005.

Kearns, Catherine. "Cyprus in the Surging Sea: Spatial Imaginations of the Eastern Mediterranean." *Transactions of the American Philological Association* 148, no. 1 (2018): 45–74.

Kees, Hermann. *Ancient Egypt: A Cultural Topography*, translated by Ian F. D. Morrow. Chicago: University of Chicago Press, 1961.

Keller, Catherine. *The Face of the Deep: A Theology of Becoming*. London: Routledge, 2003.

Kelly, Gavin. "Ammianus and the Great Tsunami." *Journal of Roman Studies* 94 (2004): 141–67.

Kemal, Bahriye. *Writing Cyprus: Postcolonial and Partitioned Literatures of Place and Space*. New York: Routledge, 2020.

Klehm, Nance. "To Dig a Hole (You Create a Heap)." *The Learned Pig*, 20 April 2020. https://www.thelearnedpig.org/to-dig-a-hole-you-create-a-heap/7877.

Kügle, Karl. "Glorious Sounds for a Holy Warrior: New Light on Codex Turin J.II.9." *Journal of the American Musicological Society* 65, no. 3 (2012): 637–90.

Kymäläinen, Päivi, and Ari A. Lehtinen. "Chora in Current Geographical Thought: Places of Co-Design and Re-Membering." *Geografiska Annaler: Series B, Human Geography* 92, no. 3 (2010): 251–61.

Ladouceur, John. "Christians and Pagans in Roman Nea Paphos: Contextualizing the 'House of Aion' Mosaic." *UCLA Historical Journal* 29, no. 1 (2018): 49–64.

Langgut, Dafna. "The Citrus Route Revealed: From Southeast Asia into the Mediterranean." *Horticultural Science* 52, no. 6 (2017): 814–22.

Langhorst, Joern. "Re-Presenting Transgressive Ecologies: Post-Industrial Sites as Contested Terrains." *Local Environment: The International Journal of Justice and Sustainability* 19, no. 10 (2014): 1110–33.

Latz, Peter. *Rust Red: Landscape Park Duisburg-Nord*. Munich: Hirmer, 2016.

Leary, John Patrick. "Detroitism: What Does 'Ruin Porn' Tell Us about the Motor City?"

Guernica/15 Years of Global Arts & Politics, 15 January 2011, https://www.guernicamag.com/leary_1_15_11/.

Leclerc, Pierre, and Edgardo Martín Morales. *Jérôme: Trois Vies de Moines*. Sources Chrétiennes 508. Paris: Les Éditions du Cerf, 2007.

Lenski, Noel. *Constantine and the Cities: Imperial Authority and Civic Politics*. Philadelphia: University of Pennsylvania Press, 2016.

Liverani, Paolo. "Reading *Spolia* in Late Antiquity and Contemporary Perception." In *Reuse Value: Spolia and Appropriation in Art and Architecture from Constantine to Sherrie Levine*, edited by Richard Brilliant and Dale Kinney, 33–51. Farnham, UK: Ashgate, 2011.

Macaulay-Lewis, Elizabeth. "The Archaeology of Gardens in the Roman Villa." In *Gardens of the Roman Empire*, edited by Wilhelmina F. Jashemski, Kathryn L. Gleason, Kim J. Hartswick, and Amina-Aïcha Malek, 87–120. Cambridge: Cambridge University Press, 2018.

Maier, F. G., and V. Karageorghis. *Paphos: History and Archaeology*. Nicosia: A. G. Leventis Foundation, 1984.

Makhairas, Leontios. *Recital Concerning the Sweet Land of Cyprus Entitled "Chronicle*," translated by R. M. Dawkins. Oxford: Clarendon Press, 1932.

Malpas, Jeff. "Place and Singularity." In *The Intelligence of Place: Topographies and Poetics*, edited by Jeff Malpas, 65–92. London: Bloomsbury, 2015.

Marder, Michael. *Dump Philosophy: A Phenomenology of Devastation*. London: Bloomsbury, 2021.

———. "The Garden as Form." *The Learned Pig*, 21 November 2018.

———. *Plant-Thinking: A Philosophy of Vegetal Life*. New York: Columbia University Press, 2013.

Mary, Lionel. "Reconnaissance par les gouffres: Métaphysique des séismes et poétique de l'histoire chez Ammien Marcellin." In *Connaissance et représentations des volcans dans l'antiquité*, edited by Éric Foulon, 171–90. Clermont-Ferrand: Presses Universitaires Blaise Pascal, 2004.

Megaw, A. H. S. "Reflections on Byzantine Paphos." In *ΚΑΘΗΓΗΤΡΙΑ: Essays Presented to Joan Hussey for Her 80th Birthday*, 135–50. Camberley, Surrey, UK: Porphyrogenitus, 1988.

Meis, Morgan. "Timothy Morton's Hyper-pandemic." *New Yorker*, 8 June 2021.

Melville, Herman. *Moby Dick; or, The Whale*. New York: Harper Brothers, 1851.

Mena, Peter Anthony. *Place and Identity in the Lives of Antony, Paul, and Mary of Egypt: Desert as Borderland*. London: Palgrave Macmillan, 2019.

Mendelsohn, Daniel. *An Odyssey: A Father, a Son, and an Epic*. New York: Vintage, 2017.

Mengual, Estelle Zhong. "The Point of View of the Mountain." In *Critical Zones: The Science and Politics of Landing on Earth*, edited by Bruno Latour and Peter Weibel, 250–53. Karlsruhe, Germany: ZKM/Center for Art and Media, 2020.

Mertz, Henriette. *The Wine Dark Sea: Homer's Heroic Epic of the North Atlantic*. Chicago: [Self-published] 1964.

Michaelides, Demetrios. "Mosaic Decoration in Early Christian Cyprus." In *Church Building in Cyprus (Fourth to Seventh Centuries): A Mirror of Intercultural Contacts in *the Eastern Mediterranean*, edited by Marietta Horster, Doria Nicolaou, and Sabine Rogge, 213–44. Münster: Waxmann, 2018.

———. "Mosaic Workshops in Cyprus from the Fourth to the Seventh Centuries CE: Two Parallel Lives?" In *From Roman to Early Christian Cyprus*, edited by Laura Nasrallah, AnneMarie Luijendijk, and Charalambos Bakirtzis, 93–110. Tübingen: Mohr Siebeck, 2020.

Mitford, Terence Bruce. "The Cults of Roman Cyprus." *Aufstieg und Niedergang der römischen Welt* 18, no. 3 (1990): 2176–2211.

Mollison, Bill, and David Holmgren. *Permaculture One: A Perennial Agricultural System for Human Settlements*. Ealing, London: Transworld, 1978.

Morris, Christine E., and Giorgos Papantoniou. "Cypriot-Born Aphrodite: The Social Biography of a Modern Cultural Icon." In *Il Trono Variopinto: Figure e Forme Della Dea Dell'Amore*, edited by Luca Bombardieri, Tommaso Braccini, and Silvia Romani, 183–202. Alessandria: Edizione dell-Orso, 2014.

Morton, Timothy. *The Ecological Thought*. Cambridge, MA: Harvard University Press, 2010.

———. *Hyperobjects: Philosophy and Ecology after the End of the World*. Minneapolis: University of Minnesota Press, 2013.

Mudie, Ella. "The Spectacle of Seismicity: Making Art from Earthquakes." *Leonardo* 43, no. 2 (2010): 133–39.

Nagel, Alexander, and Christopher S. Wood. *Anachronic Renaissance*. New York: Zone Books, 2010.

Oberhummer, Eugen. "Charbyris." *Paulys Realencyclopädie der classischen Altertumswissenschaft* 3.2 (1899): 2124.

O'Nolan, K. "A Note on the *Bacchae*." *Classical Review* 8, nos. 3/4 (1958): 204–6.

Opelt, Ilona. "Des Hieronymus Heiligenbiographien als Quellen der historischen Topographie des östlichen Mittelmeerraums." *Römische Quartalschrift für christliche Altertumskunde und Kirchengeschichte* 74, no. 3/4 (1979): 145–77.

———. "Note al viaggio in Italia di S. Ilarione siro." *Augustinianum* 24, no. 1/2 (1984): 305–14.

Pabel, Hilmar M. *Herculean Labors: Erasmus and the Editing of St. Jerome's Letters in the Renaissance*. Leiden: Brill, 2008.

Papacostas, Tassos. "Decoding Cyprus from Late Antiquity to the Renaissance: Discordant Visions, Saints, and Sacred Topography." In *Cyprus and the Balance of Empires: Art and Archaeology from Justinian I to the Coeur de Lion*, edited by Charles Anthony Stewart, Thomas W. Davis, and Annemarie Weyl Carr, 187–201. Boston: American Schools of Oriental Research, 2014.

———. "The Economy of Late Antique Cyprus." In *Economy and Exchange in the East Mediterranean During Late Antiquity*, edited by Sean Kingsley and Michael Decker, 107–28. Oxford: Oxbow Books, 2015.

Papadakis, Yiannis. "Aphrodite Delights." *Postcolonial Studies* 9, no. 3 (2006): 237–50.

Papantoniou, Giorgos, and Athanasios K. Vionis. "Landscape Archaeology and Sacred Space in the Eastern Mediterranean: A Glimpse from Cyprus." *Land* 6, no. 40 (2017): 1–18.

Parthog, Gwynneth der. *Byzantine and Medieval Cyprus: A Guide to the Monuments.* New Barnet, UK: Interworld Publications, 1994.
Pelttari, Aaron. *The Space That Remains: Reading Latin Poetry in Late Antiquity.* Ithaca, NY: Cornell University Press, 2014.
Pirazzoli, P. A., J. Laborel, and S. C. Stiros. "The Early Byzantine Tectonic Paroxysm." *Zeitschrift für Geomorphologie* Supp. 62 (December 1986): 31–49.
———. "Earthquake Clustering in the Eastern Mediterranean During Historical Times." *Journal of Geophysical Research* 101, no. B3 (10 March 1996): 6083–97.
Pollan, Michael. *Second Nature: A Gardener's Education.* New York: Grove Press, 1991.
Prieto, Eric. "Geocriticism Meets Ecocriticism: Bertrand Westphal and Environmental Thinking." In *Ecocriticism and Geocriticism: Overlapping Territories in Environmental and Spatial Studies,* edited by Robert T. Tally Jr. and Christine M. Battista, 19–35. New York: Palgrave Macmillan, 2016.
Purcell, Nicholas. "Periploi." In *Oxford Classical Dictionary,* 4th ed., edited by Simon Hornblower, Antony Spawforth, and Esther Eidinow. Oxford: Oxford University Press, 2012.
Radivojević, Miljana, Benjamin W. Roberts, Ernst Pernicka, et al. "The Provenance, Use, and Circulation of Metals in the European Bronze Age: The State of Debate." *Journal of Archaeological Research* 27 (2019): 131–85.
Rapp, Claudia. "Christianity in Cyprus in the Fourth to Seventh Centuries." In *Cyprus and the Balance of Empires: Art and Archaeology from Justinian I to the Coeur de Lion,* edited by Charles Anthony Stewart, Thomas W. Davis, and Annemarie Weyl Carr, 29–38. Boston: American Schools of Oriental Research, 2014.
Rautman, Marcus. "The Busy Countryside of Late Roman Cyprus." *Report of the Department of Antiquities, Cyprus* (2000), 317–31.
———. "From Polytheism to Christianity in the Temples of Cyprus." In *Ancient Journeys: A Festschrift in Honour of Eugene Numa Lane.* Stoa Consortium. http://www.stoa.org/texts/2001/01/0014/section_1/, (2001).
Regine. "A Bodily Experience of Man-Made Earthquakes." *We Make Money Not Art,* 9 April 2018. https://we-make-money-not-art.com/a-bodily-experience-of-man-made-earthquakes/.
Rice, Eugene F. *Saint Jerome in the Renaissance.* Baltimore: Johns Hopkins University Press, 1985.
Riegl, Alois. "The Modern Cult of Monuments: Its Character and Origin." *Oppositions: A Journal for Ideas and Criticism in Architecture* 25 (1982): 21–51.
Rizos, Efthymios. "The Cult of Saints in Late Antiquity." http://csla.history.ox.ac.uk/record.php?recid=E07142.
Roberts, Michael. *The Jeweled Style: Poetry and Poetics in Late Antiquity.* Ithaca, NY: Cornell University Press, 1989.
———. "The Use of Myth in Latin Epithalamia from Statius to Venantius Fortunatus." *Transactions of the American Philological Association* 119 (1989): 321–48.
Roberts, Tyler. *Encountering Religion: Responsibility and Criticism after Secularism.* New York: Columbia University Press, 2013.

Roller, Duane W. *Ancient Geography: The Discovery of the World in Classical Greece and Rome*. London: I. B. Tauris, 2015.

Roosien, Mark. *The Liturgical Commemoration of Earthquakes in Late Antique Constantinople: At the Intersection of Ritual, Environment, and Empire*. PhD diss, Theology. Notre Dame University, 2018.

Rosenberg, Elissa. "Gardens, Landscape, Nature: Duisburg-Nord, Germany." In *The Hand and the Soul: Aesthetics and Ethics in Architecture and Art*, edited by Sanda Iliescu, 209–30. Charlottesville: University of Virginia Press, 2009.

Rupp, D., R. Talbert, T. Elliott, and S. Gillies. "Charbyris: A Pleiades Place Resource." *Pleiades: A Gazetteer of Past Places* (2012), https://pleiades.stoa.org/places/711223.

Schalansky, Judith. *An Inventory of Losses*. Translated by Jackie Smith. New York: New Directions Books, 2020.

———. *Pocket Atlas of Remote Islands: Fifty Islands I Have Not Visited and Never Will*. Translated by Christine Lo. New York City: Penguin Books, 2010.

Schiller, Gertrud. *Iconography of Christian Art*. Vol. 1. Translated by Janet Seligman. London: Lund Humphries, 1971.

Serres, Michel. *Biogea*. Translated by Randolph Burks. Minneapolis: Univocal, 2012.

Severis, Rita C. *Travelling Artists in Cyprus, 1700–1960*. London: Philip Wilson, 2000.

"Shell and Exxon's €5bn Problem: Gas Drilling That Sets Off Earthquakes and Wrecks Homes." *Guardian*, 10 October 2015.

Silvas, Anna M. "In Quest of Basil's Retreat: An Expedition to Ancient Pontus." *Antichthon* 41 (2007): 73–95.

Smith, Jonathan Z. "Map Is Not Territory." In *Map Is Not Territory: Studies in the History of Religions*, 289–309. Leiden: Brill, 1978.

Smith, Steven D. *Greek Epigram and Byzantine Culture: Gender, Desire, and Denial in the Age of Justinian*. Cambridge: Cambridge University Press, 2019.

Solnit, Rebecca. *A Field Guide to Getting Lost*. New York: Penguin, 2005.

Soren, David. "The Day the World Ended at Kourion: Reconstructing an Ancient Earthquake." *National Geographic* 174 (July 1988): 30–53.

———. "An Earthquake on Cyprus: New Discoveries from Kourion." *Archaeology* 38, no. 2 (1985): 52–59.

Soren, David, and Thomas Davis. "Seismic Archaeology at Kourion: The 1984 Campaign." *Report of the Department of Antiquities, Cyprus* (1985), 293–301.

Soren, David, and Jamie James. *Kourion: The Search for a Lost Roman City*. New York: Doubleday, 1988.

Stephan, B. Richard, Iris Wagner, and Jochen Kleinschmit. *Technical Guidelines for Genetic Conservation and Use for Wild Apple and Pear*. Rome: International Plant Genetic Resources Institute, 2003.

Stephanides, Stephanos. *The Wind Under My Lips*. Athens: To Rodakio, 2018.

Stewart, Susan. *The Ruins Lesson: Meaning and Material in Western Culture*. Chicago: University of Chicago Press, 2020.

Stiros, Stathis C. "The AD 365 Crete Earthquake and Possible Seismic Clustering During the Fourth to Sixth Centuries AD in the Eastern Mediterranean: A Review of Historical and Archaeological Data." *Journal of Structural Geology* 23 (2001): 545–62.

———. "The 8.5+ Magnitude, AD 365 Earthquake in Crete: Coastal Uplift, Topography Changes, Archaeological and Historical Signature." *Quaternary International* 216 (2010): 54–63.
Stoppard, Lou. "Everyone's a Curator Now." *New York Times*, 5 March 2020. https://www.nytimes.com/2020/03/03/style/curate-buzzword.html.
Strout, Ruth F. "The Greek Versions of Jerome's *Vita Sancti Hilarionis*." In *Studies in the Text Tradition of Jerome's "Vitae Patrum,"* edited by William A. Oldfather, 306–448. Urbana: University of Illinois Press, 1943.
Stylianou, Andreas, and Judith A. Stylianou. *The History of the Cartography of Cyprus*. Nicosia: Cyprus Research Center, 1980.
———. *The Painted Churches of Cyprus: Treasures of Byzantine Art, Second Edition*. Nicosia: A. G. Leventis Foundation, 1997.
———. "St. Hilarion the Great in Paphos, Cyprus." *Kypriakai Spoudai* 41 (1977): 1–5.
Stylianou-Lambert, Theopisti. "En-Gendering a Landscape: The Construction, Promotion and Consumption of the Rock of Aphrodite." In *Photography and Cyprus: Time, Place and Identity*, edited by Liz Wells, Theopisti Stylianou-Lambert, and Nicos Philippou, 143–66. London: I. B. Tauris, 2014.
———. "Rock of Aphrodite: In 5 Photographic Acts." In *Re-Envisioning Cyprus*, edited by Peter Loizos, Nicos Philippou, and Theopisti Stylianou-Lambert, 73–87. Nicosia: University of Nicosia Press, 2010.
Summa, Daniela. "The Christian Epigraphy of Cyprus: A Preliminary Study." In *Early Christianity in Asia Minor and Cyprus: From the Margins to the Mainstream*, edited by Stephen Mitchell and Philipp Pilhofer, 226–51. Leiden: Brill, 2019.
Thirgood, J. V. *Cyprus: A Chronicle of Its Forests, Land, and People*. Vancouver: University of British Columbia Press, 1987.
Tiberghien, Gilles A. "Foreword." In *The Planetary Garden and Other Writings*, Gilles Clément, vii–ix. Philadelphia: University of Pennsylvania Press, 2006.
Trouet, Valerie. *Tree Story: The History of the World Written in Rings*. Baltimore: Johns Hopkins University Press, 2020.
Tsintides, Takis C., Georgios N. Hadjikyriakou, and Charalambos S. Christodoulou. *Trees and Shrubs in Cyprus*. Nicosia: Leventis Foundation—Cyprus Forest Association, 2002.
Viviroli, Daniel, Hans H. Dürr, Bruno Messerli, et al. "Mountains of the World, Water Towers for Humanity: Typology, Mapping, and Global Significance." *Water Resources Research* 43 (2007): 1–13. doi:W07447.
Wasserstrom, Steven M. *Religion after Religion: Gershom Sholem, Mircea Eliade, and Henry Corbin at Eranos*. Princeton: NJ: Princeton University Press, 1999.
Wdowinski, Shimon, Zvi Ben-Avraham, Ronald Arvidsson, and Goran Ekström. "Seismotectonics of the Cyprian Arc." *Geophysical Journal International* 164, no. 1 (2006): 176–81.
Weingarten, Susan. *The Saint's Saints: Hagiography and Geography in Jerome*. Leiden: Brill, 2005.
Westphal, Bertrand. "Elements of Geocriticism." In *Geocriticism: Real and Fictional Spaces*, translated by Robert T. Talley, 111–47. New York: Palgrave Macmillan, 2011.

White, Carolinne. *Early Christian Lives*. London: Penguin Books, 1998.
Wills, David. *Dorsality: Thinking Back through Technology and Politics*. Posthumanities. Minneapolis: University of Minnesota Press, 2008.
Wilson, M. "The Lukan Periplus of Paul's Third Journey with a Textual Conundrum in Acts 20:15." *Acta Theologica* 36, no. 1 (2016): 229–54.
Wolf, Burkhardt. "Muses of Cartography: Charting Odysseus from Homer to Joyce." In *Literature and Cartography: Theories, Histories, Genres*, edited by Anders Engberg-Pedersen, 143–72. Cambridge, MA: MIT Press, 2017.
Young, Philip. "The Cypriot Aphrodite Cult: Paphos, Rantidi, and Saint Barnabas." *Journal of Near Eastern Studies* 64, no. 1 (2005): 23–44.

INDEX

Page numbers in italics refer to figures in the text.

Achilles, 74, 79, 134
Acts of Barnabas, 31
Adriatic Sea, 13–14, 16, 31, 70
Agia Kyriaki. *See under* Paphos (Cyprus)
Agia Moni (Cyprus), 135, 141
Alexandria, 10, 13–15, 95, 101, 132, 144
Ambraseys, Nicholas, 55–56, 58
Ammianus Marcellinus (historian), 13–18, 127
anticipatory history, 71
Antony of Egypt (hermit), 10, 12, 13, 24, 94–102, 113, 119, 132, 144. See also *Life of Saint Antony* (Athanasius)
Aphrodite, 19–22, 24–25, 31, 38, 40–53, 87, 152; Rock of Aphrodite (birthplace of the goddess), 51, *52*; sacred grove, 24–25; sanctuary and temple (Old Paphos), 19–22, 24–25, 38, 41–42, 87, 136, 141; statue from Soloi, 48, *50*, *52*; statue from Trikomo, 47–48, *49*; stone of Aphrodite (cultic object), 87–89, *88*. *See also* Aphrodite Delights (candy); *Hymn to Aphrodite*
Aphrodite Delights (candy), 51
Apollo: Apollo Hylates (Apollo of the Woodlands) at Kourion, 31, 59, 62, 141; at Rantidi, 31
Areopolis (Greece or Palestine), 17
Athanasius. See *Life of Saint Antony* (Athanasius)

Bacchae (Euripides), 41
Ballroom Marfa (contemporary art museum in Marfa, TX), 63–68
Barker, Craig, 75
Barnabas, 46. See also *Acts of Barnabas*
Basil of Caesarea, 97–102
Bérard, Victor, 135
Berkshire mountains (Massachusetts), 107, 109, 111
Bernard, Eugène, 19, 132
Bocco, Gerardo, 93–94
Brooks, David, 66–67, *68*

Calypso, 98, 100, 134, 142, 145
Camerlenghi, Nicola, 76
Cameron, Alan, 43
Cape Maleas (Greece), 19, 134–35
Carson, Anne, 39–40
cartography and mapping, 22, 95–96, 100, 102, 126–27, 132–37, 142–44, *143*, 154
Cavafy, Constantine, 145
Cava of Ispica, 135
Certeau, Michel de, 1, 22–23, 26, 29, 155
Charbyris (Cyprus), 136–37, 144
Chin, Catherine Michael, 8, 70
chora, 29, 33, 152, 154
Clark Art Institute (Williamstown, MA), 107–9
Claudian (Latin poet), 42–45, 81

Clément, Gilles, 127, 130
Coccia, Emanuele, 129
Cock, Hieronymus, 81–83, *82*
coins, 17–18, 20, 87
Columella (agricultural writer), 116–18
consolation, 7, 84, 89
Constantia (Cyprus), 9, 18–19, 22, 58, 79
Constantia (Hilarion's follower), 115
Constantinople, 45, 69, 120, 137
Copelin, Laura, 63
copper: coins, 17–18; on Cyprus, 25, 101–2, 104, 127–28; in works of contemporary art, 103–5, 108
Crete, 17–74
Cross, Susan, 85–86
Cycladic islands (Greece), 19, 134
Cycle of Agathias (Byzantine poetry collection), 45
Cyprian Arc, 54, 89

Dalmatia, 12–13, 15–17, 30, 133–34
Davis, Thomas, 31, 61–63
decay, 8, 13, 27–28, 32–33, 39, 71–73, 84, 87, 125, 127. *See also* ruins
Demirag, Fikret, 46–47, 51
deserts, 10, 12, 63, 66, 94–98, 100, 102, 112, 119, 132–33, 142, 144
DeSilvey, Caitlin, 26–28, 33, 126
Devecka, Martin, 79
Dewey, Ryan: *Copper Boulder*, 103–5, *105*, 108, 112; on remoteness, 103, 113
DiFuria, Arthur, 81
Dinshaw, Carolyn, 151
Duisburg-Nord Landschaftspark (Germany), 122–28, *124*
Durrell, Lawrence, 138–39, 142

earthquakes: catalogs, 54–58; frequency of, 57–58, 67; human-induced, 63, 66; intensity of, 3–6, 16, 55–58, 152; in Jerome's late antiquity, 13–19, 74–75; liturgical commemoration of, 69; magnitude of, 3–4, 17, 54–56, 66–67; in museums, 58–67, *60*, *66*, *68*. *See also* Groningen (Netherlands), earthquakes; Kourion (Cyprus); Loma Prieta (earthquake of 1989); seismography and seismograms; seismology; tectonic shift; tsunamis
ecphrasis, 13, 43–45, 81
Egypt, 10, 12, 14, 24, 39, 46, 94–95, 98, 100–101, 112, 119, 132–33, 135, 142, *143*
Elsner, Jaś, 44
entropy, 30, 32–33, 39, 61, 126, 129–30
Epidaurus (Dalmatia), 12, 15, 17, 31, 133
Epiphanius (bishop of Constantia), 9–10, 18–19
Episkopi (Limassol, Cyprus), 59, 62, 70
Episkopi (Paphos, Cyprus), 101, 108, 136, 139–42, *140*
Eratosthenes (geographer and polymath), 25
Eustorgis (patron), 77–79, *78*
Ezousa valley (Cyprus), 139–40

fragments, 6, 8–9, 22–23, 26–28, 32–34, 37–46, 48, 51, 53, 55, 61, 70–71, 73, 76–77, 81, 83–84, 86–87, 89, 109, 115, 146–47, 151. *See also* ruins; *spolia*
Fukuoka, Masanobu, 120–22, *123*

Gaifman, Milette, 87
gardens, 5–6, 8–9, 23–26, 28–31, 33–34, 43–45, 70, 96, 99–101, 114–22, 125–30, 134, 136–38, 141, 146, 151–53
Garrison's Camp. *See under* Paphos (Cyprus)
Gaza (Palestine), 10, 132–34, 137, 144–47, 155
Genesis (biblical book), 12, 30, 32
Gennadios (archbishop of Constantinople), 137
geocriticism, 7, 9, 33, 37
George the Monk (Byzantine chronicler), 13
Geroskipos (Cyprus), 22, 24, 51
Gordon, Jody Michael, 102
Gregory of Nazianzus, 97–100
grief, 7, 32, 86, 145. *See also* melancholy
Groningen (Netherlands), earthquakes, 64–67
Guidoboni, Emanuela, 5, 17, 56

hagiogeography, 94
hagiography, 6, 10, 16, 31, 131–32, 136–37, 155
Hayes Valley Farm (San Francisco, CA), 5
Heemskerck, Maarten van, 80–83, *82*
Helena (Roman empress), 51

INDEX

Henderson, John, 117
Herculaneum, 30
hermitages, 12, 16, 19, 22, 24, 44, 119, 100–101, 131–32, 135, 137, 139–42, 144
hermits, 10, 19, 33, 44, 81, 93, 95, 97, 100, 102, 108, 112, 115, 119, 135, 137, 144
Hernández Lobato, Jesús, 44
Hesychius (follower of Hilarion), 25, 28, 33, 115
Hilarion (hermit), *120*; death and burial, 10, 26, 29, 115, 132, 134, 144, 146; early life, 10, 12, 100; journey to Cyprus, 12, 132–35, *143*, 144; mountaintop hermitage, 23–26, 28–32, 43, 44, 93, 100–102, 113–16, 119, 122, 127–30, 132, 135–44, *143*, 153; in Paphos, 16–23, 72, 79; tsunami in Epidaurus, 12–17, 30–31, 70. See also *Life of Saint Hilarion* (Jerome)
Hilarion's Castle, 137–39, *138*, 141
Holly, Michael Ann, 84, 112
Holmgren, David, 120
Homer, 37–39, 41–43, 98–99, 134–35, 145. See also *Odyssey* (Homer)
House of Dionysos. See under Paphos (Cyprus)
House of Theseus. See under Paphos (Cyprus)
Hui, Andrew, 89
Hymn to Aphrodite, 38
hyperobjects, 8, 63–64, 66

inscriptions, 17, 77–79, *78*, 146
islands, 94, 96, 101–2; Cyprus as, 5, 7, 15, 18–20, 22–25, 28–29, 38–39, 41–43, 45–47, 51, 53, 58, 62, 75, 79, 101–2, 128, 132, 134, 137, 139, 142, 144–47; other islands, 17, 19, 41, 47, 98, 133–35, 142
Ithaca, 134, 142, 145

Jashemski, Wilhelmina, 117
Jerome of Stridon, 9–10, 13, 19, 42, 46, 80–83, *82*, 132. See also *Life of Saint Hilarion* (Jerome)
Julian (Roman emperor), 12, 14–15, 31

Kapur, Anandana, 48
Karageorghis, Vassos, 74
Kato Paphos. See Paphos (Cyprus)

Kearns, Catherine, 25, 102
Kelly, Tessa, 109–12, *110*
Kemal, Bahriye, 46
Kouklia. See Old Paphos
Kourion (Cyprus), 18–20, 22–23, 31–32, 141; earthquake, 18, 30–31, 56, 58–63, *61*, 67, 70
Ktisis (mosaic), 32
Kypria (Cypriot Tales), 135
Kyrenia (Cyprus), 136, 138

landscapes, 6–7, 22, 33, 45, 53, 64, 66, 72, 80–83, 94, 97, 99–101, 103–5, 107–8, 111–13, 122, 125–26, 129, 139, 142, 154
Langhorst, Joern, 125
Lapithos (Cyprus), 19, 22
Latz, Peter, 122, 126–27
Libanius (rhetorician), 14, 18
Libya, 12, 15, 17, 39, 132–33, 144
Life of Saint Antony (Athanasius), 94–100, 132–33
Life of Saint Hilarion (Jerome), 6–28, 45, 55, 70, 100, 131–34, 155
locus amoenus ("pleasant place"), 24, 98, 100, 127
Loma Prieta (earthquake of 1989), 3–5, 56–57, 70
Long Now Foundation, 67
Lusignans (French rulers of Cyprus), 21, 137–39

Maier, F. G., 74
Majuma (Palestine), 144
Makhairas, Leontios (historian), 138
Malpas, Jeff, 155
Manetti, Giannozzo, 55
maps. See cartography and mapping
Marder, Michael, 103, 115–17, 129
Massachusetts Museum of Contemporary Art, 84–87
Mastheads project, 109–13
McFadden, George, 61–63
media and mediation, 7, 13, 32–33, 64, 66–67, 73, 77, 83, 87, 105, 132, 152–53
Mediterranean, 7, 17, 24, 25, 46, 55, 70, 95, 102, 129, 133, 135, 142, 144–46, 152
melancholy, 84, 87, 89

Melville, Herman, 109–22
memory, 3, 5–6, 15, 19, 23, 26–30, 33, 38, 47–48, 57–58, 61, 67, 69–70, 75, 77, 84–86, 109, 111, 125, 132, 136, 141, 144–45, 147, 152
Mendelsohn, Daniel, 144–45
Mengual, Estelle Zhong, 113
Methone (Greece), 13
Michalet, Estienne, 142, *143*
Modified Mercalli scale, 3–4, 55. *See also* earthquakes: intensity of
Moe, Ledelle, 84–87, *85*, *86*, 88
Mollison, Bill, 120
monasteries, 12, 19, 96, 135, 141, 144, 146, 152
Morris, Christine, 48
Morton, Timothy, 8, 63
mountains, 12, 24, 29, 34, 39, 42–43, 89, 95–102, 104, 111–13, *120*, 121–22, 127–28, 130, 133–34, 136–38, 144, 146; as water towers, 98, 100
Mount Olympos (Cyprus), 101
Myers, J. L., 87

Nagel, Alexander, 81
Nea Paphos. *See* Paphos (Cyprus)
Neophytos (hermit), 137, 139
New Paphos. *See* Paphos (Cyprus)
Nile, 41–43, 95–96

Odysseus, 100, 134–35, 142, 145–46
Odyssey (Homer), 37–39, 98–99, 134–35, 142, *143*, 144–45
Ogygia (island), 100, 134–35, 142, 145
Old Paphos, 20, 22, 31, 42–43, 51, 73, 87, 136, 144. *See also* Aphrodite: sanctuary and temple (Old Paphos); Panagia Katholiki (Old Paphos)
Opelt, Ilona, 135–36, 141
orchards, 5, 24, 116–17, 119, 121–22. *See also* gardens; trees
Ortelius, Abraham, 142, *143*

Pachynus (Sicily), 133, 135
Palaipaphos. *See* Old Paphos
Palestine, 10, 12, 14–15, 17, 24, 26, 93, 100–101, 129, 132, 136, 142, 147
Palladius (agricultural writer), 116–19, 121

Panagia Aphroditissa. *See* Panagia Katholiki (Old Paphos)
Panagia Katholiki (Old Paphos), 20
Papacostas, Tassos, 127, 139
Papantoniou, Giorgos, 48
Paphos (Cyprus): Agia Kyriaki, 21, 76, *76*; Chrysopolitissa basilica, 21, 32, 75–79, *76*, *78*, *88*; Garrison's Camp, 141; House of Dionysos, 73–74, 79; House of Theseus, 74, 79; theater, 32, 74–79, 89. *See also* Hilarion (hermit): in Paphos; Old Paphos
Paraetonium (Libya), 133, 144
Parkinson, Chris, 109
Paul (apostle). *See* Saint Paul's Pillar
periplous, 133
permaculture, 5, 121–22
Pharos (Egypt), 41–42
pilgrimage, 42, 46, 136, 142, 153
place: deterritorialized, 134–35; and earthquakes, 4–6, 56–58, 66–70; and hagiography, 1, 10, 94–97, 100–102, 131–32, 155; haunted, 25–26, 28, 45, 58, 100–101, 128, 134, 152; and lifestyle, 97; lived space, 22–23, 26, 29; relationship to, 8, 28–29, 32–33, 96, 131–32, 146–47, 154–55; and religion, 153–55; and representation, 33, 37, 134, 136, 145; and singularity, 155; unmappable, 23, 28–29, 33, 132–34, 142, 154. *See also chora*; gardens; geocriticism; hermitages; landscapes; *locus amoenus* ("pleasant place"); remoteness
plants, 23–25, 32, 45–46, 70, 98, 100–101, 115–30, 152. *See also* trees
Plato, 29, 154
Pliny, 128
poetry, 16, 19–20, 23, 28, 37–53, 116–19, 121, 131, 134, 145, 152–53
Pollan, Michael, 130
Pontus, 97–100, 102

Rantidi (Cyprus), 31
relics, 8, 53, 76–77, 132
religion and the sacred, 15–16, 24–25, 31, 38, 42, 44–47, 51, 53, 77, 79, 116, 126, 140–42, 152–55

remoteness, 10, 23, 28–29, 43–44, 63, 93–113, 115, 132, 136
Rhegium (Italy), 19
Richter scale, 3, 56. *See also* earthquakes: magnitude of
Riegl, Alois, 72–73, 83–84, 86–87
Roberts, Michael, 43–44
Roberts, Tyler, 155
Rock of Aphrodite. *See under* Aphrodite
Rome, 10, 19, 79–81, 102
Roosien, Mark, 69
Rosenberg, Elissa, 125–26
ruins, 5, 7, 9–10, 14, 16–24, 30–32, 34, 42, 44–45, 48, 51, 57, 59, 70, 72–84, 87, 89, 101, 116, 125–29, 139–41, 151–52

sacredness. *See* religion and the sacred
Saint Paul's Pillar, 77, 87–89, *88*
Salamis. *See* Constantia (Cyprus)
Sappho, 40–41
Saranda Kolones (fortress in Paphos), 21
Schalansky, Judith, 39–40, 89, 95, 97, 102
Schütte, Thomas, *106*, *107*, 107–9, 111, 113
seismography and seismograms, 3–6, 16, 54–55, 57–58, 64, 152
seismology, 54–56, 59, 151
Serres, Michel, 4, 56–67
ships, 12–13, 16, 18, 20, 109, 111, 128, 133, 142, 144; shipbuilding, 25, 127
Sicily, 12, 14, 17, 19, 102, 133, 144
Skippe, John (British traveler and painter), 21
Solnit, Rebecca, 112
Soloi (Cyprus). *See under* Aphrodite
Soren, David, 18, 30–31, 56, 62–63
Sozomen (historian), 15, 18, 136–37, 144
spolia, 73, 80, 83
Stephanides, Stephanos, 47–48, 51
Stewart, Susan, 21, 30, 72–73, 79–80, 83
stone of Aphrodite. *See under* Aphrodite
stone of Atsupa, 140
stones, 10, 20–21, 23, 48, 56, 64, 75, 77, 79–80, 84, 87, 89, 101, 108, 112, 117, 140, 147. *See*

also Aphrodite: stone of Aphrodite (cultic object); stone of Atsupa
Strabo, 25, 38–41, 99, 135
Stylianou, Andreas, 144
Stylianou, Judith, 144
stylite, 112
Summa, Daniela, 79

Tacitus, 87
tectonic shift, 8, 17, 54, 63–64
Tell Umm el-'Amr (Gaza), 146
Thabatha (Gaza), 10
Theophanes (Byzantine chronicler), 13
Tonn, Sissel Marie, 64–67, 69–70
Toumballos. *See* Paphos (Cyprus): Garrison's Camp
trees, 5, 19, 23–26, 29–30, 32, 43–44, 46, 57, 67, 98, 100–101, 104, 108, 111, 114–16, 119, 121, 126, 128, 130, 140–42, 151; alder, 43–44, 98, 126, 128; carob, 19; cedar, 128; citrus, 24, 121; cypress, 98, 128; and earthquake dating, 57; grafts, 76, 117; nurse log, 75; oak, 128; olive, 32, 128; palm, 43–44; pear, 126, 140–41; pine, 108, 111, 128; plane, 43–44; pomegranate, 24; poplar, 43–44, 98. *See also* orchards
Trikomo (Cyprus), 47–48. *See also under* Aphrodite
Troodos Mountains (Cyprus), 89, 101, 127–28, 135, 141
tsunamis, 12–17, 30–31, 70

vegetation. *See* plants
Venus. *See* Aphrodite
Vergil (Latin poet), 19, 41–42, 81, 117

Wallace, Terry C., 56
Wasserstrom, Steve, 155
Westphal, Bertrand, 33, 37
Wills, David, 149
Wolf, Burkhard, 134
Wood, Christopher, 81

www.ingramcontent.com/pod-product-compliance
Lightning Source LLC
Chambersburg PA
CBHW022056290426
44109CB00014B/1114